BIOGRAPHICAL SKETCHES.

Biographical Sketches and Anecdotes

of

Members of the Religious Society of Friends

Originally Published

by

The Tract Association of Friends

HERITAGE BOOKS
2019

HERITAGE BOOKS
AN IMPRINT OF HERITAGE BOOKS, INC.

Books, CDs, and more—Worldwide

For our listing of thousands of titles see our website
at
www.HeritageBooks.com

A Facsimile Reprint
Published 2019 by
HERITAGE BOOKS, INC.
Publishing Division
5810 Ruatan Street
Berwyn Heights, Md. 20740

Entered, according to Act of Congress, in the year 1870, by
The Tract Association of Friends
in the Office of the Librarian of Congress at Washington

— Publisher's Notice —
In reprints such as this, it is often not possible to remove blemishes from the original. We feel the contents of this book warrant its reissue despite these blemishes and hope you will agree and read it with pleasure.

International Standard Book Numbers
Paperbound: 978-0-7884-4706-8
Clothbound: 978-0-7884-9207-5

PREFACE.

THE following pages are chiefly compiled from a series of articles published in a religious periodical, about twenty years since, with the title, "Thomas Scattergood, and his Times." They comprise brief biographies of Friends, who lived in this country in the last and early part of the present century, who became conspicuous for their devotion to the cause of Truth. A number of incidents are given that had not been printed before.

As the work is interspersed with numerous anecdotes, and contains valuable records of religious experience, exemplifying the doctrines and testimonies of the Society of Friends, and their accordance with the Holy Scriptures, it is hoped that it will prove interesting, and instructive to those into whose hands it may come.

PHILADELPHIA, Eleventh month 10th, 1870.

CONTENTS.

	PAGE
DAVID FERRIS	9
WILLIAM HUNT	33
SAMUEL EMLEN	46
JOHN CHURCHMAN	67
REBECCA JONES	80
DANIEL OFFLEY	127
WILLIAM SAVERY	149
GEORGE DILLWYN	182
ARTHUR HOWELL	227
WILLIAM JACKSON	240
PETER YARNALL	259
ANTHONY BENEZET	296
JACOB LINDLEY	305
ELI YARNALL	326
SARAH HARRISON	344
JOHN PARKER	366
NICHOLAS WALN	381
MOSES BROWN	396

BIOGRAPHICAL SKETCHES.

DAVID FERRIS.

IN the year 1727, a lad, in the twentieth year of his age, who resided at New Milford, in Connecticut, was passing under much inward trouble for his sins. He had been divinely favored in early youth, but not giving heed to the Light of the Lord Jesus inwardly manifested to preserve from sin, he became fond of vain company and earthly delights, and gave way thereto until he lost his good estate. He was often reproved for his sins, and became so distressed because of his condition that he fell into despair, and wished that he might die. All this time he did not forsake his evil habits, and concluded it was too late to return, that he might repent and live. One day he concluded that he should be a disgrace to his relations if he remained at home, and so determined to leave his native land, and go where he should not be known. That very day — a day of the deepest affliction and distress he had ever known — he heard, as he followed his plough, a still, small voice saying in his soul, "The blood of Jesus Christ his Son cleanseth from all sin." Not willing to receive the consolatory declaration, he replied, "It is too late; there has been a day wherein I might have been cleansed, but, alas! I have let it pass over my head forever." In the course of some minutes after, as he was musing whither he should flee, the same words passed through his mind, and took greater hold of his thoughts than at first. Still, after a time, deeming himself lost, he once more returned to his meditation on the place he should go to, and, his anguish increasing, he stopped ploughing. Now, with great power and authority, the language was a third time uttered, "The blood of Jesus Christ his Son cleanseth us from all sin." A change took place in his feelings, faith awakened in his heart, and he thought, "If all sin, why not mine?" Joyful emotions stirred within him; he saw there was still mercy for him, and, penitent and tendered, a stream of thanksgiving and praise arose in his heart. Now, through Divine mercy, trusting in the Holy Spirit, and bowing to the cross of Christ, he was enabled to press after holiness along the narrow path of self-denial.

This young man was named David Ferris; he was born at Stratford, in Connecticut, Third month 10th, 1707, and was early favored with the visitations of Divine Grace. He mentions a simple circumstance, which, with reflections growing out of it, ministered instruction to him when very young in life. He was riding on horseback through a river, against a very rapid current, and a young dog attempted to follow him. On looking round, he perceived that the dog, scarcely able to stem the force of the stream, was unable to keep pace with the horse, and appeared in great distress. David felt pity for the poor animal, who seemed almost desperate, and while gazing on it with concern, there opened to his mind a sense of the awful amazement which a poor immortal soul must be in when death is close at hand, and there appears no hope of escape from everlasting punishment and woe. This thought was of use to him for years.

David Ferris was brought up a Presbyterian, and received a college education. Before going to college, his understanding was opened to see that various points of doctrine held by Calvin were not according to the Truth, and he had many disputes with his classmates upon the subject. He had also a long and satisfactory conversation with the head of the institution on his religious views and experience. About the middle of his last year at college, he met with Barclay's Apology,*

---

* The full title of this standard work is "An Apology for the True Christian Divinity, being an Explanation and Vindication of the Principles and Doctrines of the People called Quakers." By Robert Barclay. — It is to be had at Friends' Bookstore. 304 Arch Street, Philadelphia.

and could not but unite with the doctrines laid down therein. Believing that men could give no authority for any one to enter into the exercise of the ministry of the Gospel, he now felt uneasy at taking degrees. This was a time of deep exercise and trial with him — he had been highly esteemed by those about him, and he felt that should he now leave college he would be despised. His father had fondly looked to him, as likely to be an honor to the family — but David knew if he followed his convictions of duty, his attached parent would consider him as its disgrace. Besides this, he had the prospect of an immediate settlement, a numerous congregation, and a good salary.

Having been favored with inward strength to perform his duty and leave the college, he found less difficulty than he had apprehended. His father, although he would not speak to him for some time, yet at last relented, and treated him affectionately. One after another of the testimonies of Friends had been opened to David Ferris, and he was brought, in a great cross to the natural will, into plainness of speech, and into a disuse of hat-honor to man. Now he felt drawn to attend the meetings of the people called Quakers, and accordingly, in the latter part of the Third month, 1733, he went to the public meeting held at the time of the Yearly Meeting on Long Island. He wished to feel whether they were a living people. At this meeting were several Friends in the ministry from Europe, both men and women. These were, no doubt, Samuel Stevens, Mungo Bewley, Alice Alderson, and Margaret Copeland, who were then in America.

After attending this meeting, David says of the Friends, "I was indubitably satisfied that their worship was in Spirit and in Truth; and [that] they [were] such worshippers as the Father sought and owned. I was convinced, beyond a doubt, that they preached the Gospel in the demonstration of the Spirit; and Divine authority was felt to attend their ministry. They were not like the scribes, to whom I had been listening all my life, who had neither commission nor authority, except that which was received from man; being such as the Lord never sent; and therefore could not profit the people they professed to teach. I now clearly saw the difference between manmade ministers, and those whom the Lord qualifies and sends into his harvest-field; the difference between the wheat and the chaff; and it was marvellous to me, to reflect how long I had sat under a formal, dry, and lifeless ministry." "I heard women preach the Gospel, in the Divine authority of Truth; far exceeding all the learned rabbis I had known. This was not so strange to me as it might have been to others; for I had before seen, by the immediate manifestation of

Grace and Truth, that women as well as men might be clothed with gospel power; and that daughters as well as sons, under the Gospel dispensation, were to have the Spirit poured upon them, that they might prophesy; and though I had never before heard a woman preach, yet I now rejoiced to see the prophecy fulfilled."

David Ferris found it necessary to look around for some means of temporal support; and, feeling inclined to remove to Pennsylvania, he, in the Sixth month, accompanied to Philadelphia three of the ministering Friends from England before mentioned. In this city he felt inclined to settle for the present, if he could establish himself in business. When the Yearly Meeting for the Provinces of Pennsylvania and New Jersey, which was held there in the Seventh month, was over, and he had become somewhat acquainted with the Friends of the place, he concluded to open a school, in which the Latin and Greek languages should be taught. He says, "But, as I was a stranger, and those children that were intended to be taught these languages were mostly entered in other schools, I was doubtful whether I should be able to get a sufficient number of such scholars. I therefore agreed to teach English also; and, in time, I had a school of both sexes, sufficiently large for my support. Being a stranger, I consequently met with trials and difficulties. For a while my school was small and not likely to support me; but I endeavored to be resigned, and repose with confidence in an all-sufficient Providence, from whom I had often received help in times of great trial. My difficulties were increased by the low state of my funds. The weather was now beginning to grow cold. It was customary for the teacher to find wood for fuel, and for the scholars to pay a proportion of the expense, when they paid for their quarter's tuition; and as I had but few scholars, and no money due, and not two shillings of my own remaining, I was very thoughtful how to procure wood. No one knew the state of my purse, nor did I desire to make it known; and this I should do if I attempted to borrow. I therefore omitted to buy as long as I well could. I did not like to ask for credit, and if I did, it was doubtful whether I should obtain it; so that I was closely tried. But, while I was under this exercise, the weather was more moderate than usual at that season. After I had been sufficiently tried to prove my faith and confidence in Divine Providence, a Friend came into my school, and privately gave me twenty shillings, which, he said, had been sent by a Friend, who did not wish to be known as the donor. For this unexpected favor I was thankful to the Lord, whose mercies endure forever. Having now the means, I soon purchased some wood; and the weather, in a short time, becoming colder, I had a renewed sense of the kindness of Providence, who had so seasonably relieved me. But afterward, when my stock of wood was nearly exhausted, I was brought into the same difficulty and trial as before, and as much needed a renewal of my faith. I strove to be quiet, and to have my dependence placed on Him who fed a great multitude with a few loaves and little fishes; and just as I began to suffer, another twenty-shilling bill was privately presented to me by an unknown hand; but I received it as coming from the Lord, who knew all my difficulties. Thus I was again relieved, and never afterward received anything more in this way; nor did I ever need it, as I was sufficiently supplied by the proceeds of my business. This was a confirmation to me that I had been assisted by a watchful Providence, who knows all states and conditions, both internal and external, and is able and willing to turn the hearts of his people, and constrain them to help the needy, as, formerly, he sent the ravens to feed the prophet."

There are many authentic anecdotes of the interposition of Divine mercy on behalf of his faithful children when suffering from poverty or want of food. Thomas Chalkley gives us an account of an interesting incident of this kind which occurred while he was on a passage from Bermuda to Philadelphia, in the year

1716. The wind proved slight, and thus the time occupied in the voyage was protracted to twice its usual length. With twelve persons to feed, their store of provisions was at last reduced to one piece of beef. Pressed with hunger, and disheartened by a head wind, those on board began to relate sad and sickening accounts of seamen similarly circumstanced eating one another. The murmurs increased, particularly against Thomas Chalkley, to whom the vessel was consigned, and he felt his mind clothed with inward exercise. At last, after seriously considering the matter, he told them that if there should be a necessity for one to die for the rest, they need not cast lots, for he was free to offer his life to do them good. At this, several of those addressed said they would die before they would eat him. Thomas says, "I can truly say, that at that time my life was not dear to me, and that I was serious and ingenuous in my proposition. As I was leaning over the side of the vessel, thoughtfully considering my proposal to the company, and looking, in my mind, to Him who made me, a very large dolphin came up to the surface of the water, and looked me in the face. I called to the people to put a hook into the sea and take him, 'For here is one come to redeem me,' said I to them. They put out a hook, and the fish readily took it, and they caught him. I think it was about six feet long, and the largest that ever I saw. This plainly showed us that we ought not to distrust the providence of the Almighty. The people were quieted by this act of Providence, and murmured no more. We caught enough to eat plentifully of till we got into the Capes of Delaware. Thus I saw it was good to depend upon the Almighty, and rely upon his eternal arm, which, in a particular manner, did preserve us safe to our destined port, blessed be his great and glorious Name, through Jesus Christ, forever." *

The next important movement of David Ferris was that of seeking a wife. He was a man of a fine person, and it would appear was at least willing to find a wife with similar attractions. Near his residence in Philadelphia, a young woman dwelt, whose family was respectable, and their outward circumstances prosperous. She was blessed with good natural talents, had been educated in plainness, and was withal quite comely in appearance. These circumstances drew his attention to her, and friends who are generally ready in encouraging matrimonial connections which appear outwardly suitable, urged him to make proposals to her. Taking the hint from them, and not waiting on the Divine Guide for direction, he concluded to do so, and for that purpose paid her a visit. After chatting sociably for half an hour, he felt within him a word

---

* This incident is narrated in the Journal of Thomas Chalkley. See also Friends' Library, edited by William and Thomas Evans, Philadelphia, vol. vi., p. 32.

of reproof. The language was uttered, "Seekest thou great things for thyself? Seek them not." He felt the rebuke, and, confused and perplexed, he was no longer fit for conversation, and so withdrew. This was the first and last attempt to bring about that, to appearance, so desirable connection. It was well for him and his peace of mind that he had proceeded no further in his own will before he was checked by the inward Reprover. Some have gone on even until they thought themselves ready to proceed in marriage, and have then discovered that they had in no wise taken counsel of Him who has a right to direct the movements of his children. This must bring them under great trial and exercise. Some have gone on, because they could not see how to withdraw, and have paid by a life of discomfort for the haste with which they have run into an affectionate engagement.

Some months after David Ferris had been turned back from his own choice as before narrated, he was sitting at table in a Friend's house, and noticed a young woman sitting opposite to him. He did not remember ever to have seen her before, but he says, "A language very quietly and very pleasantly passed through my mind in this wise, 'If thou wilt marry that young woman, thou shalt be happy with her.'" David believed this intimation was from the Source of all good, but finding that the young woman was lame, he was much displeased at the thought of marrying a cripple. He passed through many exercises before his will was brought in this thing to submit to the Lord's requirings, but in a belief that it would tend to his own happiness, he at last gave up. When his will was made subject, then everything connected with his marriage seemed bright and happy. They were married Ninth month 13th, 1735, and at the close of forty years he said he had never repented his choice. A blessing had rested upon him and on his posterity. He says, " I have lived to see my children, arrived to years of understanding, favored with a knowledge of the Truth; which is the greatest of all blessings; and some of them, beyond all doubt, are landed in eternal felicity. I have been blessed with plenty, and above all with peace. I am, therefore, satisfied and thankful to my gracious Benefactor, for his kindness to me in this concern, as well as for all his other favors."

Thomas Ellwood gives an interesting account of the manner of his proceeding in relation to marriage. He found his feelings drawn toward a young woman named Mary Ellis, in whom he thought he saw the "fair prints of Truth and solid virtue." He was then residing with Isaac and Mary Penington; and as they stood in the place of parents to him, he opened the matter to them. He says, "They having solemnly weighed the matter, expressed their unity therewith:

and indeed their approbation was no small confirmation to me. Yet took I further deliberation, often retiring in spirit to the Lord, and crying to him for direction, before I addressed myself to her. At length, as I was sitting alone, waiting upon the Lord for counsel and guidance in this, in *itself* and to *me*, so important affair, I felt a word sweetly arise in me, as if I had heard a voice, which said, 'Go, and prevail.' And faith springing in my heart with the word, I immediately rose and went, nothing doubting.

"When I was come to her lodgings, which were about a mile from me, I desired the maid to acquaint her mistress that I was come to give her a visit; whereupon I was invited to go up to her. And after some common conversation had passed, feeling my spirit weightily concerned, I solemnly opened my mind unto her, with respect to the particular business I came about; which I soon perceived was a great surprisal to her. For she had taken in an apprehension, as others also had done, that mine eye had been fixed elsewhere, and nearer home. I used not many words to her; but I felt a divine power went along with the words, and fixed the matter expressed by them so fast in her breast, that, as she afterward acknowledged to me, she could not shut it out.

"I made but a short visit. For, having told her, I did not expect an answer from her then; but desired she would, in the most solemn manner, weigh the proposal made, and in due time give me such an answer thereunto, as the Lord should give her; I took my leave of her and departed, leaving the issue to the Lord.

"I had a journey then at hand, which I foresaw would take me up about two weeks. Wherefore, the day before I was to set out, I went to visit her again, to acquaint her with my journey and excuse my absence; not yet pressing her for an answer, but assuring her, that I felt in myself an increase of affection to her, and hoped to receive a suitable return from her in the Lord's time; to whom, in the meanwhile, I committed both her and myself, and the concern between us. And indeed, I found at my return, that I could not have left it in a better hand; for the Lord had been my advocate in my absence, and had so far answered all her objections, that when I came to her again, she rather acquainted me with them, than urged them.

"I continued my visits to my best beloved friend, until we married; which was in the year 1669. We took each other in a select meeting, of the ancient and grave Friends of that country, holden in a Friend's house; where, in those times, not only the Monthly Meeting for church discipline, but the public meeting for worship was sometimes kept. A very solemn meeting it was, and in a weighty frame of spirit *we* were; in which we sensibly felt *the Lord with us, and joining us;* the sense whereof remained with us all our lifetime, and was of good service and very comfortable to us on all occasions."

In a year or two after David Ferris was married, the subject of removing from Philadelphia and settling in Wilmington, claimed his attention. He took a lot of ground there, and yet the way did not at once appear clear for him to remove thither, and his wife seemed unwilling to consent. Various exercises attended his mind in the consideration of a change of residence, and he thus notes down some general reflections on the subject: "To move from one place to another, in our own time and will, I believe is a matter of serious consequence. A change of residence appears to me next in importance to marriage, and, therefore, requires the same Divine Wisdom to direct us aright. We may be qualified for service in one place, and by removing to a distance, unless we are directed by unerring counsel, the design of Providence respecting us may be frustrated, and our usefulness lessened."

Most of those who have taken notice of the things passing around them, have seen instances of persons who have been very useful in one Monthly Meeting, who yet have, on removing to another, been apparently without any qualification for rightly taking part in the discipline of the church. If we are not in our places, we need not expect to find the proper business of our day before us; and we shall look in vain for Divine aid, if we attempt to perform that which rightfully belongs to others.

At last the way opened clearly for David Ferris to remove to Wilmington. His wife cheerfully acquiesced, and he felt the comfortable assurance that he had the approbation of his Divine Master in the proposed change, and that the Lord's blessing would be with them. He removed in the Third month, 1737, and opened store in that place. Keeping closely to the restraining influence of Divine grace, in his buying and selling, he was directed safely, and, in time, accumulated a competence.

Soon after he had been admitted into membership among Friends, he believed he was called to appear as a minister of the Gospel. This was a very solemn and important call, and he had much reasoning on the matter. From time to time, as he believed himself required to stand up and minister in religious meetings, he was not faithful, under the hope that at a future meeting he would have more strength. During a long-continued time of disobedience, David Ferris was favored with many warnings and incitements to faithfulness. The Holy Spirit called him to obedience, as did many of the Lord's servants, who were dipped into a sense of his state; and sometimes in visions of the night, instruction was administered. He says:

"One night I dreamed that I saw a large, spacious building in an unfinished state; and the master builder, who appeared an excellent person, came to me, as I stood at a distance, and desired me to go and take a view of it, to which I agreed; and as we were surveying it, and examining the particular parts, I observed that among the many pillars erected for the support of the building, there was one lacking. I queried of him what was the cause of that vacancy. He replied, it was left for me, and that I was specially designed and prepared for the place, and showed me how I fitted it, like a mortise is fitted to its tenon. So that I saw in my dream that all he said was true. But, notwithstanding all this, I objected to my capacity and fitness to fill the vacancy, and was, therefore, unwilling to occupy it. He endeavored, by the most convincing reasons, to remove all my objections, and to demonstrate that I was fitted for the place. He further told me, that they had not another prepared for it, and that the building would be retarded if I did not comply with the design. After he had reasoned with me a long time, and I still refused, he appeared to be grieved, and told me it was a great pity that I should be rendered useless in the house by my own obstinacy;

and then added, 'But it must not be so; for if thou wilt not be a pillar, thou shalt be a plank for the floor.' He then showed me how I might be flatted and prepared for that purpose. But I refused that place also, on the ground that it looked too diminutive to be a plank to be trod upon by all who came into the house At this the master was troubled, seeing I would accept no place that was offered me; but, after a long debate, he concluded to leave the propositions he had made, for my further consideration; and so we parted.

"The next day I was at a meeting on Long Island, and a concern came heavily upon me to say something that was presented to my mind. The burden of the word was weighty, and more difficult to remove than usual; but I contended with it, and, at length, refused to comply. I was then in company with two women Friends. The following night one of them dreamed that she saw me sitting by a pleasant stream of water; before me a table was spread with all manner of dainties; but I was chained, so that I could not reach any of them, at which she was troubled, and asked the master of the feast why I was deprived of the liberty to partake of the good things on the table. He answered, that the time had been, when, on certain conditions, I might have enjoyed them to the full; but that I had refused the terms, and therefore was now justly deprived of them. She inquired of him whether this must always be my case. He answered, perhaps not; that if I would yet submit, and comply with the terms, it was not too late to partake of all the good things she saw. The interpretation of this dream, and of mine the night before, was easy and plain. They rested on my mind for several years, as cause of humbling instruction and excitement to future care, diligence, and obedience."

Individuals who have been called to the work of the ministry, and have refused obedience, have sometimes been left by their Divine Master in a state of darkness, their spiritual vision has been obscured, and they have fallen into the snares of the enemy.

David Ferris, after rebelling for twenty years against the Divine call to the ministry, at last yielded obedience to the requirings of duty. Comfort Hoag * and Elizabeth Dean, from New England, in the year 1765, attended the Yearly Meeting in Philadelphia, and, when that was over, the meetings generally in these parts. David Ferris accompanied them, and Comfort was dipped into sympathy with him, and felt from meeting to meeting that he was called on to speak. "David, why didst thou not preach to-day?" she asked him, after one of the meetings. He smiled and put by the ques-

---

* Comfort Hoag, afterward well known as Comfort Collins, was born about the year 1711, came forth in the ministry at an early age, and continued faithfully laboring in the gift committed to her to a very advanced period of life.

tion. The next day she again addressed him in the same words. He endeavored to get off without replying, but she told him it was useless to endeavor to evade it; she was assured he ought to have spoken, and his disobedience had almost prevented her service. David then confessed that for twenty years he had been unfaithful in this respect to apprehended duty. Comfort, after expressing her wonder at the depth of Divine kindness still manifest toward one so long in rebellion, administered such counsel and advice on the subject as she was furnished with from the Source of true wisdom. The next day they were again at meeting. Once more a call for obedience was made to David. He says: "I again felt a concern to speak to the people, but endeavored to evade it. A man of some note was sitting before me, and this increased my reluctance to speak. I supposed he would not be present at the next meeting, and then I would obey the call of the Lord to that service. Thus I spent the greater part of an hour. At length, my Divine Master, the great Master Builder, thus addressed me: 'Why dost thou still delay, desiring to be excused until a more convenient season? There never will be a better time than this; I have waited on thee above twenty years; I have clearly made known to thee my will, so that all occasion of doubt has been removed; yet thou hast refused to submit, until thy day is far spent; and if thou dost not speedily comply with my commands, it will be too late; thy opportunity will be lost.' I then clearly saw that if I were forsaken, and left to myself, the consequence would be death and darkness forever! At the sight of the horrible pit that yawned for me, if I continued in disobedience, my body trembled like an aspen-leaf, and my soul was humbled within me! Then I said, Lord, here am I; make of me what thou wouldst have me to be; leave me not in displeasure, I beseech thee. All my power to resist was then suspended; I forgot the great man that had been in my way, and was raised on my feet I hardly knew how, and expressed, in a clear and distinct manner, what was on my mind. When I had taken my seat, Comfort Hoag rose, and had an open, favorable opportunity to speak to the assembly. After meeting she told me that during the time we had sat in silence, her whole concern was on my account; that her anxiety for my deliverance from that bondage was such that she was willing to offer up her natural life to the Lord, if it might be a means to bring me forth in the ministry; and that, on making the offering, I rose to speak. On which her anxiety for me was removed, and her mind filled with concern for the people present.

"At that time I was made a real Quaker, and was not ashamed to be seen trembling before the Lord,

Under a sense of so great and merciful a deliverance, I saw and felt ample cause for it. It was with me as with Israel of old, when the Lord caused their captivity to return, saying he would build them as at the first, and they should fear and tremble for all his goodness, and for all the prosperity he would procure for them. My soul rejoiced in the Lord, and I magnified his excellent name, who is worthy of all honor, glory, and renown forever.

"It appeared to me wonderful that I should thus be lifted out of this horrible pit of my own digging; and I was so absorbed in the love and mercy of my heavenly Benefactor, that I was filled with thankfulness and praise, attended with a desire that, in future, I might diligently watch and wait for the pointing of his holy finger to every service he might be pleased to allot me, that so no opportunity might be lost of manifesting my gratitude by obedience to his will. My feelings were like those of a prisoner who had been long in bonds and was set at liberty."

David Ferris was, according to the testimony of his Friends, useful in the ministry, his Gospel labors sound and edifying, and tending to advance the cause of truth and righteousness. Yet they believed his long unfaithfulness had stunted his growth in his gift, and caused him to go in measure halting all the days of his life. In reference to this he says: "Having so long rebelled, I had no reason to expect that I should be so useful as I might have been had I rendered early obedience to the heavenly call. However, it appeared necessary, if little were committed to my care, to be faithful to that little." He had some closely proving dispensations to pass through. At one long-extended period he had no concern to labor in the ministry, and he who had refused to do the Lord's work when called to it, found all ability for service taken away. He thought, and his friends thought, the gift had been withdrawn. It was, however, the will of his Lord once more to restore it, and to the end of his days he appears to have endeavored to walk in humility and faithfulness.

He was diligent in the attendance of meetings, and in those for discipline was of good service. He did not allow his temporal affairs to keep him from his meetings, shutting up his shop that he might attend there on week-days. He was religiously concerned to educate his children in the fear of the Lord, and in Christian simplicity and plainness. He was hospitable to his friends, and charitable to the poor. He was tried with bodily weakness and frequent sickness during the last three years of his life, under which he was preserved in much patience. His mind, in the prospect of eternity, appeared tranquil and trustful, and he was enabled to say, "All is well." His

Master was with him in his sufferings; and at one time, when he had been sitting in silence with some Friends who had gathered by his bed, he was strengthened, in the fresh feeling of life, to exclaim, "To me, to live is Christ, and to die is gain." Thus sustained and supported, his close was in peace. His death took place Twelfth month 5th, 1779, he being seventy-two years of age.

WILLIAM HUNT.

WILLIAM HUNT, of whom Richard Jordan once said, he was the greatest man North Carolina ever held, was born at Manoquacy, in Maryland, in the year 1733. His parents had removed thither from New Jersey. William, very early in life, was made sensible of the visitations of Grace, and submitting thereto, had, at eleven years of age, remarkable openings in Divine things. His mind was unusually mature, and he was enabled to perceive that the works of creation and of Providence were full of wonderful harmony. When about fourteen years old he received a gift in the ministry, in which he labored with fervency and heart-awakening power the short period allotted him on earth. It has been the will of the Lord Jesus to commit his precious gifts at times to such as are very young, and to make them able ministers of his Gospel. Some such, having fulfilled their portion of service in his cause on earth, have been gathered home to their heavenly rest, while yet in childhood; others have been withdrawn from the conflicts of time in the dawning of manhood; and a few have remained bright monuments of the Lord's power and goodness, testifying of his Grace and good Spirit, to advanced age.

George Newland, in his twelfth year, was called to the ministry of the Gospel by the Giver of all spiritual gifts, and was favored to labor in the churches in his native country, Ireland, to the comfort and edification of his elder Friends. His understanding was bright, his life was innocent, his conversation exemplary, and his ministry sound. Six years of labor for his Divine Master were soon over, and then a lingering illness came upon him. He said he had passed through much inward exercise, known only to the Lord — and he did not know but he had rather die than live — yet he durst not desire death. "I have felt more of the Lord's love to me since I was sick, in a wonderful manner, than ever before. I strove to serve the Lord in my health, and now I reap the benefit of it. I can look forward, and that is a mercy." The sensible evidence of the love of God to his soul overcame him, and he said, "Oh! if the earnest be so precious, what will the fulness be?" With the praises of God on his tongue, and the love of God in his heart, his sickness was stripped of gloom, and the hour of death brought no bitterness of spirit to him. On the 24th of Eighth month, 1708, being then not nineteen years of age, his earthly course was finished, and he went rejoicing to his rest.

Ellis Lewis of North Wales, in Britain, when a child, being favored with the visitations of Divine love, submitted thereto, and about the thirteenth year of his age appeared in a public testimony to the truth. His first communication was delivered in English, a language to which he was not accustomed, and it was "remarkable and tendering." Having engaged in the service of his Divine Master, faithfully did he labor in the work of the ministry, at home and abroad, adorning, by a holy life and circumspect demeanor, the doctrine he was called and qualified to proclaim and defend. His Master saw meet to continue him long as a bright example of the blessed effects of preserving grace upon the willing and obedient; and being full of love to the brethren, and clothed with the meekness and gentleness which adorn the Christian mind, he laid down his head in peace in the Eleventh month, 1764. He was then eighty-seven years old, and had been in the ministry seventy-four years.

Robert Barclay's daughter Christiana, in her fourteenth year was engaged to labor in calling others to repentance; and thus she continued to her seventy-first year, when, her labor on earth being over, she received the welcome message, "Come, ye blessed of my Father, inherit the kingdom prepared for you from the foundation of the world."

Many members of our Society, in their fourteenth, fifteenth, sixteenth, and seventeenth years, have been constrained to enter into the Gospel field of labor, and to preach with power and authority the universality of the love of God, the heart-cleansing visitations of his grace, the holy certainty and saving efficacy of that Divine Light which lighteth every man which cometh into the world. Whether these died young, in the meridian of life, or in advanced age, they never regretted having given up the bloom of their youth to the Lord's service. James Parnell and Edward Burrough — youthful martyrs in the cause of Truth and righteousness — died in prison. What to them, in the hour of death, was the suffering their cruel enemies had inflicted on them?

In that hour, James Parnell could say, "I die innocently." "I have seen glorious things." Edward Burrough, after praying for his persecutors, in a sweet feeling of acceptance with God, declared, "Though this body of clay must turn to dust, yet I have this testimony, that I have served God in my generation, and that Spirit which hath lived, and acted, and ruled in me, shall yet break forth in thousands."

It would break too much upon this sketch of William Hunt's life, to tell of many of those early dedicated ones who like him were led to traverse sea and land to fulfil their Master's bidding, and who, being faithful to the close, were crowned with a happy and trustful death. Most of these instances occurred in the earlier periods of our Society, but not entirely so. The Lord's precious gifts are bestowed, and his merciful calls are yet extended to the very young, and some of them, even in these days, have been strengthened to proclaim his goodness to others. And why should not the call to the ministry be given as early now as in former days? Why should not the Lord's power be manifested or break forth through the labors of as youthful instruments? Surely, if the instances be few, it is only for want of dedication in the visited children, and the deadening influence of the example of those in elder years.

William Hunt travelled much in the work of the ministry, and being watchfully attentive to the openings of Truth on his mind, he was enabled to preach in the demonstration of the Spirit and with power. His vigorous intellect was sanctified by Divine Grace. Wisdom in him seemed in advance of experience, and in early youth he exhibited the ripeness of maturity. When Herman Husbands departed from the principles of our Society, and sought greater liberty in doctrine than the Truth allowed, William Hunt was his most unflinching opponent. He did not deem that it was detraction to unfold the unsoundness of those who were likely to lead others astray; neither did he think it a breach of Christian charity to withstand them with true-hearted zeal.

About the commencement of the year 1767, William Hunt felt a concern to visit Friends both to the south and to the north, and he believed it would be right for Zachariah Dicks, also of North Carolina, to accompany him. Under this conviction he wrote the following letter to that Friend:

"DEAR FRIEND, — Not having an opportunity to converse, I send thee this ambassador, to convey some fruit I lately got from the holy land, a little spikenard and myrrh, the choice spices with which our Lord was anointed before he passed through that painful dispensation of suffering. My mind had been in a true calm and profound quiet for some days, free from sorrowing and tempest of any kind; so that I was ready to conclude I should have no more to do, but sometimes to eat this pleasant fruit and drink of the well that stands in the midst of the court of God. But as I was thus musing, with deep admiration and humble adoration to the Great Name that had thus brought me through all my great and sore trials, which the Lord knows were many and grievous to be borne, I thought I espied a little spring, like unto that thou knowest lies under the threshold of the house of God, and it ran toward the south, and pointed toward the north, like the glancing of a candle by a glass window, [intimating] that some of these fruits must be conveyed to some of those inhabitants. And as I apprehend thou art a chosen companion to me of God, in the moving of that endearing love and good-will which hath subsisted between us from the beginning, I give thee a hint to the end thou mayest keep steady under the preparing hand, that when the full time is come thou mayest gird on the vestments of war, and appear as a soldier well disciplined therein. I am at all times, and in all things, thy assured Friend, WILLIAM HUNT.

On the 25th of Fourth month, 1767, the meeting at New Garden in North Carolina furnished William Hunt and Zachariah Dicks with certificates of unity with their prospect of religious service. They were together at the Yearly Meeting of Philadelphia, toward the close of the Ninth month of that year, soon after which Zachariah Dicks believed it was in accordance with the will of his Divine Master for him to return to his home. William Hunt continued his travels to the north. Perhaps it was during this journey that he made use of an expression which has been often repeated. "My concern is to be devoted to the service of Christ so fully, that I may not spend one minute in pleasing myself."

Great was his labor as he travelled from place to place. Though he was often engaged to minister at a considerable length, yet the powerful baptizing influence which accompanied the word preached, so effectually reached the hearers that they listened with unwearied attention. The plainness with which he reproved them, the blows of the "sharp threshing-instrument" which his Master put into his hands, did not offend them. Those who were desirous of doing right were glad to hear of their faults, and anxious that the whole counsel of God should be shown them; and those who were lukewarm realized the truth of a saying of Robert Walker, "People love to *hear* preaching, but they do not *love* the cross." In regard to the line of labor in which he was led, and the close rebukes he had to administer, William said, "Most of my work is rough; but rough work brings good pay, if it is well done."

In the Second month, 1768, William Hunt, at a Monthly Meeting held at Flushing, Long Island, having spoken largely to the states of Friends assembled, felt his mind clothed with a concern that slavery should be abolished. Toward the close of his testimony, after expressing his desire that all the poor oppressed African bondmen and women should be set at liberty, he said, " I verily believe the jubilee year is at hand, and I desire those that have slaves may not put it off for their children to set them at liberty; for we know not what our children may prove to be. I earnestly desire that none may put it off beyond the appointed time; for if they do, I am firmly of the mind they will be plagued, as sure as ever Egypt was for retaining Israel."

During the time that William Hunt was on his journey to the north he wrote the following letter, addressed to James and Ann Mitchell:

"SALEM, near Boston, 13th of Twelfth mo., 1767.

"DEARLY BELOVED FRIENDS, — Precious in the sight of the Lord is the fellowship of his children, and sweet their remembrance one of another, because the odor of his ointment sends forth a fragrant smell. This my joy is full in every remembrance of you, in that love which first gave birth to the covenant of life in our spirits, making them truly one, in the pure hope and feeling of Gospel power. In this we have had a near union and sympathy, with full assurance that the Lord Almighty hath called us out of darkness into the true light of his dear Son, through whom we have seen wonderful things and unutterable. We have likewise sorrowfully to behold the deluge of apostasy that covers our Sion, as with a thick cloud. But, dear Friends, in Goshen there is light, which makes the dwellings of Jacob beautiful, and the tents of Israel goodly. . . .

"This day, as I sat in meeting, a language passed through my mind, 'Hasten, hasten to visit my seed through the land, that thou may go where I send thee.' Whether this be to the grave, or to a distant land, I leave; — only petition the great Name to preserve me worthy to do all that he hath allotted me, so that I may be fit to be gathered home in due season.

"Dear youth, the affectionate feeling of my spirit

toward you I shall never forget, but often fervently desire that you may come into the house of the Lord, to behold the beauty of true holiness forever. I conclude with mine and companion's dear love, your often very poor, but true friend,   WILLIAM HUNT."

Some years before the Revolution, William Hunt had, in common with many other Friends, a deep and settled conviction that a time of trial and suffering was coming on America. On the 18th of Second month, 1770, being at a meeting at Centre, in South Carolina, he was earnestly engaged in exhorting those present to examine the foundation on which they were building before a time of trial came; adding, "The Lord will visit this land with his judgments, and then it will be known who hath built upon the sure foundation, and who hath not. In that time of deep trial, the hypocrites, formalists, and nominal Quakers will not only suffer, but many will perish and come to nought; while those who have built upon the sure Rock of Ages will be preserved by him in the midst of these trials, as it were in the hollow of his hand. There are many grown, and now within the audience of my voice, that shall see these times come."

In the testimony concerning Susanna Lightfoot we are informed, that at "divers meetings" previous to the breaking out of the American Revolution, she proclaimed, in an awful manner, that a stormy day was approaching — a day which would shake the foundations of men, and in which many of the formal professors in our Society would be blown away.

William Hunt was again on a religious visit in the northern provinces in 1770. He attended the Monthly Meeting of Philadelphia on the 26th of Fourth month in that year, and, during the sitting for discipline, said, "The man's part, the creaturely part, has no right to meddle with the business of the Monthly Meeting; neither can it do any good."

In the year 1771, William Hunt paid a religious visit to Friends in Great Britain and Ireland.

William Hunt and Thomas Thornburg, about the close of Seventh month, 1772, went to Holland, accompanied by Samuel Emlen and Morris Birkbeck. After visiting the Friends there, he embarked for Scarborough, but by stress of contrary winds, not being able to reach that place, he was landed at Shields on the 25th of the Eighth month. The next afternoon he went to the house of James King, near New Castle, where on the 28th he was taken ill. On the fourth day of his sickness the disorder appeared to be the small-pox, and William, addressing his companion, said, "This sickness is nigh unto death, if not quite." On Thomas Thornburg saying he hoped it might not be so, William continued, "My coming hither seems to me providential, and when I wait, I am enclosed, and see no farther." He said at one time, "One would wonder all the world does not seek after a quiet mind—it is such a treasure now." He was full of peace, and notwithstanding the distressing nature of his complaint he manifested no impatience—nothing but resignation to the Lord's will. In the fulness of contented faith he exclaimed, "It is enough; my Master is here." A Friend saying we might find cause of thankfulness in all our afflictions, he said, "Great cause indeed. I never saw it clearer. Oh the wisdom!—the wisdom and goodness—the mercy and kindness, has appeared to me wonderful; and the farther and deeper we go, the more we wonder. I have admired, since I was cast on this bed, that all the world does not seek after the enjoyment of Truth, it so far transcends all other things." Thus patiently he endured the disease that lay heavily upon him; being always hopeful, and sometimes rejoicing in hope, and making inward melody to the Lord. Just before his close he triumphantly exclaimed, "Friends, Truth reigns over all!"

Thus died William Hunt. He was of a meek and retiring spirit, yet was sharp in opposing error, and unbending in support of the Truth. He was an example of patient, silent waiting in meeting for the arising of life, and a skilful divider of the word, when the Lord called him to minister. To the babes in Christ, his doctrine dropped as the rain on the tender grass; to the self-willed and unfaithful, the backsliding and rebellious, the word in his mouth was as a two-edged sword. Although but in his thirty-ninth year, he stood as an elder in experience and stability, even as a father in the church, worthy of double honor.

SAMUEL EMLEN.

DURING the period of the American Revolution, and for many years after, a neatly built man of slender person, and a light, quick step, might have been often seen treading the streets of Philadelphia. His dress was generally of a drab color, and very neatly made. When the weather rendered an overcoat necessary, he wore one of a dark mixture, which he was wont to keep folded over his breast, by the pressure of his left arm. This man was Samuel Emlen. Sometimes, while passing along the street at his usual quick pace, he would suddenly fall into a slower motion, and his steps almost cease. On such occasions he would frequently turn into some neighboring dwelling; and soon — sometimes while still in the entry — commence ministering in Gospel power, and in the true spirit of prophetic discernment, to those within.

This man was considered the seer of that day. So remarkably was he at times favored with an insight into the character and condition of those he met with, that many who were conscious of secretly withstanding the operations of grace in their hearts, were afraid to meet him. Many instances are recorded of his quickness in detecting, and promptness in rebuking evil. A young man of a high, proud, self-sufficient spirit, has recorded in a letter, a short sermon preached to him by Samuel Emlen. His residence was near the northern line of Pennsylvania, but being in Philadelphia, he called at the counting-house of an elder of the Northern District Monthly Meeting, where he found this man of spiritual discernment sitting by himself. As he drew near, Samuel, whose eyesight was very defective, perhaps thinking he was some one with whom he was acquainted, thus addressed him : " Who art thou of lofty stature?" By the time these words were uttered, he was dipped into the state of the young man, and without waiting for an answer, continued his discourse, " An empty vine, thou bringest forth fruit unto thyself!" A few more sharp, pithy sentences, followed. Most emphatically true was this character, given by a man who from outward information knew him not. He brought forth fruit to himself, in a youth characterized by a headstrong following of his own inclinations; and he brought forth fruit unto himself, in a maturity of disgraceful servitude to the love of strong drink.

Samuel Emlen was born in Philadelphia, on the

fifteenth day of the First month, 1730. His parents, having themselves submitted to the restraints of religion — the cross of our Lord Jesus Christ — felt the obligation of endeavoring to preserve their children from evil. As ability was furnished them from above, they labored for the good of their offspring, seeking to bring them up in the nurture and admonition of the Lord. The temptations of Satan were presented to the mind of the youthful Samuel, and in measure obtained some hold there; yet, through the watchful care of his friends, and the preserving grace of the Most High, he was kept from gross evils. Very early in life he was acquainted with the visitations of the Holy Spirit, very early did he love inward communion with his Maker, and receive instruction in heavenly things.

He was blessed with excellent natural gifts. As a scholar he was apt, and especially in the acquisition of languages, being acquainted with Latin and Greek, besides several of the tongues spoken by the modern nations of Europe. He was thus qualified in after-life to address foreigners in their own language, when he was sent among them by the Bestower of all spiritual gifts, to preach in Gospel power the unsearchable riches of Christ.

After receiving his education, he was placed as an apprentice in the counting-house of James Pemberton, where he acquired a knowledge of mercantile business; but having a sufficient patrimonial estate, he never engaged in trade on his own account. Soon after he arrived at manhood, he accompanied Michael Lightfoot to the meetings of Friends in Virginia and North Carolina. In 1756, he paid his first visit to Europe, sailing in a vessel for Ireland, with Catharine Payton and Mary Peisley, who were returning from religious labor in America, and with his relative, Abraham Farrington, who was going to visit the churches in Great Britain. In Ireland he accompanied his cousin to many meetings, and while with him first spoke as a minister. He returned to America in 1758. It is needless, in this brief sketch, to trace his labors minutely; but we may say, that he subsequently visited England six times, in only two instances remaining over two years.

Samuel Emlen was of a cheerful temper, and having his memory stored with interesting anecdotes — which in conversation he freely brought forth — his society was very pleasant to young people.

Of the many anecdotes told of the spirit of discernment which characterized him, we may relate a few. A valuable Friend, a member of another Monthly Meeting, paying a visit to Philadelphia, brought his son with him. The young man, having heard that Samuel Emlen could see into the inward state and condition of those he was with, was particularly desirous of avoiding an interview, having, as he thought, sufficient reasons for not liking to be seen just as he was. The father attended the Northern District Meeting, to which Samuel Emlen belonged, and the son could not refuse to accompany him, although he felt no little fear at the prospect of being in the same house with this discerner of spirits. He kept, however, as far from the gallery as possible, and felt comforted at the close of the meeting, that he had so far escaped a public rebuke. But he soon found cause for fresh uneasiness; for Samuel Emlen kept close to his father, and said, when the latter accepted an invitation to dine with William Savery, "I will go along." Dinner passed sociably and pleasantly, and when the company afterward gathered into the parlor, the young man took the farthest corner of the room from the spot where the object of his dread had located himself. All his plannings, however, were in vain. Soon Samuel fell into silence, and the word of exhortation and reproof was put into his mouth. He addressed himself at once to the trembling youth, with such a soul-searching testimony as unveiled all that the latter most wished to be hidden. But there was consolation as well as rebuke in the testimony, and holy resolutions were awakened, which, through the Lord's assistance, were measurably kept.

SAMUEL EMLEN.

We have alluded to the dimness of outward vision of this extraordinarily gifted man. We have also spoken of his inward quickness of perception. The following anecdote shows that his inward sense was more to be depended on for direction than the outward sight of others.

A Friend, late a valuable elder in this city, when young in years, waited on a stranger somewhat advanced in life, to pay Samuel Emlen a visit. While sitting together, Samuel fell into silence, became religiously exercised, and soon began to preach powerfully to the state of some person young in years. There were but three persons in the room, and the youthful elder knew that the communication was fitted to neither of them. He became nervous and uneasy. He thought his spiritually gifted friend had for once made a mistake. At last, as Samuel continued his discourse, his uneasiness became so great he could no longer retain his seat. He arose and quietly approached the half-opened door to make his escape, when he perceived standing behind it, in the adjoining room, a young man weeping bitterly. Relieved of all his faithless fears, the elder returned to his seat with the substance of this text impressed on his mind: "The testimony of Jesus is the spirit of prophecy."

Samuel Emlen and his friend George Dillwyn often travelled together in great spiritual oneness, it being their lot many times in Europe as well as America to be led to the same meetings, and to labor in harmonious exercise. At one time, while they were sitting together in a meeting in London, in which George Dillwyn had been under great concern of mind, in a feeling that he was preparing for religious service, but knew not where it was to be performed, Samuel turned round to him and said, as if answering a question, "Thou must go with me to Holland." He who had been fitting George for the labor had prepared Samuel for a similar work, and unfolded to him the service to which they were called. The whole matter was now clear to both. They joined together, and, with the unity of their friends, visited the land whereto they were called, to their own peace and the edification of the gathered church and many other seeking minds there.

Samuel Emlen was sitting one day at a window in Burlington, which overlooked a tavern yard, where a number of persons were entering. The minister was too blind to see their countenances, but in the fresh putting forth of Gospel power, he commenced speaking, "I have a message to thee, O captain!" One of the company, who was a captain, gazed at the speaker with much earnest interest, astonished at such a salutation. Samuel immediately continued, "I have a message from God to thee, O captain!" Having thus drawn attention, the Gospel message flowed freely to the startled hearer. So effectually did it reach his state, that it was the means, in the hands of Providence, of opening his spiritual eyes to see the things belonging to his soul's peace, and from that time a change took place. He witnessed true repentance and amendment of life, and was himself concerned to call others to the Lord Jesus Christ, who had had mercy upon him.

His friends testify of Samuel Emlen, that he was a man fearing God and hating covetousness. He was no bigot, but he was a close reprover of those who, to shun the cross, were following the vain fashions, customs, and opinions of the world. He was often drawn to condemn the eager pursuit of riches, and yet he was constrained to encourage honest industry within the limitation of Truth. When engaged in the most lively conversation, he seemed ever on the watch for the openings of the Holy Spirit, and ever ready to drop a word in season. Although different in many respects, yet in fervent dedication he resembled our late dear friend, Sarah Cresson, who once observed, that when entering into company, she never was free to engage in general conversation until she had first felt inwardly to know whether her Master had anything for her to do there.

Samuel Emlen was a true comforter to those who were dedicating themselves to the Lord's work. His wisdom and his knowledge were great, and through Divine favor he seemed almost always furnished with a word in season for them. Job Scott very truly characterizes him in a letter to a Friend: "Mention, if thou pleasest, my love to my dear friend, Samuel Emlen. His kindness is heartily and thankfully acknowledged. I know he is a hearty lover of the blessed cause, and therein his reward will not fail him. Except that, I know no probability of his getting any. But that being almost his whole delight, I conclude he wants no other."

That honest elder, Increase Woodward, of Crosswicks, N. J., who deceased Sixth month 1st, 1822, in the eighty-first year of her age, has this passage in her diary: "Dear old Samuel Emlen, in his usual salutations, generally had something to say to the state of those he met with." She then says he told her one day, that her last days would be her best days. This she acknowledges had been verified at the time she wrote the account. It was also her happy experience to the end of her life, when she was enabled, in peace and faith, to yield up her spirit in the confidence of exchanging this earthly scene of trial for the joys of heaven.

In the year 1793, William Lewis, of Bristol, England, a serious seeker after righteousness, who had been led by the dispensations of Divine Providence, to feel and acknowledge the truth of many of the principles and testimonies of the Society of Friends, was brought under close exercise in reference to the adoption of plainness in his attire, manners, and language. Like many other individuals who dislike to bear the cross which a non-conformity with the customs of the world imposes, he found arguments against obedience. He gives an interesting account of the manner in which he was led to feel the importance of faithfulness in the maintenance of these testimonies. As respects using the plain language he says, "The very idea of a change in this particular, caused such a shrinking, and almost dread of mind, as induced an attempt to sift and prove groundless their arguments in proof of its being a genuine Christian testimony against that corruption in speech, which, as to the letter, I could not deny to be very evident, in that commonly adopted. . . . . The first passage that met, and arrested my attention, was the apostolic injunction to be in the use of 'sound speech that cannot be condemned.' This pressed and pinched in some degree at first, but I got from under its weight by reasoning after this manner. Sound! that is surely so, which, proceeding from a heart without rottenness and divested of all deceit, seeks not to leave a false impression on the minds of hearers. But 'hold fast the form of sound words,' came from the same authority, and appeared to inculcate that substantial rectitude of heart, with every other effect of the Light of Christ therein, should shine forth in its native garb before others, and that in the real possession of Truth *inwardly*, every appearance of evil must be abstained from *outwardly*. This, for a time, lay with more weight than the former; but at length, appeared to contain, in substance, nothing that added to its force. I came at last to the Lord's message unto his people through the prophet Malachi, charging them with such withholding, as was even robbery in his sight, and which was committed by keeping back 'tithes and offerings.' Reflecting upon this charge, and remembering that in these offerings, mint, anise, etc., were included, things as insignificant in themselves, when compared with the weighty matters of the law, as a form of sound words could be to substantial truth in the inward parts, and yet that Divine wisdom made them of such importance as to condemn those who refused compliance with what was enjoined respecting them, in the awful manner noticed, I began to fear — I say, *to fear* — that Friends were right; and that it was my duty, as an individual, to join them in testimony against the corruptions crept into modern language, and to go back to the primitive simplicity and plainness of speech. A sore exercise of mind now took place, and while under it, falling in company with a ministering Friend from America, a communication from his lips was a seal thereto."

This minister was Samuel Emlen; and of those assembled on the occasion William Lewis refers to, some had departed from and given up the testimonies of Friends. Samuel spoke to this import: "Robbery, robbery! it is a crime of no small magnitude with respect to things pertaining to men; how great then is its turpitude, when the rights of the Most High are invaded, and the creature holds back what is due to the Creator! Some of old were charged with this atrocity; they had the impudence to query, Wherein? but an answer was ready, 'In tithes and offerings.'" Samuel enlarged on the subject, and addressed a person present. At the close of his testimony he inquired who William Lewis was. On being informed, he addressed this short sermon to him: "Well, William! bring *all* the tithes into the store-house." This communication, in connection with his previous exercises, had a powerfully convincing effect on the listener's mind. He gave up to what he believed to be the Truth, and meekly bore the cross his Master laid upon him. After a time he was admitted into the Society of Friends, received a gift in the ministry, and walking in the Light, experienced sweet fellowship with the brethren, and the favor of his Divine Master, to the close of his life.

Well would it be if our members who are inconsistent in their attire, were brought to participate in that kind of feeling which troubled Thomas Ellwood, when he heard a persecutor of Friends say of him, because he wore a high black velvet cap, "Let him alone; don't meddle with him; he is no Quaker, I'll warrant you." This, he says, was worse to him than if they had beaten him as they did the Friends, and put him out of conceit of his cap. If those who profess to be Quakers, and yet do not conform to the testimonies of the Society, were blessed with a sound, discriminating judgment, they would not fail to perceive the incongruity of their conduct. People who are not members among Friends, have often a keen appreciation of what consistency requires. Robert Nesbitt, in 1791, while laboring in the Yearly Meeting of Philadelphia, told an anecdote to this effect. During the war of the American Revolution, a member of the Society of Friends was laid hold on by a body of soldiers, who told him that he must go with them to the war; in other words, join the army. His clothes were no index to a peaceable profession, or he would not have been disturbed. He told the soldiers, however, that he was a Quaker, and could not fight. "You a Quaker!" said they; "you have not got the marks of one." However, on his repeated assurance that he was a Quaker, and earnest solicitation to be released, they let him go, but not before they had cut off his hair, which he wore tied behind, his cross-pockets, and large fashionable buttons — thus in a smmmary way reducing him somewhat nearer to their idea of the true standard of Quaker plainness than he had before exhibited.

We have spoken of Samuel Emlen's knowledge of languages. On one occasion, in his public ministry of the Gospel, he addressed a learned audience in Latin; and during his travels on the continent of Europe, his French and German were frequently called into exercise. During one of his visits in England, a female in his presence, amused herself highly with his primitive dress and diminutive person. Speaking in French, she thought the object of her ridicule, though perhaps conscious that she was laughing at him, was yet ignorant of what she was saying. At last she closed her foolish remarks about him with, "I wonder if *it* can talk?" "Yes," said Samuel, turning his intelligent eye on her, "Yes, *it* can talk a little Latin, a little Greek, a little Hebrew, a little Spanish, a little German. Which of these wouldst thou like to converse in?" Samuel Emlen's reproof was felt by the poor girl, and in her confusion she was fain to betake herself to the quietness which became her. She was no doubt more careful in future in her speeches about others, and perhaps had a conviction impressed upon her mind, that simplicity in dress and manners was no proof of feeble intellect or limited knowledge. Those who are accustomed to speak their minds freely, had need to be very watchful, before they draw up the floodgates of restraint, and let out the pent-up stream of thought, opinion, and prejudice. Many an individual has unintentionally hurt the feelings of others, and many have brought on themselves severe rebukes for want of attending to this.

Samuel Emlen was fervent in his public ministrations. His voice was clear and harmonious, and his labors acceptable to Friends and others, being accompanied with baptizing power. His constitution was infirm, and his bodily afflictions often rendered travelling trying to him. But although very frequently unwell, he was yet generally able to be moving about, visiting the sick and afflicted, for which service he was remarkably qualified. He could enter into sympathy with them, he could console them with the precious promises of Him, whom he had found to be a faithful High Priest, touched with a feeling of our infirmities. During one of his visits in England, being very ill, he made use of this expression, which, while it manifested his humility, sets forth the ground on which his soul reposed: "Thanks be to the Lord, for the *hope* I have in his mercy!"

Many of Samuel Emlen's letters are very instructive and interesting, containing pithy passages worthy of preservation. Those composed during the latter years of his life were written by others at his dictation, because of his inability to see; yet he generally endeavored to sign his name to them. In one dated Seventh month 7th, 1794, addressed to his fellow-townswoman, Sarah Harrison, then in England on a religious visit, and to her companion, Sarah Birkbeck, is this passage: " My hope is that mercy and goodness will follow her [Sarah Harrison] for present comfort and support, and that at last she will be found, through adorable condescension, worthy to dwell in the house of the Lord our God forever and ever; — the prospect of which should be powerfully encouraging in a care to learn that exalted anthem, 'Thy will be done, O Father who art in heaven!' I wish dear Sarah Birkbeck preserved from sacrilege, — that she may not be a robber of churches as she goes along, but obedient to holy commandment, giving unto the people that they may eat, without improperly adverting to the quantity or quality of that which may be intrusted to her by the good Lord of the family."

Toward the close of his life, though his weakness of body increased, and his pains augmented, yet were his spiritual faculties in lively exercise, and his industry in the fulfilment of his religious duties, whether of a public or private nature, continued unabated. He had the assurance, he said, that he must shortly put off this earthly tabernacle, and he desired to be found at his post of duty, with his loins girded and his light burning.

In the year 1798, he first became affected with spasms in the arm and chest; these were believed to be of a gouty character. Attacks of this nature, although very violent while they lasted, were soon over, and did not confine him to his house many hours at a time. In the summer of 1799, while on a visit to his son Samuel, who resided near Burlington, he thought himself sensible of a slight paralysis. Its effects were quite transient; and on his return to Philadelphia, he resumed, at the promptings of love and duty, his visits of Christian benevolence.

In the Twelfth month of that year the gouty spasms became more frequent, yet he still ventured to meeting. On First-day, the 15th of that month, he attended his own meeting, (the Northern District,) and was engaged in earnest fervent labor in the ministry of the Gospel of life and salvation. As his service was about terminating, he felt himself suddenly taken very ill. He leaned against the rail of the gallery for support, not knowing but that his last hour was come; and then with much feeling he uttered the lines of Addison.

> "My life, if thou preservest my life,
>   Thy sacrifice shall be;
> And death, if death should be my doom,
>   Shall join my soul to thee."

The Friends assembled perceived that Samuel was ill, and the meeting closed. He was conveyed to a neighboring dwelling, where he soon partially recovered. The next day he attended the morning meeting of ministers and elders, and on Third-day was at his weekday meeting. At this meeting he was raised up in Gospel power and authority to set forth the excellency of that faith which is the saint's victory, and which is sufficient to overcome the world. This was the last public opportunity he had to advocate the cause of his Divine Master, which had been for nearly half a century so precious to him. His weakness and sufferings continued to increase, yet in the midst of his afflictions of body, he was cheerful in mind, and gladly received the visits of his friends.

Some of his beloved fellow-laborers in the Gospel of Christ Jesus being with him, he said: "Remember, 'Ye have not chosen me; but I have chosen you, and ordained you, that ye should go, and bring forth fruit, and that your fruit should remain.'"

The attributes of the Almighty seemed ever before him, and he frequently acknowledged, with thankful emotions, the rich consolation administered to his soul. These passages were uttered by him, in melodious tones: "Their sin and their iniquities will I remember no more." "I will cast all their sins behind my back.' "Ye shall have a song, as in the night, when a holy solemnity is kept; and gladness of heart, as when one goeth with a pipe to come into the mountain of the Lord." "Oh, the tears of holy joy which flow down my cheeks! Sing praises, high praises to my God! I feel nothing in my way. Although my conduct through life has not been in every respect as guarded as it might have been, yet the main bent of my mind has been to serve thee, O God, who art glorious in holiness, and fearful in praises! I am sure I have loved godliness and hated iniquity."

It was not until the day before his death that he confined himself to his chamber, and even on that day he sat up and enjoyed the conversation of his friends. He made mention of many absent ones who were dear to him, and expressed his fervent desires to the God of all grace for their preservation and growth in the Truth. He said he felt a portion of that love for them which was stronger than death.

Serene and peaceful, he seemed in a state of mind well befitting one about entering a happy immortality. In this condition he retired to rest, about ten o'clock in the evening, easy in body and in holy tranquillity of soul. He fell into a sweet sleep, which lasted about one hour, and was succeeded by a violent return of pain, which resisted all efforts at alleviation. After the physician had done all that seemed likely to be useful, without effect, Samuel desired that nothing more might be attempted, saying, "All I want is heaven; Lord, receive my spirit." "My pain is great. My God, grant me patience, humble, depending patience." "Call upon me in the day of trouble; I will deliver thee, and thou shalt glorify me." "Oh, how precious a thing it is to feel the Spirit itself bearing witness with our spirits that we are His." "Oh! this soul is an awful thing; I feel it so. You that hear me, mind, it is an awful thing to die: the invisible world, how awful!"

He now deemed that his end drew near, and desired that he might not be disturbed, except at his own request, "that my mind may not be diverted — that my whole mind may be centred in aspirations to the throne of Grace." Inquiring the hour, he was informed that it was about three o'clock; he then said, "The conflict will be over before five." He soon added, "Almighty Father, come quickly, if it be thy holy will, and receive my spirit." He now lay perfectly quiet awhile, and life seemed over; but a faint whisper was heard, "I thought I was gone!" "Christ Jesus, receive my spirit!" The end had now come! At half-past four o'clock on the morning of the 30th of Twelfth month, 1799, in a state of mind full of goodwill to man, and at peace with his God, he quietly departed.

How animating to the tribulated Christian is such a

close to such a life! All have not the same brightness of faith in the hour of death; but however the true follower of the Lord Jesus is led, his example may be useful to others. Some are cheered by tracing the deep poverty of spirit and exercise of mind in which some faithful ones tread the valley of the shadow of death, and some are animated at finding departing saints bursting out in thanksgiving, "Oh, blessed be God that ever I was born!"

JOHN CHURCHMAN.

JOHN CHURCHMAN was born in Chester County, Pennsylvania, on the 4th of Sixth month, 1705, and was tenderly brought up by religiously concerned parents, members of the Society of Friends.

He was a remarkable man. Visited by the Lord's Holy Spirit in very early age, tendered and contrited in meeting at eight years old, instructed and taught in many of the mysteries of the kingdom while yet a child, he grew up watchful and obedient to the direction of his heavenly Father and of his earthly parents. He gave, it is true, early evidence that sin had a root in him, which produced some fruit, which he mourned over and repented of. Of the visitation in his eighth year, he thus wrote: "I saw myself and what I had been doing, and what it was which had reproved me for evil, and was made, in the secret of my heart, to confess that childhood and youth, and the foolish actions and words to which they are propense, are truly vanity. Yet blessed forever be the name of the

Lord! in his infinite mercy and goodness, he clearly informed me, that if I would mind the discoveries of his pure light for the future, what I had done in the time of my ignorance he would wink at and forgive; and the stream of love which filled my heart with solid joy at that time, and lasted for several days, is beyond all expression."

Through various degrees of stability John grew up, and having given up his own will to the Divine will, he soon was made use of in the church militant. Being brought forth in the ministry, he had some sore conflicts of spirit, the enemy suggesting that the call to speak had not been powerful enough, and that in giving up thereto he had perhaps committed the sin against the Holy Ghost which would not be forgiven. Of this he says, "My exercise was great, but as I endeavored to be quiet in my mind, seeking to know the truth of my present condition, I was secretly drawn to attend to something that spake inwardly after this manner: 'If thou wast to take a lad, an entire stranger to thy language and business, however likely he appeared for service, thou must speak loud and distinctly to him, and perhaps with an accent or tone that might show thee to be in earnest, to engage his attention and point out the business; but thou wouldst expect it should be otherwise with a child brought up in thine house, who knew thy language, and with whom thou hadst been familiar. Thou wouldst expect him to wait by thee and watch thy motions, so as to be instructed by thine eye looking upon him, or pointing thy finger, and wouldst rebuke or correct such an one, if he did not obey thy will on such a small intelligent information.' I was instantly relieved thereby, believing it to be from the Spirit of Truth, that is to lead and guide into all truth."

John Churchman mentions in his journal a remarkable instance of obedience to Divine pointings in his ministry. He was at Flushing, on Long Island, where the Yearly Meeting was held. He says, "On First-day I thought I had an engagement to stand up, and considerable matter before me; and after speaking three or four sentences which came with weight, all closed up, and I stood still and silent for several minutes, and saw nothing more, not one word to speak. I perceived the eyes of most of the people were upon me, they, as well as myself, expecting more; but nothing further appearing, I sat down, I think I may say in reverent fear and humble resignation, when that remarkable sentence of Job was presented to my mind, 'Naked came I out of my mother's womb, and naked shall I return: the Lord gave, and the Lord hath taken away; blessed be the name of the Lord.' I suppose for nearly a quarter of an hour I remained in a silent quiet; but afterward let in great reasonings and fear lest I had not waited the right time to stand up, and so was suffered to fall into reproach; for the adversary, who is ever busy and unwearied in his attempts to devour, persuaded me to believe that the people would laugh me to scorn, and I might as well return home immediately and privately, as attempt any further visit on the island. After meeting I hid my inward exercise and distress as much as I could. I lodged that night with a sympathizing friend and experienced elder, who began to speak encouragingly to me; but I said to him, that I hoped he would not take it amiss if I desired him to forbear saying anything; for if he should say good things, I had no capacity to believe, and if otherwise, I could not then understand so as to be profitably corrected or instructed, and after some time I fell asleep. When I awoke, I remembered that the sentences I had delivered in the meeting, were truths which could not be wrested to the disadvantage of Friends, or dishonor of the cause of Truth, though they might look like roots or something to paraphrase upon; and although my standing some time silent before I sat down might occasion the people to think me a silly fellow, yet they had no cause to blame me for delivering words without sense or life. Thus I became very quiet, and not much depressed, and was favored with an humble resignation of mind, and a desire that the Lord would be pleased to magnify his own name and truth, and preserve me from bringing any reproach thereon. I ventured to have meetings appointed, and my particular friend and intimate acquaintance, Caleb Raper, of Burlington, being at that meeting, went as companion with me, of whose company I was glad, he being a valuable elder. We went first to Rockaway, then to Jamaica, Sequetague, Setawket, Matinicock, Cowneck, and Westbury meetings, and at most of them I had good satisfaction; the presence of the Lord in whom I delighted above all things, being witnessed to my comfort, and I believe to the edification of the sincere in heart; but the testimony of Truth was particularly sharp to the lukewarm professors and libertines in our Society. That humbling time I had at Flushing was of singular service to me, being thereby made willingly subject to the Divine openings of Truth, the motion of the eternal Spirit and pure Word of life, in speaking to the several states of those who were present in the meetings, and life came into dominion, and the power thereof overshadowed at times, to my humble admiration; blessed be the name of the Lord who is worthy forever and ever!"

How much better for the meeting, and the minister, that he should not rise to speak until he has something given him to say, and that he should not attempt to proceed when his Master withdraws his illumination and direction. Mistakes have sometimes been made by those who are rightly anointed for the work. Samuel Fothergill on one occasion, while laboring in the ministry, found the spring of life to stay, but did not immediately cease speaking. When the meeting was over, feeling that he had been wrong, and yet not quite clear wherein he had mistaken his way, he asked of that honest, clear-sighted mother in Israel, Sarah Taylor, what she had to say of his service that day. She told him that as he had spoken she had travelled in exercise with him up to a certain point in his discourse. "There," she said, "thou lost thy guide, thou thrust thy hands into thy own pockets and helped thyself!"

John Churchman was discouraged when young in the ministry by comparing himself with others, who he deemed were growing in religious attainments and in their gifts much faster than he. A dream related of Mary England may convey instruction. At the time she appeared in the ministry, eight or nine others at that meeting or neighborhood began to speak in meeting. These all appeared to Mary to be growing in their gifts, and were evidently branching out in their communications, while she found nothing required of her to deliver but a text or a few words. She became discouraged, and thought she was making little progress compared with the others. While in this state of mind, she was relieved from her depression by the following dream:

She thought she was in a room with the other young ministers, when a person of pleasing and superior appearance came in, gave each of them a stone pitcher, and bade them follow him. Glad to be near him, she at once arose, treading close after him along the path he trod, thinking the others were coming on behind. He led the way down a descent to a spring of water, the purest she had ever seen, and which might be compared to the pure river John saw issuing out of the throne. He told her to put her pitcher in the spring. She did so; and when it was filled, drew it out and set it on the ground. The water at once began bubbling over the top, and continued doing so until the pitcher was empty. Her guide then told her to put it in again. She did so, again withdrew it, and set it down, and once more the water flowed out. The command was several times repeated, and she perceived that the longer she allowed the pitcher to remain in the spring, the more water remained in the bottom of it after the bubbling out ceased. Her guide now told her to hold the pitcher in the water till *he bid* her take it out. She did so, and as it was some time before the command to withdraw it came, and both hands were requisite to hold it, she became almost overcome with fatigue. At last the word was given to lift it out. She set it down, and it remained full. Now she remembered that her director had never before bid her withdraw it. On looking round, she now noticed that not one of those who had been called when she was, had accompanied the guide to the spring.

Mary England was instructed by this dream to keep under exercise till the command was given to hand forth to the multitude. And she afterward felt, in her baptisms and exercises previous to engaging in the ministry, similar feelings of fatigue to that she had experienced when holding the pitcher in the spring, awaiting direction to withdraw it. The young speakers referred to, all branched out into words, and never became established as Gospel ministers.

Gospel love, while it takes all bitterness from the tongue, removes all flattery also. It ever tends to make the Christian give utterance to plain, honest truth, but clothes even his chiding with a feeling which gives evidence that he longs for the good of him reproved. Some people are so sensitive that a gentle hint will reach them, and powerfully stir their feelings. Others are so hardened in a continual round of wickedness, or so sunk in the lethargy of indifference, or so immersed in the spirit of the world, that to reach them requires a direct and sharp address — a " Thou art the man!" When John Churchman, in ministering to the people at North Wales, had, as he tells us, " with a zeal that exceeded my childish knowledge, laid on some strokes with the strength of the man's part, more than with the humbling power of Truth," he soon felt inward darkness and dejection of mind. He was enabled to see his error, and makes this remark, "If we deliver hard things to the people, we should ever remember that we are flesh and blood, and by nature subject to the same frailties. This would lead us closely to attend to the power, and to minister only in the ability of Truth, in the meekness, gentleness, and wisdom which it inspires." This reflection did not make him lower the standard of Truth, deliver its testimonies deceitfully, or tend in anywise to make him one of those who sew pillows under armholes. In a subsequent visit he thus wrote: "One meeting we were at was remarkably hard, and my companion was exceedingly exercised, under a sense that the people were too rich, full, and whole in their own eyes; but he sat the meeting through, and suffered in silence. I had something to say which was very close, and felt a degree of the strength and power of Truth to clear myself in an innocent and loving manner; and remembering they were brethren, I did not preach myself out of charity toward them, and so had peace. We went home with an elderly Friend, who, in a stern manner, asked me from whence I came, and said I was a stranger to him. I answered him with a cheerful boldness. He asked me what my calling was; I told him husbandry. He queried if I was used to splitting wood; I let him know

I had practised it for many years. He asked me if I knew the meaning of a common saying among those who were used to that business, "'T is soft knocks must enter hard blocks.' I told him I knew it well; but that to strike with a soft or gentle blow at a wedge in blocks of old wood that was rather decayed at heart, would drive it to the head without rending them, and the labor would be lost, when a few smart, lively strokes would burst them asunder. Whereupon he laid his hand on my shoulder, saying, 'Well, my lad, I perceive thou art born for a warrior, and I commend thee.' Thus we came off better than we expected; for I thought he pointed at my service that day. He was ever afterward very loving to me, and I was thankful that the Lord was near to me, for which I praise his sacred name. To be becomingly bold in the cause of Truth at times is particularly necessary, otherwise the weight of the testimony thereof would be lessened, and a carping spirit be set over it."

The following is narrated by John Churchman in his journal. He was told the anecdote by John Kilden, of Masham, Yorkshire, England. A knight in that county, calling to see one of his tenants who was a member of the Society of Friends, found him actively employed. After a time the landlord thus addressed the tenant:

"So, John, you are busy."

Tenant. Yes; my landlord loves to see his tenants busy.

Landlord. But, John, where were you, that you were not at your Quarterly Meeting at York the other day? I saw most of your staunch Friends there, but you I missed.

Tenant. Why, thou knowest I have a curious landlord, who loves to see his tenants thrive and pay their rent duly, and I had a good deal in hand that kept me at home.

Landlord. Keep you at home? You will neither thrive nor pay the better for neglecting your duty, John.

Tenant. I perceive my landlord was at Quarterly Meeting. How didst thou like it?

Landlord. Like it! I was at one meeting, and saw what made my heart ache.

Tenant. What was that?

Landlord. Why, the dress of your young folks; the men with wigs, and the young women with their finery, in imitation of fashions. I thought I would try another meeting; so next day I went again, and then I concluded there was little difference, but the bare name, between us whom you call *the world's people*, and some of you; for you are imitating us in the love and fashions of the world as fast as you can. So that

I said in my heart, these people do want a Fox, a Penn, and a Barclay among them.

John Churchman was faithful to his Divine Master, through his long life, and his blessed Saviour was very Faithfulness and Truth to him in the hour of his death, giving him a glorious close, and a certain foretaste of the joys in store for the righteous. Exemplary in youth, offering its bloom to his Divine Master — faithful in maturity, dedicating its ripening fruit to the Lord's praise — heavenly-minded in age, bringing all of his stores of wisdom and knowledge to the altar of God, John Churchman stood pre-eminent in his day. The Lord, whom he had served his life long, kept him green to old age, gave him large place in the esteem of the living in Israel, and amid all the exercises he caused him to bear for the sake of the church, sustained him in holy hope, in fervent faith, in cheerful resignation, even to a joyful putting off the shackles of mortality.

John Churchman, like many others of the Lord's deeply exercised servants, was cheerful in conversation, and spread a pleasant influence wherever his lot was cast. A happy turn for innocent pleasantry, circumscribed by an ever-watchful regard to the limitations of Truth, made his company agreeable to young and old, and enabled him to give instructive hints and seasonable admonitions to hearts ready to receive them.

Watchful and careful in youth, John Churchman

was appointed an elder when but twenty-six years old, and soon after received a gift in the ministry. Faithful to the gift, he grew in it — labored in the Gospel of his dear Lord in America and Europe; and having walked in great innocency and circumspection, and performed his day's work with acceptance to his Divine Master, he was not affrighted when death came to remove him from earthly comforts and hopes. As he grew weak, his spiritual exercises were continued to him — he felt stripped of good; but knowing that all this was to bring him more perfectly into the image of his Master, he was content to bear it, even until he could say, "I now experience my life and my will to be slain, and I have no will left." Then came his time of rejoicing. Light broke forth in his darkness — and in the midst of great pain, sweet melody sounded forth in his voice, and aspirations of praise went up from his soul to the Lord God of glory and grace. He knew that when relieved from the body, for him there was, through the Lord's goodness, nothing but peace; and that if then taken, he would be spared many deep trials which he saw coming on the faithful laborers remaining in the church militant. His close took place on Second-day, the 24th of Seventh month, 1775.*

* For a further account of this Friend, see Journal of John Churchman, in Friends' Library, vol. vi., p. 176.

REBECCA JONES.

AS Catharine Payton was entering one of Friends' meeting-houses in Philadelphia, in the Third month, 1755, a girl of fifteen or sixteen years of age slipped what appeared to be a letter into her hand. As at that time she could not examine it, she transferred it to her pocket, and took her seat in the gallery. When the meeting closed, the paper was opened, and proved to be a communication from one who was passing through much religious exercise. The writer was already convinced that she must bear the fire of the Lord in its inward burning until it should consume all the corruptions of her heart, that she might be prepared to feel true peace and spiritual enjoyment; for she expressed her conviction that she should only receive consolation as she was fit for it. No name was attached to this letter, and Catharine Payton, whose heart was dipped into sympathy with this unknown lamb, who was bleating for admittance into the fold of Grace, was at a loss to know where she should find her, and how she should recognize her. Tradition says she applied to her friend, Anthony Benezet, who, on reading the letter, and being asked if he could tell the author, answered, " I don't know—unless it be romping Beck Jones."

Rebecca Jones, to whom Anthony referred under the above characteristic title, was born in Philadelphia, Seventh month 8th, 1739. She received a good education, and her mother, who was zealously attached to the forms and doctrines of the Church of England, endeavored to bring her up in the same profession. But the child soon manifested a partiality to the meetings of Friends, which she often solicited permission to attend. Her mother frequently consented, thinking no harm would result to her daughter, who, she deemed, was too young to judge in matters of religion. Tradition says that sometimes Rebecca wandered at that early age into the meetings of ministers and elders, whose members did not think it needful to turn out such a child, who sat down quietly and made no disturbance. Although fond of sitting in silence in the meetings of Friends, Rebecca was yet a child full of animal spirits, whose earnestness in play won her the title in good old Anthony's mind of " Romping Beck."

As she grew older, to her mother's inquiry, what she went to Friends' meetings for, she replied, " I don't know; but I believe they are a good people, and I like their way; for there is not so much rising up and sitting down among them as at church." She says her mind was secretly drawn "toward this people, not only to go to their meetings, but I loved even the sight of an honest Friend. I was at times under the influence of another spirit; and though I loved the people, and very early discovered a beautiful order and becoming deportment in their meetings, I could not give up my days to lead such a life of self-denial as the Divine Instructor in my own breast at times plainly directed me to. I loved vanity and folly, and to keep unprofitable company, by which I was led into many evils, and quenched the blessed Spirit from time to time, yet not wholly; for oftentimes, in the midst of my career, I was favored with its secret smitings, and from which it was impossible to fly. Frequently when in bed, or alone, my heart was made uneasy for the multitude of my transgressions, so that I often promised to amend; for I greatly feared to die. But, alas, though I made covenant, I soon forgot it, and returned to the same things for which I had been reproved, and thus added sin to rebellion for some time, yet kept close to meetings, both First and week days, when I could get away without my mother's knowledge — though I knew not why I went; for I liked not their way of preaching, but was always best pleased with silent meetings.

"In the year 1754, and in the sixteenth year of my age, came from Worcestershire, in Old England, on a religious visit to the churches of Christ in America, Catharine Payton, in company with Mary Peisley from Ireland. I was at divers meetings in this city with the aforesaid Friend, and heard divers testimonies which she bore, with which I was much pleased; but like many others, I only heard, and sought not to learn the way to salvation in sincerity. But forever blessed and praised be the great Minister of all ministers, and Bishop of souls, who in his abundant compassion to a poor creature, in the very road that leads to the chambers of death, was graciously pleased through his handmaid to set my state and condition open before me, and enable her, in one of our First-day evening meetings, to speak so pertinently to my situation, in showing the consequence of trifling with Divine conviction, and proclaiming God's love through Christ to all returning sinners, that I cried out in the bitterness of my spirit, 'Lord, what wilt thou have me to do to be saved?' So effectually was my heart reached that I was made willing to forsake everything here, to obtain peace;—yea, my natural life would not have been too great an offering if it had been required—that I might have inherited eternal salvation."

"Oh, the many days of sorrow, and nights of deep distress, that I passed through! How frequently did I cry out, 'Lord, save me, or I perish!' I almost despaired of finding mercy;—for sin, not only appeared exceedingly sinful, but my soul's enemy almost persuaded [me] that my sins were of so deep a dye, and so often repeated, that I had neglected the day of my visitation, and that, though I might, like Esau, seek the blessing with tears, I should not obtain it. But forever magnified be the kindness and goodness of the Lord my God—the everlasting Father—He left me not here, though I was in the situation described by the prophet,—I was greatly polluted, lay wallowing in the filthiness of the flesh, without any succor from temporal connections, and a stranger to the Lord's family. 'Not washed at all, nor salted at all, but cast out as in an open field, void of any enclosure;—none eye pitied me, to do any of those things to me,' when the sure Helper passed by, beheld me in my deplorable condition, cast his mantle of Divine love over me, and with a most powerful voice said, Live! Yea, he said unto me, Live! I was again encouraged by the renewal of Divine favor to enter into solemn covenant with that gracious Being, whom I had so highly rebelled against, and so justly offended; and fervent were the breathings of my soul, that I might be enabled to stick close to the terms made in this, the day of my humiliation."

Such was the condition of mind of the young maiden, who was rightly judged by Anthony Benezet to have written the letter to Catharine Payton, before referred to. Catharine, on considering the matter, felt most easy to answer that communication, which she did, and gave what she wrote into the hands of Anthony to deliver. Rebecca Jones's mother had become very jealous of Friends, and very much opposed to her daughter's attending their meetings, and Anthony found it a matter of some difficulty to place the document in the young girl's hand.

In regard to her letter and this answer, Rebecca Jones writes: "My love to this instrument [C. P.] in the Lord's hands was very great, and on a certain time, being reduced very low in my mind, under the consideration of my many and deep transgressions, I took up my pen, and opened a little of my condition to her, though I was afraid to sign my name to it. I watched an opportunity and slipped it into her hand just as she was going into meeting, and in two days afterward I received, by the hands of one of her friends, the following answer, which, as it had a blessed effect in encouraging my mind reverently to confide in the Lord's infinite mercy, I here transcribe at large: peradventure it may revive the hope of some afflicted soul.

"'PHILADELPHIA, Fourth month 1, 1755.

"'DEAR CHILD, — I have carefully read over thy letter, and from a tenderness of spirit which I feel towards thee, conceive much hope that thou wilt do well if thou keep to that Power which has visited thee; which, as it has already appeared as a Light to convince thee of sin, will, if thou wilt suffer it, destroy it in thy heart. Which dispensation being already begun is the reason of that anguish of spirit which thou feelest, which will lessen gradually, as thou art assisted to overcome.

"'And be not too much discouraged, neither at what thou hast committed against the Lord, nor yet what thou mayst have to suffer for him; for though thy sins may have been as scarlet, he is able and willing to make thy heart as snow, upon thy sincere repentance and humble walking in his fear, and also to give thee strength to do whatsoever he commands thee. If thou art willing and obedient for the future, thou shalt eat the good of the land in the Lord's time; and as thou hast been already instructed that "thou shalt only receive consolation as thou art fit for it," wait patiently, and let the administration of condemnation be fully perfected; so shall the administration of light and peace be more clear and strong, which will assuredly come upon thee if thou abidest faithful to that Power which has visited thee. Thou desirest me to explain some portions of Scripture to thee which I had to mention, which I am willing to do as far as the mentioning of them respects thy state, which I believe was to bring forth the fruits of purity and love to God, which will be manifested only by thy obedience; and that thou may not rest in anything short of the knowledge of His power revealed in thy heart as a Refiner and Teacher, nor place thy happiness in anything short of his salvation.

"'I go out of town to-morrow, and not knowing thy name by thy letter, know not how to get to speak to thee, and have therefore committed the care of this to A. Benezet, who, I believe, will use his best endeavors to convey it to thee.

"'Farewell! and may the Lord continue to bless thee. I conclude, in much haste, thy sympathizing Friend, CATHARINE PAYTON.*

"'P. S.—I had rather thou kept this to thyself; and be sure be careful how thou tellest thy condition to such who have no knowledge of it.'

"On the receiving and reading this letter, my heart was melted into great tenderness before the Lord, and my mind encouraged to trust in his boundless mercy thus extended to a poor unworthy creature. My resolutions were daily strengthened in remembering that 'at what time soever the wicked turneth from his wickedness, and doth that which is lawful and right, he shall save his soul alive.'"

The case of Rebecca Jones is one among many in-

---

* A further account of Catharine Payton (afterward Phillips) may be seen in a memoir of her life published in Friends' Library, vol. xi. A journal of Mary Peisley (afterward Neale) will also be found in the same volume.

stances of young children, not members of the religious Society of Friends, who have been glad to attend their meetings. The case of Samuel W. Clark, of Rhode Island, will probably suggest itself to some of our readers. His parents were Baptists; but about his seventh or eighth year, at his particular request, they permitted him to sit with Friends in their meetings. After a time the members of the Monthly Meeting at Greenwich, at his request, granted him the privilege of attending those for discipline. This young lad ripened soon for heaven, being gathered by death in 1815, when only nine years old.

An anecdote is told of a little boy of about eight years of age, who was a pupil at a school in Pine Street in Philadelphia, the teacher of which attended Friends' meeting close by on Fourth-day, with his scholars. The mother of this child was a Moravian by education, who, having lost one of her children by death, was greatly affected therewith, and endeavored to find consolation in attending places of worship. She went to many, but did not obtain relief, and thought, in her religious exercises, she should find no one to sympathize, no body of professing Christians with whom she could unite. She was sitting one day in great distress, shedding many tears, when her little son entered the room. He went to her, took her by the hand, and began to weep aloud. No words passed to unfold to him the feelings of his mother. At last he asked what ailed her — what made her cry so much, adding, "I wish you would come to one of the meetings our school goes to; I am sure it would do you good." The child had found consolation there, and the mother, strongly stirred by the affectionate invitation, could not but accept it. She found that for which she had sought, doctrines which she could own — a people with whom she could unite. She is said to have been ever after a diligent attender of Friends' meeting, to have found consolation in earthly sorrow, and to have been enabled, through Divine Grace, to die in peace, full of faith and hope.

Rebecca Jones now attended meetings constantly, although she could not do it without much opposition from her mother, and was subjected to many very trying things in fulfilling this duty. She was, however, enabled to rejoice when meeting-day came; and even the evening before, her mind, she says, "seemed under the preparing power for the solemn performance of Divine worship, of the necessity whereof I was now truly convinced, as well as of my unfitness therefor without the daily influence of the blessed Spirit. The heart-tendering power of Truth in a very singular manner attended, insomuch that if I was not in the enjoyment thereof, my meeting seemed in vain."

"I frequently compared my situation about this

time with that of the children of solid Friends, many of whom I perceived walked widely from their holy profession. I thought if I had been favored with the like privileges many of them enjoyed, I had not had so much work for repentance. Oh, that they did but see and rightly understand the manifold obligations they are under to the everlasting Father, and also to their pious parents! Oh, the unspeakable advantage of an early education in virtue and the fear of the Lord! Certainly, in the great day of decision, it will but add to the weight in the scale against them, who pursue lying vanities, forsake their own mercies, and rebelliously turn their backs on the admonitions, counsel, and instruction of tender, pious, heart-aching parents. I esteemed myself as a branch broken off from the wild olive and grafted into the good olive-tree, and was secretly instructed that I stood by faith, and that the goodness of God would be toward me, while I continued in his fear — otherwise I should be cut off. I often fervently desired that those who had erred and strayed among the youth, whom I compared to the natural branches of the good olive-tree, might be grafted in again, for God is able to graft them in again. 'Be not high-minded, but fear,' was the solemn admonition frequently sounded in the ear of my soul."

We may often observe children of the family — the sons and daughters of faithful men and women, who have not truly profited by the privileges they have enjoyed. Some of them have run into evil courses, and lost, even among men of the world, their reputation and standing;—some, seeking for a less cross-bearing and more self-pleasing religion than that of their fathers, join some of the form-laden and ceremony-encumbered professions around them;—some retain their membership among Friends, yet give the energy of their minds to the acquisition of wealth, and demonstrate that they love the present world, and are not as pilgrims seeking for a better, that is an heavenly. In vain for these has been the holy example, the Christian discipline, the pious advice, the secret prayers and wrestling of soul of their parents on their behalf. While such are not prizing their privileges, we see some brought into our Society as from the highways and hedges, and made to sit among the princes of the people—raised up as from the very stones of the street to be, first, spiritual children, and then, as they advance in knowledge, to be fathers and mothers in the church. Yet the Lord's blessing continues to be to children's children of those that fear him; and he is still raising up and qualifying some of these to occupy the places of dignified and faithful ones, whom he has taken home to their eternal rest. It is heart-cheering to behold how, in divers instances, the blessing seems eminently to rest, from generation to generation, on the seed of the faithful. Some may deem that our Society has effected all the good it is capable of doing in the world, and be prepared to believe it will fall; some may think that to those brought in from other societies we must principally look for supporters of the primitive principles of Truth; — we cannot believe either. We look hopefully for a brighter day to come for our Zion, a day of spiritual grace and enlargement; and we firmly believe that the Lord will continue to bestow his gifts upon her children, from generation to generation.

Toward the close of the last century, an individual, called in from another profession, preached in one of the meetings of Friends in Philadelphia. When he had closed his communication, one of the ministering Friends present rose with these words of Isaiah: "Strangers shall stand and feed your flocks, and the sons of the alien shall be your ploughmen, and your vine-dressers." Instantly Samuel Emlen, who, though knowing the gathering mercy of God was toward all, yet felt his heart clothed with love to the children of the family, and warmed with a present assurance that the Lord's peculiar blessing was not to be taken from them, broke forth in an animated voice with the succeeding verse of the prophet, "But YE shall be named the priests of the Lord; men shall call YOU the ministers of our God."

Rebecca Jones, though suffering many things from former acquaintance, yet was strengthened to persevere, and her resolutions, she says, " were confirmed to serve the Lord, the little time that remained to me in this life, which I then often thought would not be long."

In 1756, Catharine Payton, with Mary Peisley and Samuel Fothergill, returned home to England. A new temptation of Satan now assailed Rebecca Jones — she began to feel indifferent about attending meetings. She was sorely tried with suggestions that her repentance had been vain, and that her sorrow was feigned, her tears insincere, and herself under a delusion. She says, "The Lord, my only Helper in this night of probation, saw meet in his wisdom for the trial of my faith to hide his face from me. Thus spoke the deceiver, 'Why art thou thus? Surely, if thou wert the visited of God, he would not have left thee thus poor, stripped, and helpless. Thou art not on the right foundation, for if the Lord had been at all with thee, he would have remained with thee forever.' Oh, the grief and distress of my poor soul! The Divine presence was withdrawn. I had no friend upon earth to speak to, nor any to whom I could make my complaint. Yet I was favored, under all, with strength to pray that I might be favored to see clearly whence this distress and doubting arose. Blessed forever be the God of my life, whom though I thought afar off, was near, and had only withdrawn as behind the curtain — He heard, and graciously answered me in the needful hour. I resolved if I perished to perish at his feet. Thus spoke my only Friend and Helper: 'I will thoroughly purge thy dross, and take away all thy tin!' My soul replied, 'Amen! so be it, blessed Lord!' Here I could feelingly say as did David, 'I know, O Lord! thy judgments are right, and that thou in faithfulness hast afflicted me.' Hope revived as an helmet of salvation. I saw mine accuser, and he fled! Oh, my soul, forget not thou the loving kindness of thy God, who thus graciously appeared for thy help, not only when the floods of the ungodly made thee afraid, but when in close combat with the Prince of the power of the air — the Lord's arm brought salvation, and his right arm got the victory!"

After her deliverance from the temptation of the enemy, Rebecca Jones found her love to the Lord's people renewed, and she says, "Through much difficulty and strong opposition I attended meetings both on First and week days, and should have rejoiced had I been worthy to sit at meetings of discipline — a privilege not yet granted me. I frequently went to Monthly and Quarterly Meetings, and stayed the first sitting, but withdrew when Friends entered on business. I knew I had no right to stay longer. Besides, in one of the Yearly Meetings for business, I was desired to withdraw by a Friend whom I afterward loved; and though I left the meeting under much distress, (being at the time very low in mind,) yet no hardness got in — blessed be the Lord! My love rather increased, not only to this mother in Israel, but to the whole flock; and I admired the care used to keep such meetings quite select, saw that it was necessary to do so, and never after attempted to stay until I was invited by some who, I thought, tenderly loved me, and were authorized to do it."

Rebecca Jones, we have stated, was born of parents in connection with the Church of England. She had, however, been an attender of the meetings of Friends from childhood, was of an exemplary character, and as she now manifested, by her life and conversation unity with the doctrines professed by them, she was invited to attend their meetings for discipline, although she made no application to be received into membership. At this time there were not many among the young in Philadelphia who had, by submitting to the cross of Christ and the powerful operations of the Holy Spirit, become qualified, and drawn to take part in the discipline of Society. The meetings felt the lack of such spirits. The elder and more experienced Friends are expected to give sentiments on important matters in such meetings, and sometimes, it may be, it is done from custom or to answer the expectation of others. Where there are young persons who, broken under the humbling power of Truth, are constrained to speak a word to matters under consideration, it is apt to affect solemnly and beneficially the minds of the hearers. The late Benjamin Kite, in one of his letters, speaking of meetings of discipline, says: "I often think that if some of our goodly young men were now and then to put a shoulder to the wheel, they would be of singular service. Oh, it is of good savor when words spoken to the discipline are not from habit, but necessity." It is true, young people are sometimes too zealous, and may put the hand too freely to the work; but in this, as in all other cases, true wisdom is profitable to direct. It is said that Samuel Bownas, perhaps toward the close of his time, when the holy zeal of some of those elders who succeeded George Fox had begun to grow somewhat slack, came to a meeting in which this was in some measure true. Among the young people a zeal had sprung up to revive the discipline, and perhaps they were too energetic and eager to move forward in the concern. After the meeting was over, some of these came round Samuel and complained that their elder members were too slothful and lukewarm in carrying out the discipline. "Ah! my young friends," he said, "it is well for you that there is some prudence in your elder friends, or you might set the house on fire!" Pretty soon, some of the more aged members complained to him of the forward activity of their younger brethren. Samuel, in answer, remarked, "It is well that there is some zeal in the younger members, or you might all go to sleep!"

At the time when Rebecca Jones was first admitted to sit in meetings of discipline, very little complaint could have been made because of the zeal of the young. She says, "And here I would mention the observation I made of some of our youth, after I was favored to sit in meetings of business. I frequently looked at them with love and tenderness; but I admired to see so little sense appear among them of the nature and design of such meetings. I found many attended through curiosity, and some from other motives, but very few whose shoulders were preparing for the burden and exercise that lay weightily on divers mothers in the family, who were far advanced in years, and, in all probability, would ere long finish their course. I mourned at the little prospect there was of a succession, and wished the spirit of Elijah might rest on Elisha. At these seasons I often felt an holy zeal to cover my spirit, and an engagement sometimes attended that the Lord's work might go on and prosper; but in that weak state I concluded that if the youth would not come up to the help of the Lord, (I mean children of believing parents,) the cause would drop; and was sometimes favored to understand the Lord's proclamation, 'I will work, and who shall let it?' Very frequently I was seized with an apprehension that if I was faithful to the manifestations of Divine Grace, the baptizing influences thereof would be witnessed for the cleansing, purifying, and preparing my spirit rightly to engage in the Lord's work; at which my heart trembled within me, and I greatly feared I should push forward Uzzah-like. And though in meetings, both for worship and discipline, my duty was often clearly pointed out to me, yet the fear of the Lord's work, a sense of my own weakness, the situation I was placed in in the world, the prospect of much suffering awaiting me, but, above all, a sense of the purity and stability necessary for those that fight the Lord's battles, and a sight of my own state and lonesome condition in the family — I say all these things mightily humbled me, and reduced me to the brink of the grave. I went alone; I kept silence; I refrained from my natural food, and my sleep departed from me; 'I was stricken of God and afflicted.' In this situation I attempted several times to break my mind to some Friends by writing, and to let them know how it was with me, but was always stopped from doing so; and once, when I went to the house of an honest-hearted, faithful servant of the Lord, with an intention to open my case to him, the ear of my soul was saluted with this prohibition, 'See thou do it not. The work is the Lord's.' My mind was fervent with the Lord (than whom none else knew my condition) that he would be pleased to favor me with the distinct sight and knowledge of his will, that I might not be deceived by the enemy of my soul — whom I had before seen in some of his artful transformations — but that light might so attend as that I might make no mistake in darkness. I carried my burden from one month to another and from meeting to meeting, until Seventh month 9th, 1758. In an evening meeting, finding no excuse would longer do, and that faithfulness was required, after William Rickett had finished a testimony, in which he expressed much sympathy and had great encouragement for some who were under preparation for the Lord's service, I stood up in great fear and trembling, and expressed a few sentences very brokenly, and returned home with the promised reward of peace, which I had long sought in vain; but now that I had given up to the Lord's will, [I] was favored to obtain it. This was my first public appearance; and I greatly desired, as a sign, that if I was yet mistaken, I might be visited and advised by some Friends; but as I met with no opposition from Friends, and, contrariwise, some spake encouragingly to me, I found need to watch self with a jealous eye, and was fervent in spirit, that I might be preserved in true humility and Divine fear, the only safe situation for a Gospel minister."

On Fifth month 12th, 1760, Anthony Morris informed the Second-day morning meeting of ministers and elders that the Monthly Meeting of Philadelphia had approved the public ministry of David Estaugh and Rebecca Jones. It was concluded to admit them to sit in the Second-day morning meeting, and Anthony Morris and Catharine Callender were appointed to inform them of it. Anthony and Catharine were most easy to give the information to Rebecca Jones in the presence of her mother. They accordingly did so. On hearing it the mother was much affected, and said, "Beck, your friends have placed you on a pedestal; take care you don't fall!" From that time Rebecca had no difficulties thrown in the way of her attending meetings. The mother's heart seemed to open toward her daughter; she became very affectionate, and treated all Friends who came to visit them with kindness and respect.

Rebecca Jones deemed herself very unworthy to sit in the meeting of ministers and elders, and she says she "attended the first meeting of that sort under strong apprehensions of my own weakness and the necessity of laboring after true humility."

She continues her narrative:

"In the spring of the year 1761, my dear mother began to decline very fast in her health, and could scarce keep about house. She grew weaker and weaker, insomuch that she needed constant attendance all the summer. I had a large school on my hands (the only means for our subsistence) to take care of, and her to nurse both night and day, till the Ninth month, when she grew so ill that I was obliged to break up the school. I also was much reduced in my health, and, by such constant exercise both of body and mind, received a weakness that I fear I shall never be rid of. She deceased near the end of the Ninth month, 1761. And here I seem free to add, that she was a woman of good natural understanding, of a noble disposition, had many good qualities, and lived a peaceable life among her neighbors, and I have good grounds to believe was under a religious exercise of mind for many months before her decease. She was favored with an easy passage, which she often in her illness prayed for as a sign of acceptance with the Lord, and was buried in the burial ground of the Church of England, (so called,) among whom she always made profession. In her illness she desired to see Daniel Stanton; he came, and had a heart-tendering time in supplication, particularly on her account, (whom he had known from a young woman,) that she might be favored with patience, and might obtain mercy with the Lord. After which she seemed easy, and said he was a servant of the living God."

After the decease of her mother, Rebecca Jones began seriously to consider whether it would be best for her to continue keeping school for a livelihood, or whether she should make a change. She says, "But as our Yearly Meeting was coming on, [I] concluded to leave it till that was over; and in waiting to know what was best, I seemed most easy to continue in the same way, as being what I was most used to; and a suitable Friend offering, made it easy — Hannah Cathrall, a religious, prudent young woman, who joined me in the business. I esteemed this a favor from kind Providence, for I was now grown so weakly, I could not have attempted to have undertaken it alone, and she [was] of an affectionate disposition to me. We soon had a large school, and were blest with a sufficiency to live comfortably. I had been very little abroad; not only because I was confined by my business, but was at times under great discouragement in my own mind on account of my weakness, both of body and mind; but whenever my aforesaid companion apprehended me under any engagement of that sort, she always encouraged me, and did all in her power to make things as easy as she could; for which I feel grateful acknowledgments and esteem for her. In 1762 I went, in company with E. Smith, of Burlington, and some other Friends, to the general meeting held at Shrewsbury; and after that, at different times, with Esther White, Mary Evans, Hannah Harris, etc., several little turns, to some Quarterly, Monthly, and particular Meetings, within the compass of our Yearly Meeting.

"In 1769, I found a draught of love in my mind toward the Yearly Meeting of Long Island, and obtained leave of our Second-day morning meeting of ministers and elders. I made preparation, and was in readiness; but when the time came, my mind was so beclouded and distressed, that I was glad to give it up. The cause afterward appeared very plain to me, and I was made thankful for the secret intelligence afforded from on high.

"In 1770, the engagement for that meeting was renewed, and my Friend Hannah Foster, of Evesham, having sent me word she intended [to be] there, I gave up, and though much discouraged, being poorly in my health, and not used to ride on horseback, yet was favored to hold it pretty well as far as Rahway, where my kind friends Joseph Shotwell and wife provided a chair for my accommodation, and went with us to Flushing. I was much assisted in this journey, or I could not have held out, for I was not only indisposed in body, but my mind was very low, insomuch that I apprehended I should not live to return, and accordingly settled my outward affairs, and took a very solemn leave of my dear companion, who was also fearful on my account. However, the Lord was near, blessed be his Name, and made the weak strong. We were mutually comforted together at that meeting; and I returned home better every way; for which I bow before the Almighty, and acknowledge nothing is impossible with him; praised and magnified be his great Name, both now and forever!

"Soon after my return, my mind was bowed very low by reason that a beloved friend and father in the Truth, Daniel Stanton, was taken from works to rewards. He had been eminently favored in his public appearances for many months before, insomuch that many Friends were apprehensive of what he sometimes expressed, 'that he thought he had not many days longer to labor among us.' This was a great stripping to the church, a near trial to many individuals, and the loss not likely to be soon made up. Such was the prospect of things among us; yet there were still left some honest laborers, and a remnant clothed with the same spirit of true zeal, which was the covering of this great and good man, who deceased the 28th of Sixth month, 1770, in the sixty-second year of his age, and had disinterestedly labored among us upward of forty years, approving himself called of God, a workman that needed not to be ashamed, rightly dividing the Word to every class in the family. 'Precious in the sight of the Lord is the death of his saints.'" *

---

* A journal of the life and Gospel labors of this faithful minister of Jesus Christ is published in Friends' Library, vol. xii.

Rebecca Jones endeavored faithfully o fulfil her varied duties as an instructor of children, and as a minister of the Gospel of Christ. Yet she was not forward to move in her religious exercises; and her friends sometimes thought that, through discouragement, she tarried more at home than was best. Young ministers are often exercised not to be in the way of those of elder years and more religious experience; and the exercise is doubtless right; yet, carried too far, this feeling sometimes prevents their moving in the order of Divine appointment, and hurts the service of the meeting.

In the spring of 1784, R. Jones, Samuel Emlen, Thomas Ross, George Dillwyn, and Mehetabel Jenkins, were all prepared with certificates of the unity of their Friends to go to England on a religious visit. They were anxious to reach London in time for the Yearly Meeting held there, toward the close of the Fifth month. Report says, that on considering in what ship they should take their passage, most of them were inclined to go in a new one then about to sail. They, however, went in a body and sat down in it; when Samuel Emlen almost immediately intimated that that ship would not do. They then repaired to the ship Commerce, commanded by Thomas Truxton, and on sitting down in her, Samuel almost as quickly expressed his conviction that that was the ship they must go in. They took their passage. When Truxton found they were going with him, concluding that no gaming could be allowed in the ship while they were on board, he took a pack of cards which he had, and dashing them down the hold of his vessel, bid them "lie there in death and darkness."

They sailed towards the latter part of the Fourth month, and Truxton learning their wish to attend London Yearly Meeting, informed them that it was not to be hoped for, as his vessel was a dull sailer.

One day on their passage, Rebecca Jones sat with George Dillwyn, who appeared to be in deep inward thoughtfulness. After a time he asked her if she could keep a secret; she replied, that her Master had at times communicated his secrets to her, and that she had not revealed them without his permission — and she thought she could keep the secrets of another. "Well," he then added, "I have one to tell thee: We shall see England this day two weeks." On the same day being seated by Thomas Ross, he turned to her and said, "Rebecca, canst thou keep a secret?" She answered him in the same words she had used to George; and Thomas then added, "we shall see England this day two weeks." That morning two weeks Rebecca rose early, and found that George was up before her, and had climbed to the round-top. Soon he shouted out "Land!" which brought the mate to his side, who not being able to see any, found fault with him. After a little space George cried "Land" again, and Truxton, who was then on the quarter-deck, mounted the rigging as his mate had done before, and nothing being visible, he also remonstrated with George for giving a false alarm. To this the self-appointed lookout man, as if secure in the consciousness of being right, paid no regard. Soon, in stentorian voice, George cried out, "Land! and breakers ahead!" Now, other eyes could see breakers near at hand, and the ship was safely put about. The captain afterwards declared, that if George had not been able to see what they could not, they would have been on the rocks and suffered shipwreck. England was soon plainly visible. The ship had made an uncommonly quick passage for her, and the passengers were able to reach London in time for the Yearly Meeting. The new ship referred to did not arrive until some time after.

Captain Truxton was much pleased with his passengers, and had acquired a very high estimate of them, particularly of Rebecca Jones. An anecdote is related strongly illustrating this. On his arrival, he had some contention with one of the public officers connected with the customs, who, in a pompous manner, during the dispute, frequently made use of the phrase, "Wisdom of Parliament." Truxton, losing his patience, exclaimed, "Wisdom of Parliament! Why I have a Quaker lady on board my ship who has more wisdom in her little finger than you have in all your Parliament put together!"

When the Friends reached London, they found that the women Friends who had collected there to the Yearly Meeting of ministers and elders, were under concern and exercise that a Yearly Meeting of business for those of their own sex should be established. In the year 1753 or '54, a proposition was first made in the men's Yearly Meeting for the establishment of a similarly organized meeting for women Friends. At that time Samuel Fothergill rose and said, "I see it, but not now; I behold it, but not immediately nigh." In the year 1783 it was revived; but the meeting was even then not prepared to adopt the measure. One of the men who opposed it declared, in the Yearly Meeting, that a body with two heads would be a monster. On which a woman Friend remarked that though a body with two heads might be a monster, she could see nothing incongruous in a body with one head having two hands. William Matthews, from America, had a deep concern in his mind for the establishment of this meeting, and he visited the women collected in London to spread it before them. They also were under the concern, and thought it would be right again to lay the matter before the men's Yearly Meeting. Esther Tuke, Elizabeth Robinson, Rebecca Jones, and nine others were selected to go on this important embassy. The women were admitted, and Joseph Gurney Bevan, observing the noble figure of Esther Tuke as the delegation entered the men's apartment, had this passage of Scripture instantly and forcibly brought to his remembrance: "What is thy petition, Queen Esther? and it shall be granted thee: and what is thy request? and it shall be performed, even to the half of the kingdom." When her request was made known, the current of true unity therewith was so strong that all opposition was borne down, although some difficulties were raised by a few. A Yearly Meeting for women Friends was established. Its first session was in 1785.

Rebecca Jones, in her travels through England, was often much discouraged at the low state of things in our religious society there. Her letters bear testimony to this.

"Seventh month 1st, Norwich. The Quarterly and Yearly Meeting here ended yesterday. William Matthews and Elizabeth Gibson, with divers others from a distance, attended. Though in many instances there is abundant cause of lamentation and mourning, yet the precious visitation of Divine love was remarkably extended to the young people, many of whom were bowed under it. . . . Upon the whole, it may be said with thankfulness, there is yet a solid number in this place who are, under the present low state of things, much depressed. Among them are, particularly, worthy Edmund Gurney and his sister Mary. He has not gone into the gallery once during the meeting, but sat low, and appears so, both body and mind. Much plain dealing has been used in public and select meetings for the help of 'the men who are settled on their lees.' I trust the servants are clear."

In this same letter she says that the young people at Norwich and London, had widely departed from the primitive standard of plainness.

Rebecca Jones returned to her own country in 1788. In the Yearly Meeting of Philadelphia, in 1792, Rebecca was earnestly engaged in pressing on old and young the necessity of weightiness of spirit in religious meetings. In the course of her remarks she said, that if members were truly weighty in spirit during the time of the meeting, they would not exhibit the lightness which is so much apparent in some before they are out of the house, and round about it. The solemnity on the countenances of Friends would indicate that they had been with Him whom they met professedly to worship, and in meekness and humility they would feel and show themselves to be his humble servants.

How little is known by many of that state of true introversion, in which the mind being drawn from outward things, is properly prepared to understand the motions of the spirit, and through the fresh aspirations thereof, effectually to cry "Abba, Father!" Instead of waiting upon God in earnest desire to draw near him in spirit, many in religious assemblies let their minds out in consideration of their business or their pleasures. How common is this sin! A Friend of Philadelphia, who was by profession a tanner, once dreamed that he was sitting in a religious meeting, wherein he was surprised to observe the congregation with tables before them, at which they were pursuing their usual avocations. The merchant had his books there, the retailer his goods, the mechanic his tools. Indignant at such employment, among those professedly assembled for the awful and soul-important purpose of Divine worship, he was about rising to reprove them sharply, when, incidentally placing his hands behind him, he found a bundle of calf-skins suspended from his own shoulders! How much easier it is to discover the errors of others than our own, and how often we richly deserve the very condemnation we mete out to our neighbors. The wilful indulgence of wandering thoughts in meeting, is sin, and it will be felt to have been so, whenever the soul comes really and truly under a concern to be saved. Perhaps there are few things which have a greater tendency to encourage such unsettlement of mind, such dwelling on outward things, than a lifeless, formal ministry. A true Gospel minister, when clothed with the baptizing power, and called to labor in word and doctrine, is often enabled to awaken the sleepy spirit, recall the wandering thought, and to bring many, at least, to a transient sense of the awful importance of working out their soul's salvation with fear and trembling. A lifeless discourse, on the contrary, often disturbs the true seeker after good, turns the thoughts of the weak and unstable outward, and it is to be feared, the hearers, finding no spiritual nourishment, sometimes willingly encourage thoughts of their business to pass away their time. A ship-carpenter, not a thoroughly religious man, but an acute observer of men and things, once characterizing the ministry of two individuals, remarked, that under one of them he could build a ship from stem to stern, but under the other he could not lay a single plank.

In the Tenth month, 1793, Rebecca Jones was seized with the yellow fever, which at that time was raging to a fearful extent in Philadelphia. On the 23d, Thomas Scattergood, calling to see her, found her scarcely able to speak through extreme suffering. On the 24th he says, "Dear Rebecca Jones appeared under much discouragement respecting getting about again, but was in a heavenly frame of mind and glad to see me, telling me that I felt like bone of her bone.

On my telling her that I had not seen but that she might be raised up to bear testimony to the Lord's goodness and Truth, she replied, 'I am a poor atom, unworthy to be employed in the Lord's work. Dear Thomas, many have fled from the Truth, but the Lord will meet with them. I have been an exercised woman for thirty years past, and often grieved to see the pride and forgetfulness of many in our Society, the multiplying of pleasure-carriages, formal visiting, etc.' At another time, when with her, she said, 'There is another dispensation in store for this people, depend upon it,' repeating it more than once, 'if the people are not humbled by the present.'"

Those who are acquainted with the state of things in Philadelphia for the next few years, will know how fully this prediction of Rebecca Jones was verified. On the 25th, Thomas Scattergood in the morning again called to see his sick friend, and was distressed to find her so low as to take no notice of him. About noon she was somewhat revived, and told him she had seen him in the morning, but was unable to speak to him. She added, "I am in waiting; there is nothing to do." Before narrating what further took place on this occasion, we may say that Thomas Scattergood had long been wading under heavy exercise, in a prospect that it was required of him by his Divine Master to pay a religious visit to England. He had told no one of his concern, although he now deemed the time for laying the subject before his friends drew near. But although Thomas had not opened his prospect, the Lord himself had unfolded it to Rebecca Jones, bringing her into heartfelt sympathy with his poor servant, whom he was anointing to send forth in his name. Rebecca, as she lay, was too weak to do much more than look round with love and sweetness on her friend. At last she said, "Go, and the Lord go with thee." Later in the day, Thomas being there again, she said, "Dear Thomas, if the Master renews thy commission, and should send thee over the water, mind the time; do not deal it out to individuals, but spread it before thy Friends, and thou wilt find sympathizers. When thou gets there, remember the poor servants in families; they are too often neglected. The Lord dealt bountifully with me in that land, and I have had comfortable seasons with such." Thomas then asked what she meant by her address to him when previously with her? She answered, "I could not tell thee before J. J., though I love him, but I alluded to thy going over the great waters. The Lord has in some instances intrusted me with his secrets, and I have not betrayed them." This conversation proved very consoling to Thomas Scattergood, confirming his faith that it was indeed the Lord who was calling him to labor in a distant part of his vineyard.

Such secret sympathy with others and inward participation in their thought and exercise are not always confined to those in advanced years. The late Daniel Haviland, feeling drawn to attend a meeting not very distant from his residence, took his daughter Hannah, then quite young, with him. Soon after the meeting was gathered, she seemed to enter into sympathy with her father, thought it would be right for him to appear in the ministry, and saw clearly the text he should speak on. After a time her father arose, and, to the great comfort of the child, commenced with the passage of Scripture that had impressed her mind. As he spoke, she was enabled to follow him in great unity of feeling for some time. At last he reached a point at which the opening on her mind closed, and she thought he ought to stop. He did not, however, cease speaking, but, to her great distress, continued his discourse. When the meeting was over, they went home with a Friend to dine. After dinner, Daniel took his pipe, and got into a corner by himself, apparently uneasy and desirous of avoiding observation. On their ride homeward, the little girl asked her father how he felt; but as this did not lead him to unburden his feelings to her, she told him honestly how it had been with her. As she described how her mind had been impressed in the early part of the meeting, how she had travelled on with him as he had ministered, where she thought he ought to have stopped, and her distress at his proceeding, he became deeply affected, saw clearly the mistake he had made, and exclaimed to his child, "My dear daughter, 'flesh and blood hath not revealed this unto thee, but my Father which is in heaven.'"

Soon after the return of John Fothergill from his last visit to America, he went to the Quarterly Meeting at York, which was large, and attended by many Friends from different parts of the nation. His company was very acceptable; and the occasion was, in a peculiar degree, solemn and instructive.

Here he met his son Samuel. Tradition has handed down (and there is no other record of it) a remarkable circumstance connected with this, their first interview, after the return of the father to England. It is said that, from some accidental circumstance, John Fothergill did not arrive in York until the morning of the day of the meeting, and that it was late when he entered the meeting-house: after a short period of silence he stood up and appeared in testimony; but after he had proceeded a short time, he stopped, and informed the meeting that his way was closed; that what he had before him was taken away, and was, he believed, given to another. He resumed his seat, and another Friend immediately rose, and taking up the subject, enlarged upon it in a weighty and impressive testimony, delivered with great power. It is added, that at the close of the meeting John Fothergill inquired who the Friend was that had been so remarkably engaged amongst them, and was informed that it was his own son *Samuel!*

Their thus meeting together, under circumstances so different to those in which their last memorable interview had taken place, previous to John Fothergill's departure from England, was peculiarly moving and affecting to them both. The good old man received his son as one restored from the spiritually dead, and wept and rejoiced over him with no common joy.

Our late worthy ministering Friend William Williams, in his religious labors in the State of Delaware, appointed a public meeting, to which came the Governor of the State and many other persons of eminence. The subject that opened on the mind of William, was the unlawfulness of war. He felt tried to be called on to speak on that subject, fearing his inability to do it justice, and for a long time thought he could not give up to the requiring. At last, however, trusting to Him who is might and wisdom, tongue and utterance to his dependent children, he stood up, and the Lord was pleased to favor him eminently that day, in matter and manner. After the meeting was over, as William was sitting on the porch of a Friend's house, Solomon Bayley, a pious colored man, came near. The owner of the dwelling, who knew and respected Solomon, invited him to walk in. He declined doing it, but said he wished to speak to the Friend. Addressing William, he said, "Thy Master commanded thee to preach; but thou wert afraid; but when thou submitted, He brought thee off victorious." This touched William's feelings deeply; he felt this colored man's participation with him in his exercise of spirit, as a token of the Lord's mercy, and he was thereby quickened to endeavor after a livelier and more unshaken faith.

How low and humble the condition of mind in which Rebecca Jones was kept by her Divine Master! Often the true minister of the Gospel must go mourning in the tribulated path of obedience; and we may receive it as a certain truth, that those who know not inward conflicts and fiery baptisms, are not walking in the favor of the Lord, nor advancing toward that city where sorrow is unknown. That wise woman and sound minister Sarah Harrison, wrote thus in 1796 from England: "When I last met with Nicholas Waln at York, he was in a very tried state, not having opened his mouth in testimony since he left Ireland, nor for some time before. Poor man! he has to travail in the deeps; and I wish with all my heart, that it was the case with *some* others. Then I believe the *grace* would be more magnified, and the *creature* less gratified both in visitors and visited."

Sarah Grubb says in one of her letters, "I remember to have heard that Samuel Fothergill, in the last journey he took, was often so exceedingly stripped and tried, particularly after his public appearances, that the unity or approbation of the least child in the family would have revived him; [this] led him to acknowledge he was never more weak, and apt to doubt the rectitude of his ministry; [yet] a Friend of much religious worth and spiritual discernment, who was often with him, told me that it was never more pure and baptizing."

Thomas Cash had a saying to this purport, "We cannot think too lowly of ourselves, if we do not despair." This doctrine was beautifully and very characteristically set forth by our simile-loving Friend, James Simpson: "Friends, be as little as the snow-birds, and then the Devil can't hit you."

A young Friend of Philadelphia, who was passing through great exercises of mind, was much depressed. He felt as though he were of no value or importance to any one; in short, that no man cared for his soul. While in this condition, feeling his mind drawn to call upon that honorable elder William Wilson, he went in fear, thinking it almost presumption in him to venture to intrude on a father in the Truth. When he was introduced into the room where the worthy old Friend sat, he was cordially received and greeted with a salutation in substance as follows: "I take it very kind indeed of thee, to call and see an old man who did not know that there was anybody in the world thought him worth coming to visit. It is very kind indeed!" This unexpected reception immediately afforded relief to the disconsolate youth, and they were comforted together. "He that watereth shall be watered also himself."

Rebecca Jones sometimes preached very short sermons. The following note from Richard Baker, that valuable minister of Dover, England, inserted in a letter from Thomas Scattergood, gives us one of them. "Richard Baker desires his very dear love to be remembered to Rebecca Jones, who frequently has revived in his remembrance profitably, and wishes her to be informed, for her encouragement, to attend to impressions that may sometimes appear small; that the single sentence she delivered to him in a street has been made more profitable to him than some whole volumes he has read, which was this: 'Blessed are they that mourn, for they shall be comforted.'"

In the meeting at which Robert Barclay was convinced of Friends' principles, we are told that but three sentences were spoken, viz.: "In stillness there is fulness. In fulness there is nothingness. In nothingness all things." Our late pithy friend, Samuel Atkinson, of Rancocas, New Jersey, once delivered the following short, thought-awakening discourse: "Shepherds and shepherdesses, take care of the lambs; wolves are very hungry in snow-time." At another time he uttered this short text, and still shorter comment: "'Put off the old man with his deeds.' A long job for some of us!"

In the summer of 1799, Rebecca Jones, with Jane Snowdon for a companion, visited Friends in New England. She writes from Nantucket, under date of Seventh month 10th, that she and her companions, seven in all, were then waiting for a fair wind to take them to New Bedford, which, according to a received opinion among Friends there, would remain ahead as long *as anything further was to be done.*

The reference above made to the prevalent idea at Nantucket, that the wind will not become fair for ministers to leave that island until they have performed all the service required of them there by their Divine Master, recalls to mind an anecdote, in which a horse refused to go into a boat to leave a place where his mistress had not discharged her duty. The account was given by a ministering Friend, the late Samuel Gummere, who said he received it from the mouth of the female minister herself. About the time of the last war with England, the Friend, having a concern to visit Canada, passed there in a sloop which plied regularly as a ferry-boat. The horse of her companion being led on board, her horse, to the surprise of the witnesses, followed of its own accord. When her labor in those parts was nearly completed, she felt a concern arise in her mind to have a religious meeting with the inhabitants of Kingston. But it was court time, many military officers and great men were there, and her faith failed her. Jonah-like, she took her passage, intending to cross the lake, and thus escape drinking this bitter cup. The sloop in which she had come to Canada was to convey her back, and the man who had led her companion's horse into it on the American side, now did it again, expecting to see her horse follow. But the animal showed no disposition to stir. Efforts were then made to lead him on board, but he stoutly resisted; and, after many vain attempts, the tackle of the vessel had to be employed, whereby he was fairly hoisted in. This difficulty over, they started with a fair wind, and the captain said he thought they might reach their port in half an hour. But presently the wind arose boisterous and contrary, and the vessel beat about for some time, but made no progress. The poor deserter from duty felt like Jonah indeed, and was now willing, could she return to Canada, to perform her Master's bidding. She desired the captain to put her back; but he told her it was impossible, with that wind and such weather, to reach the place he had left. There was a point of land on the Canada side not very distant which he could make, but it was one of the English military posts. At her request, the captain hailed the sentinel, and inquired if a passenger might be landed there. The sentinel replied he dared not permit it under pain of death. The woman Friend, recollecting she had been born a subject of the king of England, and had never forfeited her allegiance, desired the captain to inquire if there was any officer at the post. An officer was called, who granted her permission, as "one of his majesty's subjects," to land. The landing was effected after they had been tossing from eight o'clock to twelve on the water. Being now again on shore, the woman Friend was prompt to take the necessary steps to enable her to fulfil her apprehended duty. She applied to an English naval officer, stating her desire of having a meeting with the inhabitants of Kingston. He readily offered his services in procuring a suitable place, and endeavored to obtain the Episcopal meeting-house for that purpose. The clergyman was, however, from home, and it was said the key could not be found. In the mean time, the Chief Justice, hearing of the Friend's concern, procured a large ball-room, and had it fitted with benches. The meeting was held that very evening, and, it was thought, three thousand persons were present. When the meeting closed, the Chief Justice sent to the Friend's lodging to inquire if he might pay her a visit. On her assent being given, he came. In the course of his conversation he informed her that he had tried being a Roman Catholic, an Episcopalian, and a Presbyterian, and now he found he had all to learn yet. He said he had heretofore been harsh towards Friends who had been brought before him for not obeying military requisitions, because he had believed their refusal proceeded from obstinacy, but that now he thought otherwise. The next day the Friend crossed over to the New York shore, her horse going on board the sloop without leading. The captain, observing the action of the horse, said, "It will go over now, for the work is done." It may be well to add that the Chief Justice fulfilled his promise, and that no consistent Friend, up to the time this account was written, had suffered under him for conscientious scruples.

Those who remember Rebecca Jones in health and vigor, describe her as being of a fine, portly person, as having an imposing appearance in the gallery, and a countenance readily flushed by the earnestness of her feelings, as she was pleading with her fellow-candidates for immortality, that they might be reconciled unto God. There was much dignity in her demeanor and wisdom in her conversation. In meetings for worship she was clothed with Gospel power and authority, and in meetings for discipline with the spirit of wise discernment. Some years before her death, her labor for others being much over, and tried with many infirmities of body, she looked, with wistful earnestness, for the period when her Master should grant her a release from the afflictions of life's weary pilgrimage.

Rebecca Jones had experienced many trials calculated to depress her spirits. She had beheld those with whom her soul had enjoyed sweet fellowship, who had labored with her in the Gospel of her dear Lord, who had been as bone of her bone, fall from their stability, lose their spiritual gifts and graces, and even bring reproach on the blessed Truth. Her heart had been sorely wounded thereby; her faith had been closely tried, while she feared lest she also might one day fall and become a castaway from the holy fellowship of her people and the blessed favor of her God. Many of the faithful had been removed from her side, and earth offered little to induce her to desire to longer tarry amid its checkered scenes. Samuel Emlen had gone to receive the blessed reward of pure dedication. Sarah Harrison had been in mercy taken from a world of trouble. Thomas Scattergood had exchanged his earthly state of mingled weeping and rejoicing for a resting-place in that glorious city where sorrow finds no entrance. And others, near and dear to her heart, were now, like herself, aged pilgrims, waiting for their own dismissal from mortality, with little ability to salute an old fellow-traveller in the way everlasting. She could but hope over some of the younger laborers in the Lord's vineyard; yet the signs of the times seemed to her prophetic of coming sorrow, and feeling that "mourning, lamentation, and woe" were inscribed on the future, she found little room for rejoicing.

Her decease took place on the 15th of Fourth month, 1818, she being then nearly seventy-nine years of age.

DANIEL OFFLEY.

ON the east side of Front Street near Walnut Street, in Philadelphia, about the close of the Revolutionary war, was a large blacksmith's shop, in which anchors were forged. In it might be seen, standing at an anvil, hammer in hand, a strong, wide-shouldered, full-set man, of about five feet ten inches in height, whose powerful, clear voice could be heard above all the din of the roaring of fires and the ringing of iron. It was a scene to attract attention. This stout man, the proprietor and conductor of the business, was of a light complexion, of handsome features, and well-proportioned in every part of his muscular body. When the gazer, while beholding the many ponderous hammers descending on the partly-finished anchors, and feeling almost stunned by the noise, heard the voice of the owner rising distinct and clear above all, directing the workmen in their various labors, it was wont to excite surprise. That voice was peculiar, and in a meeting for worship, when the speaker was under deep religious exercise and concern for his fellow-believers, it was remarkable for its melody. It was exceedingly rich in tone, and he seemed to speak without effort. This man of the fine face, the well-proportioned frame, the powerful arm, the far-extending voice, was Daniel Offley.

He was the son of Daniel and Rachel Offley, and was born in Philadelphia, on the 29th of the Eleventh month, 1756. Being of an animated and joyous disposition by nature, not regulated by Divine Grace, he rushed, in his youth, into many of the vanities and follies which beset his path. He was gay and light-hearted, but was far, very far from partaking of true peace and heart-comforting happiness. These can only be enjoyed by those who, through the mercy of the Lord Jesus Christ, witness a pardon for past sins, and grace to enable them to live a life of piety and virtue. One of his most intimate friends, and the partaker with him in vanity and frivolity, was Jonathan Evans. This, his strong-minded associate, was as averse to religious things as himself, until brought, through the secret convictions of Grace operating by a providential incident, to repentance and amendment of life. From the memorial of Jonathan Evans, and the account given by some of his friends, we learn some of the particulars of his convincement. In search of something he wanted, he was examining the contents of an old chest, when, picking up a book which he found there, he opened it. His eyes caught the words "The Light of Christ." There was nothing in this sentence attractive to him, so the book was thrown down, and he went about his business. But although the book was closed and left behind him, and he occupied by his worldly concerns, he could not forget that sentence, "The Light of Christ." At last he determined to examine the book further, and, on taking it from the old chest, found it to be William Penn's "No Cross, no Crown." He read this book, and, through Divine mercy, was now thoroughly reached and awakened to a sense of his lost and undone condition by nature, and was prompted to seek earnestly for deliverance from the shackles of sin. As he could no longer enjoy the company of his former associates, he withdrew from them, keeping himself much retired. Some of those who loved his society were not disposed to give him up, and Daniel Offley undertook to reason the matter with him. Daniel supposed this withdrawal from a gay life was but the effect of a melancholy fit, which would soon depart if he would mingle with his former associates; and in arguing with him he told him so. This opened the way for Jonathan, who so clearly set forth the sinfulness of the course they had both been pursuing, that Daniel Offley was himself convinced. He too now felt strong convictions for sin, and, through the mercy of his Saviour, he also experienced repentance toward God and a saving faith in our Lord Jesus Christ. Being brought under the power of judgment and condemnation for his past transgressions, in a sense of his lost condition, except he could find one mighty to save and able to deliver, he was deeply humbled. But as he patiently bore the chastening of the Lord, he was favored to experience the glad tidings of the Gospel of Jesus, who saveth his people from their sins. Then was there opened to him, for his comfort, the dayspring from on high, and, in the midst of conflicts, he had joy and peace in believing.

He was not yet free from trials. He who had redeemed him from evil, now called him to labor in the work of the ministry. Strong baptisms of spirit were therefore upon him; — and under their operation, his will was subjected to the Lord's will — and before many months had elapsed, he opened his mouth in religious meetings to the comfort of his Friends. In a very short time afterwards, his friend Peter Yarnall appearing in the same way, a strong sympathy of spirit was superadded to their former friendship for each other.

Peter Yarnall being at Concord trying to establish himself in business as a physician, Daniel thus wrote to him:

"PHILADELPHIA, Twelfth month 20th, 1780.

"DEAR FRIEND, ... Thine, by favor of Jonathan Evans, contained a very seasonable apology for thy not calling to see me, when last in town. Since which [time] many favors conferred upon us, claim our deep and humble acknowledgment to the great Author. It still continues to be my lot, to dwell mostly in a state of deep proving, and humbling exercise. I am desiring to be made fully acquainted with my own infirmity, and the workings of the enemy of our happiness, which I believe many of us have been favored to see, are deep and hidden. I think I have also been favored to see the indispensable necessity of our dwelling deep, and being often brought under the baptizing power of Truth, which has a tendency, as it is patiently abode under, clearly and distinctly to discover the snares which Satan, or his emissaries, have laid for us. I believe these snares and baits are always suited to our various natural inclinations.

"As respects us, who have believed ourselves called, and not only called, but chosen of God, to bear a public testimony to his goodness, oh! that I, in particular, oh! that all who are thus called, may dwell so deep as to be preserved from all the snares of the enemy, and kept under that Power which gives authority, and which 'maketh his angels spirits, and his ministers a flame of fire,' that neither the stubble nor the chaffy nature can withstand. For I do verily believe, if there be but, on our part, a proper waiting for the fresh anointing, that the Lord will raise up 'threshing instruments.' Oh! how necessary it is to guard well against the working of self-imagination, compassing ourselves about with sparks, but not of the true fire; and by impatience (when perhaps the anointing Power was at work, and would have properly qualified) there has been strange fire offered; which I believe, without breach of charity, has been offensive in the sight of God, who will not accept 'robbery for burnt-offering.' There must be a waiting in holy silence, and ceasing from self-activity, until we feel the command, 'proclaim my word which I have given thee, to this people.'

"When there is such a clear discovery, it is an awful thing, and its consequences are fearful to disobey. Notwithstanding it is so, there has been at times, in myself, and it may be so with others, a reluctance to yield obedience; and then we are brought under chastisement and close rebuke; which may work in us a disposition of willingness to do anything, in order to be relieved from the deep distress of mind that we feel. Here is the enemy again, presenting a way for us, working upon the unmortified nature, and proposing many things to us, in order to get from under this trying dispensation; which in these beclouded times, makes the trial still deeper and more exercising. I have ever found it safest for me, in the course of my small experience, to bear the indignation of the Lord, till it be overpast, and his mercy again revealed, with a clear evidence of his being again reconciled.

"I cannot tell the reason why I should be thus led; but hope these remarks may, by no means, be a discouragement to thee, whom I love and esteem. But if thou should have to travel in any of these trying paths, thou may remember that others have trodden therein before thee. So, in dear love to thee, in which my wife joins, I remain thy assured friend,

DANIEL OFFLEY, JR."

The comparatively trifling occurrence made use of in the Divine hand in the convincement of Jonathan Evans, and, through him, of his friend, Daniel Offley, is in accordance with the working of Providence in awaking many others. The following anecdote is an incident in point. A gay, thoughtless, unregenerate woman, in looking over the shoulder of a religious servant, to find out what she was reading, had her attention arrested by the word "eternity." Eternity!—a word of but eight letters—yet how much is comprised in it! The Holy Spirit set this word home on the heart of the careless beholder. She began to feel what eternity, to an immortal, accountable being, implied—future unending happiness to those who on earth should walk in obedience to the law of the Spirit of life in Christ Jesus; hopeless, irremediable misery to those who, like herself, were gratifying the desires of the vain mind. That night sleep forsook her eyes, deep exercise of spirit came upon her, and from that time, as she submitted to the inward baptisms of the Holy Ghost and fire, her heart grew more and more tender, and her spiritual understanding more enlightened. That one glance had produced, through the Saviour's blessing, a train of reflections, of inward conflicts, of submissions on her part, which resulted in a change of heart, manifested in a change of life.

Edward Andrews, of the province of New Jersey, the son of faithful parents, in his early years took great delight in music and jollity. By giving way to his evil propensities, he stifled the reproofs of instruction, until at last the Lord's Holy Spirit seemed no longer to strive with him. After a time a series of losses and crosses, as respected worldly things, came upon him, and yet little change for the better was wrought in him thereby. His residence had been among Friends at Mansfield, but he now removed to the neighborhood of Egg Harbor, on the sea-shore, where his principal companions were Indians, and their chief business seemed to be getting up idle diversions, wherein the fiddle had the principal place. He was far from any meeting of Friends, and the principles of his education seemed to have lost all hold on his mind. In the twenty-seventh year of his age a renewed visitation of the Lord's mercy was manifested effectually, savingly to him, and very simple indeed did the first moving thereof appear. He saw, one day, as he was walking in his field alone, a bone of a man's leg. He had often handled it, and had at times made use of it as a club to strike with and to throw; but now there came a thoughtfulness over his mind as he looked at it, with an impression that it would be right to bury it. This, after a time of inward debate, he did, and felt peaceful in so doing. From this time the witness for God stirred in him again, recalling the days he had spent in vanity and estrangement from good, and raising in him desires for deliverance from sin. Step by step he trod the path of self-denial and the daily cross, until he was led out of his former evil habits, and was brought into inward conformity to the will of his God. It was in the Fourth month, 1704, that he found this bone, and as he continued faithful to that which reproved him, he was led for a time through many conflicts, and experienced largely of weeping and mourning, and then came a season of inward comfort in the assurance of the Lord's favor. Now his blessed Saviour filled his heart with love for others; he was brought to long for their spiritual welfare, and then a gift in the ministry of the Gospel of life and salvation was committed to him. He labored as the Lord opened his way. A blessing attended his ministry; many were convinced, and a meeting of Friends was soon established near his residence. Through faithfulness under his exercises, and to his openings, he grew in spiritual grace and wisdom.

He was honest and sharp-sighted as a watchman on the walls of Zion, bearing a true testimony against wrong spirits in the church, whilst ever ready to pass by and forgive trespasses against himself. He did not live long to labor, and being taken sick, was sensible that his end had nearly come, telling his friends the Lord had brought him through all his exercises. The evening before his death, his heart was tendered by the sweet incomes of the love of God, and in living prayer he committed himself and family to the Lord's keeping. On the 26th of Tenth month, 1716, having been favored with the Lord's comforting and sustaining presence to the last, he joyfully departed.

Daniel Offley continued to labor faithfully in the ministry to which he was called. To his friend Peter Yarnall, at Concord, he thus wrote:

"PHILADELPHIA, Eighth month 7th, 1781.

"DEAR FRIEND, ... I have often thought, and had to marvel at the long forbearance and mercy of our God; and a language, similar to that formerly expressed respecting some other places, has often run through my mind. Oh, Philadelphia! Philadelphia! had the many powerful visitations, which have been extended to thee, been reached forth unto Sodom and Gomorrah, they would have repented long ago, in dust and ashes. Therefore the men of these cities shall rise up in judgment against thee, and, may I not say, condemn thee. But I do believe there are a living number, whose cries have entered into the ears of the Lord of Sabaoth, and he has opened a gracious ear to their mourning and sighings, as between the porch and the altar, with this language, 'O Lord, spare us a little longer. Try us yet another year.' He has long waited for fruits. But it would be no marvel at all with me, if his anger should yet rise higher, and he should pour out the vials of his wrath upon the inhabitants of this once highly favored city.

"As to my own particular state, I have been of latter weeks under much humbling exercise. Yesterday I attended our Quarterly Meeting, and believe it was favored with a covering, which clearly evidenced that something good was still with us; and that the Lord had not wholly forsaken his people — it may be for the sake of the 'ten righteous,' whom he has yet found among us. And, oh! saith my soul, may their number increase; and that we, who have put our hands to the gospel-plough, may not look back, nor, through dust gathering on our garments and becoming soiled, thereby dim the beauty of holiness, and occasion the weak to stumble, and the daring rebel to reproach the holy Truth. . . . I believe it cannot now be called a time of health in the city.

"Thy affectionate friend,   DANIEL OFFLEY, JR."

An expectation similar to that expressed by Daniel of a time of judgment on the city of Philadelphia, was felt and declared by many other Friends. The year 1793 saw the fulfilment of their fears. Then came the yellow fever, and with it fearfulness of heart and paleness of face throughout the devoted city. Then was felt the silence of desolation; the wheels of trade were at rest, and little was heard but the rumbling of the dead-cart, even more awful because of the absence of other sounds.

About the beginning of the year 1783, George Dillwyn and Daniel Offley, Jr., paid a visit to Friends in New York State. On this visit, when at Stanford, they called one evening at the house of Tiddeman Hull, the father of the late Henry Hull. Henry, then eighteen years of age, was engaged in his father's fulling-mill, and being sent for to the house, was disturbed in his mind to find he was interrupted in his business merely to come into a family sitting. He says he "could hardly speak pleasantly to the Friends." Notwithstanding this, Daniel Offley was so enabled to minister to his spiritual condition as to be the means, he records, of "turning me into the paths of obedience."

How great the influence for good or evil man possesses, and how necessary that all should be faithful to apprehended duty! No one knows, when he is doing despite to the convictions of grace, how many are evilly affected by his sin; and no one knows, when he yields himself up in perfect obedience to the Lord's will, how much of a saving ministry to others there may be in his example of humble dedication. Jonathan

Evans was faithful to the awakening call given him; he was made instrumental in the conversion of Daniel Offley, and Daniel Offley of Henry Hull. Doubtless many were stirred up to spiritual diligence — were made to cry earnestly for help to the Lord — through the baptizing power of Henry Hull's ministry. See how the circle of good influences extends. Every one who receives permanent benefit is himself a fresh centre of beneficial action on others. So is it of evil. If by my example others are encouraged in wrong, their influence is exerted in behalf of wrong. It is, indeed, an awful thing to live; for unless we retire to the solitude of some distant forest, or bury ourselves on some uninhabited island, we cannot rid ourselves of the fearful responsibility of living — of operating for good or for evil on society.

In a letter addressed to Peter Yarnall, dated Seventh month 29th, 1783, after mentioning that he was about setting out on a visit to New York, Daniel Offley adds:

"Not long since, I returned, with my friend, George Dillwyn, from the tour I now have in prospect. But, finding a too anxious desire after home, I returned too early, to my wounding. Oh, dear friend, there is need for us to mind the pointing of the Lord's finger, both in going out and coming in: to be wholly unshackled from all the cumbering things of this world, and to be given up to his appointment and direction!

If this was more the situation and state of such as are at times made use of as instruments in his holy hand, how many shining stars would there be, whose brightness would have a tendency to overawe those clouds of darkness which sometimes do overspread our Sion. I feel a necessity for myself to be more devoted in heart to run, with a becoming cheerfulness and resignation, the ways of his requiring, whereby my strength might more increase. For how subtle is the adversary in his attempts to draw us back into captivity and thraldom! So that I have sometimes, when in low, desponding moments, been ready to query, who is able for these things?

"But we have a merciful God to deal with, who, when he has tried the integrity of our hearts, will arise in his mighty power, and put to flight the enemy: and thus our souls, wearied with exercise, will be permitted to enjoy a short, but precious Sabbath. May I, with thee, dear friend, ever press forward through these crowds of opposition, which I believe neither of us are exempt from, that so, neither heights nor depths, principalities nor powers, things present nor to come, may ever be able to separate us from the love of God in Christ Jesus. As this becomes our daily concern, I humbly hope that way will be made for the remnant of God's Israel to pass through as on dry land, to the praise of his holy Name."

Many another Friend besides Daniel Offley, has retired from fields of service to which they were called before they were quite released. Henry Drinker, of Philadelphia, writing to Samuel Neale, under date Third month 10th, 1788, says: "Our valuable friend Samuel Emlen hath visited my dwelling twice this day. He is, as thou must have known him, often feeble in body, but continues to be a vessel chosen and appointed to preach the Gospel in the authority thereof, frequently animated and strengthened to the admiration of many. Ever since his last return from your land he appears at times much bowed under a sense of a too hasty escape, and an apprehension that he must yet give up to visit some parts of the island of Great Britain once more."

We are all liable to be led astray, when we allow our reason to take the place of revelation, and let our own idea of fitness govern us in things where simple obedience is required at our hands.

We are told by George Fox in his Journal, that in the year 1648, being at Mansfield in Nottingham, he felt a concern to go and speak to a company of Justices, who were there sitting "about hiring servants." The burden on the mind of George to deliver was, a warning to them not to "oppress the servants in their wages." In obedience to the will of his Divine Master, he started toward the inn where they met, but on coming near and finding a company of fiddlers in the same house, his faith failed him, and he turned back, thinking that time not seasonable for so serious a subject as he wished to bring to their notice. With the prospect of returning in the morning, he turned from the performance of present duty. In the morning when he came to the inn, he found that the justices had departed. Under the feelings produced by this information, he became so blind he could not see. The tavern-keeper informed him the justices were to sit that day at a village eight miles from Mansfield. His concern to see them still continued, and in the prospect of being yet able to perform his duty, his hope revived, and his sight began to be restored. In the present strength and vision afforded, he commenced running as fast as he could toward the village named. He reached the place, and entered the room where the justices were sitting with many servants before them. In the power and authority given him of the Lord, he delivered his warning to the justices, and then exhorted the servants to be faithful in the performance of their several duties, serving in all honesty. Those addressed received his exhortation and warning with kindness and attention.

We have but little to say of the many religious engagements of Daniel Offley during his short life. In the Eleventh month, 1786, he and Samuel Emlen left

Philadelphia for Barbadoes and some other of the West India islands. At Barbadoes they were received with kindness, and particularly so by the Governor of the island. They found that the great hurricane of 1780 had blown down all the meeting-houses of Friends, which were five in number. Preparations were, however, then making for the erection of a new one.

The memorial of Daniel Offley says that in this visit to the islands, and in his labors in many of the meetings on this continent, his service was "to the satisfaction and edification of those among whom his lot was cast; [he] being often, through deep baptism, led into close-searching labor with the indolent and lukewarm professors of the blessed Truth."

About the middle of the Eighth month, 1793, the yellow fever made its appearance in Philadelphia, and as it was evidently spreading with fearful rapidity, and was generally quickly mortal in its effects, a great degree of public terror was shown. By the 26th, vast numbers of the citizens began to remove, and for many days the public roads leading from the city were thronged with vehicles of all descriptions laden with people and furniture. Many members of the Society of Friends fled with their families; but there were others who believed it their duty to remain — some as a testimony to their belief in the superintending providence of the Most High, and others to minister to the wants of the sick and needy. Among the latter was Daniel Offley. He was not one of the original volunteers appointed by the citizens to assist the guardians of the poor in the general oversight of the greatly-increasing number of persons who were destitute of the means of living, or were taken down with the distemper; but in a few days he joined them. To walk about the street at this time with any degree of composure and peacefulness, required great command of nerves or a great faith in Him who alone can control "the pestilence that walketh in darkness, and the destruction that wasteth at noonday." To hear, while walking, the bells of the different places of worship tolling unceasingly for the members of their respective congregations who were hourly dropping, one by one, into eternity — to see the yellow flags waving on all sides, and other marks of sickness within, on windows and doors through all the streets, and to meet at every corner the hearse with its dead, or the sick-cart conveying its sick and dying to the hospital, were evident tokens of mortality sufficiently striking to appal the bravest. Yet amid all these sights and sounds, in the performance of his Christian duty, Daniel Offley continued his almost unabated labor in visiting the sick, ministering to their physical wants, and, as ability was afforded, preaching the Gospel of the kingdom to them in freshness and power. With some he could rejoice even while mourning that they were about putting off mortality. Calling on the 19th of the Ninth month on Sarah Rodman, a young woman of Newport, Rhode Island, who had been taken with the prevailing fever the previous day, he had to tell her of the comfort it had afforded him to feel that she was favored with quietness and tranquillity, and to know that she had not, at that awful time, to learn where to look for relief in her distress, or how to pray to Him who alone could deliver or save. In his visits to the sick, he called almost daily upon her. At one time he said, "The Lord is with thee, and I believe he will be with thee as thy Caretaker, thy Supporter, and thy Comforter, however the present illness may terminate." At another time he was bowed in awful supplication in her chamber to the Father of mercies, wherein, in fervency of spirit, he made intercession that she might be supported on the bed of languishing, have her spirit raised above the fear of death, and centred in safety with her God. He felt himself clothed with sympathy also with the relatives of the sick and dying. To Hannah Fisher, sister of Sarah Rodman, he was on different occasions drawn to administer the word of consolation. He affectionately desired her, on the 25th, to seek after resignation, saying, in relation to the probability of her sister's speedy decease, "It is, indeed, a close trial, and many of thy friends feel for thee; but, as I have told thee before — and now have no disposition to recall it — she is the Lord's, and let him take her. I have no doubt she will enter into the full fruition of that joy which is prepared for the righteous. She will be released from a troublesome world, and centred where the wicked cease from troubling and the weary are at rest. This is my faith concerning her; therefore try to compose thy mind, and do not give way to sorrow which may hurt thee. I know it is hard to part with such near connections, having had to experience it." The night of the next day, Sarah, having given a bright example of patience and resignation, passed quietly away; and, according to the necessary custom of that sad period, in a few hours after her body was consigned to the earth.

As the mortality in the city grew greater, the ringing of the bells to denote death, was dispensed with, but the increased activity of the hearses, and the general yellowness of the complexion of the citizens, made walking the streets as little to be desired as ever. But Daniel Offley still was faithful to his duty. His stability and unshaken confidence in God, made him a comfort to the distressed in mind, and the faint-hearted ones who seemed cast down at the prospect around them. In religious meetings, which were then small, he was often clothed upon with heavenly love, and enabled in a tender and Christian manner to exhort those gathered. He pressed upon them fidelity in the discharge of religious duty — and in thus doing, he believed a qualification would be granted them to understand the language of the awful dispensation meted out to them, and prepared, if it should be the Lord's will, to lay down their lives with joy.

It is not needful to narrate many of the heart-rending scenes which the city of Philadelphia witnessed during the Ninth and Tenth months, 1793. Many died unattended — wives fled from sick husbands — husbands abandoned their dying wives — parents deserted their own offspring in their distress — and children left their plague-stricken parents to die of neglect. But notwithstanding this, very many instances of deep affection, of faithful fidelity unto death, were also witnessed. Never were the kindnesses of human nature and the prevailing loveliness of Divine grace in tendering the feelings to the woes of others, more strongly developed, than at this season, where, in many, self appeared all in all.

Daniel Offley having, about the close of the Ninth month, been with two of his friends and associates on some errand of mercy, as they were separating, he said, "The language of this dispensation to every one of us is, 'Be ye also ready,' for at such an hour as we expect not, the messenger of death may be sent to our houses." They parted, never to meet again. Two of them were soon called home to heaven the third, our late friend, Thomas Wistar, sickened with the prevailing disorder, but was, in the ordering of Divine Providence, restored to health, and survived, many years, the death of his companions.

On the 3d of the Tenth month, Daniel Offley was taken ill. On the 4th, one of his friends came to see him, and while sitting by his side, expressed the sorrow with which he was affected, at seeing one who had been so serviceable to the sick, himself seized with the disorder, adding, that he had hoped Daniel would have been spared. The grace-supported patient cheerfully replied, "It matters little, when in our places, how we are disposed of, whether in life or death."

With a holy, happy confidence in the Lord, unshaken by the pains of his distressed body, he lay serenely tranquil, waiting the result. He knew that all would be well, and expressed his resignation to the Lord's will, whether it should be for life or death. On the morning of the 7th of the month, his wife asking him how he was, he replied, that he had had a very comfortable night, and had been overshadowed with the calming influence of Divine love, in a degree he had never before experienced.

Thus sustained and comforted, he continued to the close, departing this life on the 11th of the Tenth month, 1793, aged nearly thirty-seven years.

WILLIAM SAVERY.

WILLIAM SAVERY, who had been plucked by Divine Grace as a brand from the burning, was, in the year 1780, occasionally opening his mouth in the ministry. William was born in Philadelphia, in the year 1750. In the days of his youth he had given way to the temptations of the enemy of all good, and had become estranged from the paths of purity and peace. Yet he was not forgotten of his God. Many and many a visitation of reproving mercy was meted out to his soul. His days, which were often spent in wantonness and mirth, were followed by nights of lamentation and mourning. We learn from his own account, that he at this time frequented taverns and places of diversion, and indulged in card-playing. Having been somewhat awakened to a sense of his evil habits, he endeavored, in his own strength, to improve his moral condition. He refrained from some of his most glaring sins, and, doubtless, appeared much improved in the sight of men. He says:

"Now I struggled hard to break myself of my fondness for company, seeing the snare there was in it, being apt to relate adventures and tales to provoke mirth; and often, for the embellishment of them, to strain beyond the truth. I was much concerned to watch over myself in this particular, which is both dishonorable and sinful, yet a vice that I have observed to be very prevalent among the youth of both sexes. Even in companies that are termed polite, or well bred, the discourse is often so strained, that few sentences or narratives, if examined, would be found to be strictly true. Some fondly imagine that there is but little harm in telling untruths, unless they be related seriously, not considering our holy profession, and who it was that said, 'Let your yea be yea, and your nay, nay; for whatsoever is more than this cometh of evil.'

"Oh, the folly of thus misspending our precious time! How watchful, how careful ought we to be of our words and actions! always remembering that the holy eye of an all-seeing God pervades the most secret chambers we can retire to, and his ear is ever open to hear both the evil and the good! Insomuch that one formerly said, 'There is not a thought in the heart, nor a word on the tongue, but he knows altogether!' Yea, and many of the present day have known when the terrors of the Lord have overtaken them for sin, and they have had to taste of the spirit of judgment and of burning — that every secret thing has been brought to light, and the hidden works of darkness have been made manifest; and that even for *idle words* they have had to render an account.

"I had been employed, as before related, in bringing myself to a more circumscribed life, being pretty careful in my conduct and conversation and just in my dealings among men, and was willing to believe that I had attained to great matters, and that I might now take up my rest; for by my own strength, ability, and contrivance, I could not only keep up a fair, upright character among men, and make myself happy and respected, but (oh, the deceitful workings of Satan! oh, the mystery of iniquity!) that it would, at the close of time here, gain me an inheritance among all those that are sanctified, in the regions of purity and peace.

"How can I sufficiently adore [the Lord] for his continued regard and care over me, in that he did not suffer me to remain long in this state of delusion and error, but disturbed my false rest, and made me, at times, exceedingly uneasy with it? At length he gave me to see that, notwithstanding my regularity of behavior and all my boasted attainments, I fell far short of that purity which all the vessels of the Lord's house must come to, and that I was yet under the law, which cannot make the comers thereunto perfect, not having passed under the flaming sword, nor felt the day of the Lord to come, which burns as an oven.

"This brought great distress and anxiety of mind over me, and sometimes I was ready to doubt the truth of these Divine revelations. I was also exceedingly desirous to find, if possible, an easier way to happiness than by submitting myself wholly to the cross, of which I had, as yet, experienced but little. And one night, as I was much tossed and distressed in mind, (which was usual for me about that time,) I went to bed, and as one that was in a dark and howling wilderness, where I could see no way out, to the right hand or to the left. But at length the Lord, who, indeed, watched over me continually for good, (blessed and praised forever be his name!) brought me into some degree of composure, so that I believe I went to sleep. Be that as it might, it appeared to me that I was travelling with a friend, and we saw, at a distance from us, a very spacious house, the like I had never seen, situate on a high hill, which I believed to be the mansion of rest and happiness. We kept together along the road, and, with little difficulty, arrived within a few yards of the house, which we then perceived to be the back part of it; and in the door stood a very venerable old man, whom I thought to be one of the prophets, and who, I think, beckoned to us not to come forward. At which we stopped, and he informed us we were not right, and that this was not the right way into the house, and that if we got in that way, we should not enjoy the happiness we expected. Upon which I left my companion, and soon found myself at the front of the house. But now the difficulty appeared; for between me and it was a furnace, which all that ever arrived therein must pass through. Around this furnace, at a little distance, stood a multitude of people, who, I believed, had likewise the desire that I had of getting into the house, and were looking at the furnace, but were afraid to enter. I pressed forward and got near the mouth, and it appeared exceeding hot, about four times as long as myself, and about four feet in diameter. As I stood viewing it, I believed the fire was much the hottest round the sides, but decreased in heat toward the middle, which appeared to be the best place to pass through, and where, if I could be steady enough to keep, I should receive the least hurt. My thoughts were much tossed to and fro and very irresolute, and I reasoned thus: If thou shouldst attempt to pass through, and find the fire too hot, and be obliged to come out again backward, thou wilt then become the laugh and scorn of all the multitude: and I believe my heart failed me, and I turned away sorrowful, and remember no further, but thus far dwelt exceedingly lively in my imagination, and with uncommon clearness. I immediately related it to my beloved partner, who, being acquainted with my state of mind, without much hesitation could unravel the meaning of it, which, indeed, was so plain that he that runs might read.

"Though I have not been apt to catch at every imagination that presents itself in sleep — believing, in general, that dreams are but of small import, and commonly proceed from the engagements of the day — yet I have no doubt that the Lord is pleased, at times, to manifest himself to man in dreams, as he sees meet, either for encouragement, reproof, or instruction.

"With respect to what I have related, the strong impression it made on my mind, the plain application of it to the state I was then in, and the instruction it conveyed to me, left no room to doubt its being divinely intended for my good. But as it opened my eyes more clearly to discern where I was, and that all the righteousness of my own putting on was as filthy rags, of which I must be stripped before I could experience a putting on of that purity and righteousness which is the fine linen of the saints; so it brought great distress and anxiety of mind over me."

The dream of William Savery, in which a state of acceptance with the Lord, is typified under the form of a house enclosed and of difficult access, recalls to recollection one of a somewhat similar kind, the dreamer of which was a young Carolina girl. The circumstance was narrated by William Williams during one of his religious visits in this city.

This young girl was a member of the Society of Friends, a child of careful, religious parents. Having gone one day to a neighboring factory, she was tempted during the absence of the owner from the apartment she was in, to steal an earthen cup of little value which she saw lying there. She committed the sin, and returned home with the cup secreted in her dress. The owner almost immediately after missed it, suspected her of the theft, and was able to prove it upon her. The Devil who had led her to commit this disgraceful act, now sought to harden her in crime, and prompted her to refuse to acknowledge her sin. The case was brought to the Monthly Meeting; and when the committee who had, in conjunction with her concerned parents, unavailingly labored to bring her to a state of humble acknowledgment and contrition, reported their want of success, there seemed no way for the meeting to act but to disown her. This would no doubt have been the case, if William Williams had not been, in the ordering of Providence, at that meeting. He felt his mind clothed with love for the child, and with an apprehension of duty to visit her. He told his feelings to the Friends, and way was made for his visit, the meeting deferring a definite judgment in the case for another month. His visit was attended with a very different result from that of the committee. The Good Shepherd who still loves to seek and to save those who are lost, had prepared the way before him, and opened her heart to receive the word of exhortation and tender entreaty. Her proud spirit was humbled, and in the depth of abasement she made a full and complete acknowledgment of her transgression. It was a melting season of heartfelt sorrow and contrition. "Now, mother," said the weeping girl, " shall I tell him the dream I had last night?" Being encouraged by her mother, she gave a narrative, of which the following is the import.

She thought she was alone in a wilderness, around which there was an impenetrable hedge of briers, except on one spot from which a path led up a very steep hill. To escape from the wilderness she commenced ascending the hill, and although many difficult and steep places obstructed her passage, she reached its summit. Here she found a beautiful mansion, within whose wall she much desired to be. Indeed, a fervent and uncontrollable longing for admission took hold of her mind, and she sought to enter. Her wishes, however, seemed vain. The door was so high from the ground she could not reach it — and no one appeared to offer her any assistance. She walked round and round the building in vain, disconsolate and hopeless

At last her persevering desire for admission was granted, for William Williams came to the door, and stooping down to her low condition, laid hold of her hands and lifted her in.

Such was the dream. The interpretation was plain. He whose mercies are toward all his works, thus opened her heart to receive with humble alacrity the word which he had put into the mouth of his servant for her good. Rightly humbled, she sincerely condemned her evil act, to the satisfaction of the meeting she belonged to; and she grew up, respectable and respected. How applicable the passage of Scripture, " God speaketh once, yea, twice, yet man perceiveth it not. In a dream, in a vision of the night, when deep sleep falleth upon men, in slumberings upon the bed, then he openeth the ears of men, and sealeth their instruction, that he may withdraw man from his purpose, and hide pride from man."

William Savery having through the merciful visitations afforded his soul been made willing to bear the yoke of Christ, was brought into great circumspection of conduct, and watchfulness over his thoughts and conversation. He now felt the necessity of doing his Master's will, and not his own. In 1779 he left the comforts of his home, and the pursuits of worldly business, to accompany a ministering Friend to visit the meetings in Virginia and Carolina. This visit was paid at a time when it was dangerous to travel, on account of the war that was waging, and the warlike spirit that was in full force in many of the inhabitants. Among the cases of suffering in support of the doctrines of peace furnished during that eventful period, William Savery narrates one with which he became acquainted on this journey. A Friend who had been drafted for the army in one of the Southern States, refused to serve because of his conscientious scruples against war. For this he was tried by a court martial, and condemned to receive forty lashes on his bare back with a whip of nine thongs. The punishment was inflicted in the midst of many witnesses. The poor mangled sufferer bore it all with unflinching patience, and was enabled by the grace of his Divine Master, to remain firm to his faith and consistent to his principles. He was offered different employments in the army, such as waiting on the sick, etc., but as he was satisfied that he could take no post there with peace of mind, he was proof against persuasion and threats. In his difficulties, his honest wife encouraged him in faithfulness to his religious duty, and was much tried at hearing a report, which, however, was false, that he had been induced to comply with the wishes of his persecutors. When the period for which he had been drafted had expired, he was permitted to return home in peace.

Very many instances of suffering among Friends

occurred in the Southern States during the war. In the Ninth month, 1777, fourteen members of Hopewell meeting, in Frederick County, Virginia, were taken from their habitations by files of soldiers, and carried to Winchester. They refused to perform military service, and for this, they were very roughly treated by Marquis Calamis, lieutenant-colonel, by James Barnet, the captain of the company they were drafted into, and several other officers. These drew their swords on the Friends, and with the points of them pushed them into rank, declaring they would kill them if they did not comply. The unresisting prisoners were preserved in meekness and patience, so that they allowed the officers to push and drag them about at will, neither saying or doing anything which might provoke them to further injury. They had, after a time, an opportunity of opening and explaining their views of war to those who had thus ill-treated them, which for a time seemed to give them some relief. They were, on the 23d of Ninth month, sent from Winchester, to join the army under Washington, which was then lying north of Philadelphia, watching the English who had possession of that city. Various efforts were made on their march to induce them to take part in military operations, without effect, although they were again harshly treated, and on three of the youngest men, guns were fastened.

When they reached the camp where Washington lay with his army, which was on the Skippack Road, twenty miles from Philadelphia, their appearance drew the attention of Clement Biddle, a colonel in the army. His sympathies were perhaps aroused, and he made application to the General, who ordered them to be instantly discharged, with a pass to return home. The same favor was shown to a number of young Friends forced in the same manner from Loudon County, in Virginia. When the Friends from Hopewell were about setting out for their homes, they thought it right to bid farewell to the officers who had brought them, and who had ill-treated them. It was now found that their patient, Christian spirit, had produced a great change of feeling in these men toward them. They received them kindly, and generally expressed their satisfaction at their release, and also their friendly desire that they might get well and safely home. This they did about the 1st of Eleventh month, thankful in heart to the Lord, who had preserved them in faithfulness, and had opened the way for their comparatively speedy deliverance. While with the army, they would not partake of the military stores, and had it not been for the kindness of Friends at different places on their march, they must have suffered extremely if they did not perish of hunger.

The faithfulness of Friends throughout the whole

of the provinces, in support of their testimony against war, had at length a powerful influence upon the thoughtful and reasonable people of other professions. Some of them did not hesitate to declare that Friends ought not to suffer, for they had not attempted to deceive; that they had from the beginning opposed war; and that the consistent ones among them would under no circumstances bear arms.

During this journey to the South, William Savery met with an observation made by a great woman, a member of the Church of England, which he noted down. It was to this effect: "She observed some of the Quakers' children had departed from the plainness of their profession, and got about half-way into the fashions of the world, which rendered them ridiculous in the eyes of others, and a reproach to their own Society."

One of the striking characteristics of William Savery's ministry was its full and forcible acknowledgment of the divinity and various offices of our Lord Jesus Christ. He had no sympathy with infidelity in any shape. While on a religious visit in Europe, in 1797, he makes this note in his diary, dated at Paris, Second month 23d: "I do not doubt that with all the vices and infidelity which reign in Paris, there are many of Sion's true mourners there; with such I was favored frequently to feel a secret sympathy. May the great and universal Shepherd of the heavenly fold stretch forth his arm to this nation, and gather many thousands to the standard of truth and righteousness, where their tossed souls may lie down in safety, and none be able to make them afraid. In the evening, David Sands and myself fell in with Thomas Paine, and spent about an hour and a half in conversation about his opinions and writings. He made many assertions against Moses, the prophets, Jesus Christ, etc., which had much more the appearance of passionate railing than argument, to all which we replied. I felt zealously opposed to him, and believe that nothing was said by my companion or myself that gave him the least occasion to exult. We bore our testimony against him firmly."

At Dunkirk, Fourth month 30th, he writes, "Had meetings morning and evening; at the latter, through the condescension of the good Shepherd of the sheep, it was a time of refreshment and comfort, I believe, both to the laborers and the auditory. For my own part, having felt for a number of days like a dry and withered branch, I was rejoiced to feel again the circulation of that life and virtue, by which alone all the branches of Christ, the true Vine, are nourished and supported to bring forth fruit to his praise. The Truth as it is in Jesus, appeared to rise into dominion. The erroneous and destructive opinions of deism are subtilely making their way into many minds, who will be robbed and spoiled, whether they be of our Society or others, that indulge it, of the most inestimable jewel, the most powerful consolation to the soul, both in life and death, that ever a Being, infinite in mercy and boundless in his compassion, conferred on mankind. Oh! that he may protect and preserve our Society from drinking in this deadly poison to the soul — that the watchmen on the walls may be enabled faithfully to sound an alarm to the careless, to whom it may be offered as a gilded bait, and the poor wounded receivers of it [not] be left to lament their folly in that day when its fatal consequences will be forever irretrievable."

In Ireland there was at that time much secret infidelity among some members of the Society of Friends, and it is, therefore, not a matter of wonder that William Savery should often feel his mind drawn to set forth the danger of deistical opinions while in that land. When Nicholas Waln attended, in 1795, the province meeting held at Mount Mellick, through the immediate openings of the Holy Spirit, his mind was impressed with the conviction that there was a spirit at work in that place which would divide and scatter Friends. He believed it would draw many of those who even filled high stations into self-sufficiency and a disbelief of the truths of the Gospel of Jesus Christ. As he honestly unfolded his view, it was a matter of surprise to many of his hearers, and some wished to have him publicly censured. Now in the First month, 1798, when William Savery attended a meeting at the same place, his mind was also opened to discover the workings of the same unbelieving spirit, and he faithfully labored against it. At many meetings on his travels, wherein he was constrained to bear testimony to the Truth as it is in Jesus, fully and emphatically, he afterward found that avowed deists were present. In one of his meetings at London he spoke to the following import: "One of the brightest young men I ever knew was the delight of his acquaintance, the pride of gay company, the life, or, as some say, the soul of every place he visited for gayety, humor, and wit. The Lord, in his wisdom, laid his hand upon him — laid him on a sick-bed. When he was brought to see that he had not many days to continue, he wished to see some who he thought were religious. Oh, how was his heart tortured, and what were his expressions? Why, upon this wise: 'I have seen abundance! I know men and things! I have been at different courts! I have tasted a great deal of that which the world calls enjoyment! I have been educated in some religious principles, but they were too narrow for me! I read Bolingbroke and Hume, and encouraged myself in their views. But now it has pleased the Lord to bring me upon the bed of sickness, where medical aid cannot help me.'

"While he was in this state I went to him, and found him wet with tears. He told me his former companions neglected him, but added, 'If they had not neglected me, they would have yielded me no comfort; they would have been stings to my conscience, and as daggers to my heart. What would you have me to do? I want to believe; but I have been so dark, and encouraged these principles so long, I cannot believe as I ought to do.' This was a sorrowful and afflicting scene to me! The Lord, no doubt, is rich in mercy, and I trust he visited the soul of this young man even in the last few days of his life. I cannot say that Infinite Love did not, even at that late hour, accept him. But, oh! my friends, let us, while we have strength and liberty — let us, with all our hearts, apply them to those things which will be something to lean upon in such an hour! This is the end of all religion, so to live as not to be afraid to die! — and so to die, when it shall please the Lord to separate us from this body, that we may live before him forever!"

After William Savery had returned to America, the spirit of infidelity and curious speculation in Ireland still further increased and spread, through the efforts of Hannah Barnard, a person in the ministry from the

State of New York. When this woman laid her concern to visit England before her Monthly Meeting, a committee was appointed to consider the subject — which committee feeling doubts and misgivings, did not report to the meeting for nine months. Had they reported that a way did not open with clearness to set her at liberty, much trouble and exercise might have been spared the church. We shall not follow her in her various movements in England and Ireland, but shall briefly state that her unsoundness at last claiming the consideration of Friends, she was prevented travelling as a minister. She appealed to the Yearly Meeting at London, in 1801, which confirmed the judgment of the subordinate meeting. During the period intervening between the judgment of the one, and the confirmation by the other, William Savery thus wrote to a Friend near London:

"Many of my friends in and about London are very often sweetly in my remembrance, and of latter times you have had my near sympathy, under your divers trials; but nothing has been more exercising to me, than the concern my countrywoman, Hannah Barnard, has occasioned in the church. I look forward to your Yearly Meeting as a time that will require the whole armor of light to be sought for, as much as at almost any preceding period. Ye cannot doubt of the kind care of the Shepherd of Israel over you, who has long blessed Friends of your nation many ways; and will be, in every needful time, 'a spirit of judgment to those who sit in judgment, and strength to them that turn the battle to the gate.' The longer I live, the more unshaken confidence I think I obtain, that the doctrines laid down by Robert Barclay and our first Friends, founded on the New Testament, and still maintained by the Society at large, are invulnerable to the efforts of vain philosophic sophistry and curious speculation, so long as we retain a belief in that most excellent of books; and am of the mind, that all such as depart from that foundation, will wither and be confounded."

Hannah Barnard had obtained a number of adherents to her views in different parts of England, but the Yearly Meeting very decidedly condemned her doctrinal sentiments. A charge was presented to her Monthly Meeting at Hudson, by which she was disowned.

Hannah Barnard's appeal was heard at her Quarterly Meeting, and then at her Yearly Meeting, both of which bodies confirmed the judgment of the Monthly Meeting. After this she lived very many years, a poor, isolated person, who having separated herself from the Holy Head of the church, was separated from the unity and fellowship of the faithful.

An interesting incident in which William Savery

bore a part, is told relative to Whitehead Humphreys, an infidel who had once been a member among Friends in Philadelphia. Sarah Harrison one night dreamed that she was sitting on a low chair in her parlor with a white apron on. Soon a tall person entered the room, and coming up to her, threw something heavy upon her lap. She looked at it, and inquired of him who brought it, what it was. He answered, "It is a soul in hell; but touch it with the end of thy finger and thou wilt find there is life in it!" She did as she was bidden, and the soul began to move about in her lap. She became greatly agitated, and her husband finding her very much disturbed, awakened her to inquire what ailed her. She said she could not tell him, but she expected to be called shortly to witness some awful scene.

Whitehead Humphreys was at that time very ill, and his friends, believing his close drew near, were very anxious about him, knowing the infidel principles he had professed. His brother, who was deeply concerned, asked him if he would not like to see some Friends. The dying man did not appear to feel his situation, and declined to have an interview with any one, until the morning after Sarah Harrison's remarkable dream. He then consented to see Arthur Howell. His brother hastened to Arthur's residence, and not finding him at home, left a message, and went to Samuel Emlen's house. Samuel also was out. On his way back to his sick brother, he met Sarah Harrison and William Savery, and requesting them to accompany him, they did so. Soon after they reached the residence of Whitehead Humphreys, Samuel Emlen and Arthur Howell came in. They proceeded to the chamber of sickness, and found the dying man full of conversation, and in a restless, unsettled state. They sat down in silence by him, and at last Samuel Emlen said, "Whitehead, Whitehead! there is no time to be idle; thou art in an awful state!" This seemed to quiet the poor man, and then Sarah Harrison was drawn under a deep and awful concern to pray for him. After this he became more composed. He acknowledged fully the absurd wickedness of his infidel profession, saying, "Tell it at the corners of the streets; proclaim it in the assemblies of the people, that I have been endeavoring to believe a lie!" After some time the Friends left the chamber, somewhat relieved from the soul-harrowing feelings which had overpowered them on first sitting down in it. As she went away, Sarah Harrison told a sister-in-law of Whitehead her dream of the previous night, and mentioning the awful impressions which had clothed her mind, at the time of the vision, and when she first saw the sick man; she added, that her feelings were much more comfortable. She thought he might be called as at the eleventh hour. He died in two or three days.

Arthur Howell has been heard, in his public ministry, with a loud voice and energetic manner rehearsing this deathbed declaration of the would-be infidel — "Tell it at the corners of the streets; proclaim it in the assemblies of the people, that I have been endeavoring to believe a lie!"

It is related that while William Savery was in Ireland, he attended one meeting in which he was unable to speak in his usual fluent manner, and yet was not easy to omit endeavoring to express his concern. Yet his ministry in this meeting, foolish as it almost seemed to him, was of excellent service, and he mentioned after his return to America, that he had heard of more good effected by it, than by his testimony in any of his large meetings where words flowed smoothly and freely. It is not the melody of sentences or the beauty of ideas which makes the true ministry of the Gospel — it is the power which accompanies the words spoken. This power may accompany broken sentences, and set home the unpolished language of the illiterate even to the saving of souls.

While Mehitable Jenkins was in England on a religious visit, perhaps in the year 1787, she attended the circular meeting held at Exeter. Catharine Phillips was also at the meeting, and in the exercise of her beautiful and acceptable gift, spoke largely to those assembled. After Catharine had ceased, Mehitable, who was an illiterate woman, and not extensive as a minister, stood up and delivered a brief testimony. Some critical Quakeress, concerned perhaps for the *literary* reputation of the Society of Friends, complained to Timothy Bevington, that such a Friend as Mehitable should speak in such a large meeting. The complainant thought that good order required that an opportunity should be taken with Mehitable to prevent the possibility of her disturbing large gatherings, and said that the Friend's gift appeared better adapted to small meetings of our own Society. Timothy Bevington, from whom the anecdote is derived, replied to her that he believed no harm had been done. It so happened, that he had invited a man of some standing in Exeter, to attend this circular meeting, who had accepted the invitation. Soon after, he met Timothy, and expressed his warm thanks for the treat he had received. Timothy said he was pleased to find him so well satisfied — adding, "My friend Catharine Phillips is considered a great minister." "Yes," replied his friend, "we know Mrs. Phillips is a very sensible woman; we therefore are not surprised to hear *her* preach a good sermon; but the few words the elderly lady from America said, were to me far more weighty and suited to my situation of mind than anything Mrs. Phillips had to say. I hope to be thankful as long as I live for the great instruction, and sensible feeling of Divine goodness I experienced from the sweet, the short sermon of your American Friend."

This anecdote is very much in accordance with the testimony of William Penn. The wife of Lord Baltimore, after attending a meeting for worship at the time of the Yearly Meeting in Maryland, told him, she did not want to hear him, and such as he, for he was a scholar, and a wise man, and she did not question but he could preach; but she wanted to hear some of the mechanics preach — husbandmen, shoemakers, and such like rustics; for she thought they could not preach to any purpose. William told her, some of them were rather the best preachers we had among us.

The account of John Steel, and his testimony against those ancient apostates, John Wilkinson and John Story, is a strong illustration of the power of the Holy Spirit in qualifying illiterate instruments for the Lord's work. His testimony was, in the words of William Penn, " Neither the wisdom of the North, nor the eloquence of the South, but the power of God through a ploughman, and marvellous in our eyes."

About one hundred and twenty-five years ago, a Friend from England, on a religious visit in America, appointed a meeting in Philadelphia. After a time of silence, a young man in his common working clothes, with a leathern band around his waist arose from his seat about the middle of the meeting, and stepping into the passage-way, began to preach with great energy and power. This youthful preacher was the illiterate Thomas Brown. The Friend who had appointed the meeting felt excused from any public labor therein, but was well satisfied with that which had taken place. After the close of the meeting some of his Friends gathered round him, expressing their sorrow that another should have occupied the time, so that he should have had no opportunity of relieving his mind. He replied, "The service fell upon the lad."

John Richardson informs us in his journal, that when a young man he attended a large Yearly Meeting, at which there were many able ministers. The principal part of the labor having fallen on him; William Penn, when the meeting was over, took him aside, and thus addressed him: "The main part of the service of this day's work went on thy side, and we saw it, and were willing and easy to give way to the Truth, though it was through thee, who appears but like a shrub; and it is but reasonable the Lord should make use of whom he pleases: now, methinks, thou mayest be cheerful."

He says that, from William Penn's remarks, "I gathered, that he thought I was too much inclined to be cast down; therefore I gave him this true answer: 'I endeavor to keep in a medium, out of all extremes as believing it to be most agreeable to my station; with this remark, 'the worst of my times rather imbitter the best to me.' William shook his head, and said with much respect, 'There are many who steer in this course besides thee, and it is the safest path for us to walk in;' with several other expressions which bespoke affection. This worthy man, and minister of the Gospel, notwithstanding his great endowments and excellent qualifications, yet thought it his place to give way to the Truth, and let the holy testimony go through whom it might please the Lord to empower and employ in his work, although it might be through contemptible instruments. I sincerely desire this may prove profitable to those whom it may concern, and into whose hands it may come, that the Lord's work may be truly minded, and given way to, when it is opened; for seeing no man can open it, let not any strive in the man's part to shut the same."

John Richardson gives an interesting anecdote, showing how the Lord, in great kindness, did condescend through an unusual incident to confirm the faith of one of his tried and faint-hearted children. He says, "One thing is worthy of notice. As I was speaking in a meeting in Virginia, a sudden stop came upon me, and occasioned me to say, 'I cannot go forward;

whatsoever the matter may be, I know not;' but giving over immediately, a friend, whose name was Edward Thomas, began to preach, who was but young in the ministry, though an elderly man, and apt to be attended with reasonings. He said, after the meeting, he had sought to the Lord with prayers, that he would condescend so far to his request as to give me a sense of him, and in so doing he would take that as a great strength and confirmation to his ministry, in this day of many exercises and great fears." John stopping in the midst of his discourse, just when Edward was under a concern to stand up, was felt by the latter to be such a confirmation of the Divine authority of his call, as greatly consoled him. John adds, "Thus we see the Lord in his great mercy condescends to the low, weak, and as it were, infant states of his children, like a tender father, and being our heavenly High Priest, is touched with a feeling of the infirmities of his people; thanksgiving and honor be given to his most excellent name, now and forever."

William Savery was frequently silent in the meetings he attended in Europe, and sometimes his communications were very brief. Mary Dudley informs us, that at a meeting in Ireland, he was silent until near its close, when he arose, and said, "I feel as I often do when in meetings with my brethren and sisters — not much to say. But I wish them well, and if they are not admitted to the communion table, the supper of the Lamb, it will not be because they are not bidden guests, but because they are in the same state as those formerly bidden, not ready; — being full of, or employed too much about other things — lawful in themselves, but pursued to the hindering their acceptance."

While William Savery was abundant in his acknowledgment of the benefit of the outward coming of the Lord Jesus Christ and his sufferings and death upon Calvary, he was no less full in his testimony to the universality of the manifestations of the Lord's Light and Grace, and good Spirit in the hearts of all men with the offers of salvation. His Christianity was that of Fox, Barclay, and Penington. It embraced the one great sacrifice for all, and the benefit of that sacrifice offered for the acceptance of all by the Holy Spirit, through obedience to its requirings. He believed, and his heart was often warmed with grateful emotions in the belief, "that the grace of God, which bringeth salvation, hath appeared unto all men." In one of the meetings he attended in London, he spoke thus:

"Light is come into the world; but men love darkness better than light, because their deeds are evil. They are not willing to bring their deeds to this glorious touchstone — this test that would try all manner of actions — Christ *in* you, the hope of everlasting glory, in which the primitive believers were settled, and found rest. Here, from the beginning, the church of Christ was built — upon this Holy of holies, and everlasting Word of Christ and of God, speaking, directing, teaching, and leading them wheresoever they should go. If men had abode under this, it would have taught them all the same thing. It would have preserved those that have called themselves Christians, as well as all others, in harmony and unity. It could have made neither rents nor divisions. It would not have told *thee* one thing and *me* another. But this is the language it would have proclaimed in thy heart and mine, 'The work of righteousness is peace, and the effect thereof, quietness and assurance forever.' Is not this written upon every man's conscience? I am persuaded it is. I have heard the wild inhabitants of America declare this was truth. They found inscribed on their hearts, according to their own expressions, ' by the finger of God's Spirit, that the work of righteousness is peace, and the way to be happy in this present life, and to be eternally happy in the world to come, is to obey his voice — to do those things which, by his law written in them, he had made known to them they ought to do.' This Divine principle I desire more people to come to; but men have been too long bewildered in following one another in darkness and confusion."

This doctrine, as "Christ within the hope of glory," was abundantly preached by our early Friends. How it was held and enforced by George Fox, we have set forth in the following narrative given by an ancient woman:

"Now, Friends, I will tell you how I was first convinced. I was a young lass at that time, and lived in Dorsetshire, when George Fox came to that county; and he having appointed a meeting to which the people generally flocked, I went among the rest; and on my going along the road, this query arose in my mind: 'What is that I feel which condemneth me when I do evil, and justifieth me when I do well? What is it?' In this state I went to the meeting. It was a large gathering, and George Fox rose up with these words: 'Who art thou that queriest in thy mind, what is it which I feel, which condemneth me when I do evil, and justifieth me when I do well? I will tell thee what it is. Lo! He that formeth the mountains and createth the wind, and declareth unto man what are his thoughts, that maketh the morning darkness, and treadeth upon the high places of the earth; the Lord, the God of Hosts is his name. It is he, by his Spirit, that condemneth thee for evil, and justifieth thee when thou dost well. Keep under its dictates, and it will be thy preserver to the end.'" After narrating this, the aged Friend was enabled to add, "It was the truth — the very truth, and I have never departed from it."

On the 30th day of the Eighth month, 1650, George Fox was committed to the House of Correction in Derby, for his faithfulness to apprehended duty. While he was in confinement, a trooper being in the parish steeple-house listening to the priest, heard a voice within him, saying, "Dost thou not know that my servant is in prison? Go to him for direction." He went to see George, who spake to his condition, so that his spiritual understanding was opened, and he made sensible of the Lord's mercy. The substance of the sermon was, "That which shows thee thy sins, and troubles thee for them, will show thee his salvation. For He that shows a man his sin, is the same that takes it away."

William Savery was an active, energetic laborer in whatever his Master called him to. He said, "In the Lord's house there is no room for the slothful;" and his actions manifested that he believed in the truth of this assertion.

He was in person about five feet nine or ten inches in height, was of a firm make, and for one inclining to corpulency, had a good figure. His features were comely and although his complexion was not fair, it was good and healthy. The expression of his face was usually placid, and when he was sitting in silence, in meeting, or the social circle, it was dignified and sedate. But when in conversation, his countenance would often suddenly brighten up, and a smile the most benignant and attractive would play over it.

He was diligent in his worldly business — liberal in administering to the wants of the needy, as far as was in his power — and faithful in the performance of his various religious duties. In 1802, and 1803, in both which years Philadelphia had slight visitations of pestilential fever, he devoted himself to visiting the sick and afflicted, and being deeply affected with their sufferings, he was enabled to sympathize with them, and minister to them at seasons comfort and consolation.

While his bodily health was declining, he did not complain, but continued attending to his outward business, with quiet cheerfulness. He found himself constrained to declare in some of the last public meetings he attended, that his time on earth would not be long, but signified, in an animating view of a blessed immortality, that it mattered not how short it might be, if heavenly rest was attained.

When unable to attend meetings, he at one time appeared anxious to get there, that he might have the opportunity once more to warn the aged who had got into the earth, and the youth who had got into the air.

The Saviour whom he loved, was with him to the close, leading him in a low, humble path, wherein all earthly dependence was shaken. His labors in the ministry — the favored seasons he had witnessed — the services his Master had enabled him to perform in the church — were not now his stay and support. "I thought," he said, "I was once strong for the work, but now I am a child, brought back to my horn-book, and have nothing to trust to but the mercy of God through Christ my Saviour." Thus leaning on the Christian's unfailing support, he drew nearer and nearer his close, and in the fresh feeling of inward comfort, he exclaimed, "Glory to God!" A short time after thus expressing himself, he quietly passed away, leaving to survivors a bright example of dedication and humility. His death took place on the 19th of Sixth month, 1804.

GEORGE DILLWYN.

GEORGE DILLWYN was born in Philadelphia, on the 26th day of the Second month, 1738. His parents were members of the religious Society of Friends. His father was removed by death when he was quite young, leaving him to the sole care of his mother, who was enabled, through the Lord's holy assistance, to exercise a wise and restraining influence over him. Her watchful care over his conduct, and pious concern for his soul's best welfare, were no doubt blessed to him, yet he was often thoughtless in his actions, and at times little outward evidence could be seen of the operation of that principle of light and Truth which was at work in his soul.

He manifested a strong tendency to foppery in dress and a great fondness for vain amusements. These, no doubt, often grieved the heart of his mother, and caused the secret prayer to arise that God would enamor his soul with such a love for the ornaments of the Christian character, and such a taste for heavenly refreshment, that all outward adorning would appear to him as less than nothing and vanity, and all earthly pleasures as trouble in disguise. Among other foolish habits he was wont to indulge in whistling. When Thomas Gawthrop, that honest old seaman, was on his second religious visit to this country, in the year 1755 or '6, he was sitting at the dinner-table in a Friend's house, when George Dillwyn entered the room, whistling in his usual thoughtless manner. Thomas ceased eating, laid down his knife, and, in accents of strong feeling, said, " I wished for the wings of a dove, to be with you; and now you make my heart sick!" This short sermon made a powerful impression on the lad to whom it was addressed, and it was remembered and repeated by him in very advanced life.

In the early part of his life George Dillwyn was in Lancaster for a short time. During that period the following occurrence took place. As he was walking in the street one day, he beheld the Deputy-Governor of the province approaching, and at the sight an intimation was inwardly given him, " Thou must address him in the singular language." He had not yet learned to take up the cross of Christ and despise the shame, and therefore he met the dignitary with the usual salutation, " How do you do, sir?" as he bowed his head and touched his hat, with that flourish of the hand, which is intended to say, "You may consider my head uncovered." Condemnation followed in the mind of the young man for this compliance with the fashions of the world, in opposition to the sense of duty which had been clearly given to him. In anguish of spirit he paced up and down the streets, despising himself for his weakness and folly. Some time after he again met the Governor, and, in a vivid feeling of his past troubles for unfaithfulness, he touched not his hat, while the simple Quaker salutation, "How dost thou do?" passed from his lips. In the latter part of his life, while relating this circumstance, and commenting on the comfort he felt for this little act of faithfulness, he said, "It was as if a pebble had been removed from the spring's mouth, so sweetly did the stream of consolation flow."

In the latter part of 1759, when but little more than twenty-one years of age, George Dillwyn married Sarah Hill of Philadelphia. He then entered into business, in which he met with many losses and disappointments. Honest in principle, he felt himself bound to pay every one of his creditors in full, which, by dint of economy and retrenchment, he effected. During these temporal trials which beset his path, and which helped to drive him to the Fountain of love for comfort, an honest Menonist, who loved him and was anxiously concerned for his best interest, one day thus accosted him: "Georgey, I heard de was in drouble, and I was very glad of it!" The speaker, no doubt, had learned, from heartfelt experience, that trouble springeth not "out of the ground;" that it is "whom the Lord loveth he chasteneth," and that it still remains to be a truth that "acceptable men" are tried "in the furnace of affliction."

As the trials of life began more and more to press upon him, his inward desires after holiness grew stronger and stronger. Through the effectual baptisms of the Holy Spirit, the process of regeneration was carried on, and in that closely proving season, he witnessed a preparation for entering upon the exercise of a gift in the ministry, which the Lord Jesus Christ had conferred upon him. This was in the twenty-eighth year of his age.

Some of his friends were slow to receive the conviction that he was really an anointed minister; but as he endeavored patiently to keep to his gift, his heavenly Master made way for him, and removed one by one the fears and the prejudices which at first prevailed against him.

He was deeply impressed with the mercy which had been extended to him, and, in looking back over the many sins and corruptions which had marked his youthful years, he was ready to query, "If I am accepted, who can be rejected?" Feeling the universality of the

16 *

love of God to every soul which he had created, and remembering his own deliverance, no wonder that he should often be led to treat thereon in his ministry. Indeed, so emphatically did he declare that God willeth not the death of him that dieth — so earnestly set forth the sufficiency of the means of grace and salvation for the redemption of all — that some mistook him, and a fear that he was tending to "Universalism" was one of the causes which prevented full unity with him for a time. As way was made for him in the minds of his friends, he was soon called abroad to travel in the work of the ministry. One of his first visits of any length was through the Southern States, with Samuel Emlen and Thomas Scattergood, the latter of whom had not then opened his mouth as a minister.

Thomas Scattergood, after his return from a journey to the East, in 1781, passed through many fiery baptisms and spiritual exercises, and was thereby prepared in humble faithfulness to wait on the gift committed to him, and to minister in the Lord's time, and under the fresh anointing, in life and power. In the First month, 1783, the elders of the meeting he belonged to called the attention of the meeting to his public appearances as a minister among them. Great unity was expressed with his Gospel labors, and a proposition was made to acknowledge his gift in the ministry by recommending him to the Quarterly Meeting of Ministers and Elders. Some Friends, though uniting with him, yet were not disposed to move along so fast, and proposed that the case should lay over another month for consideration. Others thought, that as the meeting had entered into the subject, and had fully and freely expressed its unity with him, the business had better be finished at that time. Some discordant remarks were made, and as the discussion continued, Thomas, who had been sitting under religious exercise, arose, and, after premising that though the unity of his friends was precious to him, yet the time of publicly acknowledging it was of no consequence, proceeded to labor in Gospel power and authority. So remarkably was he favored, that when he took his seat the subject of recommending him at that time being revived, not a dissenting voice was heard. It seemed as though the overshadowing of heavenly good attending was a seal of Divine approval appreciated by all present.*

Although his services were generally acceptable to Friends, George often experienced times of desertion and conflict, in which he was buffeted by Satan. During one of these seasons he was at a meeting in Philadelphia, in which a Friend from England spoke encour-

---

* A memoir of the life and religious labors of this dedicated follower of the Lord Jesus has been published. See Friends' Library, vol. viii.

agingly to his state, as he thought, yet he seemed unable to lay hold of it, and could derive no comfort or satisfaction therefrom. After meeting he wandered about the streets disconsolate, and apparently without any other purpose than an endeavor to escape from himself. Without knowing whither he was going, he had approached William Wilson's door, and, upon recognizing the place, concluded to go in and see that worthy elder. As he entered the door, William cried out, in a cheerful voice, "George Dillwyn, thou art the very man I wanted to see! I have just received a letter from Samuel Emlen, who says, 'Give my love to dear George Dillwyn, and tell him, we *know* in whom we have believed.'" This message from his dear companion came to the soul of the mourner in the very spirit of true Gospel ministry, reviving his faith, animating his love, and awakening gratitude and praise. The clouds of gloom fled away, and once more, in hope and confidence, he could look toward the Lord's holy habitation. Trials and exercises he held to be needful for all Christian travellers, but particularly for ministers of the Gospel.

During the troubles of the American Revolution, he thus wrote to a Friend, Fifth month 8th, 1781: "We were yesterday invited to the burial of Edmund Hollinshead; but it being our Monthly Meeting, and the day inclement, few went from Burlington to it. Inned, *such changes* don't appear to make the same impression on our minds now as in serener days. They rather look like escapes from approaching storm; and our concern for the departed is lost in apprehension for the living."

In 1784, George Dillwyn left America, with the unity of his Friends, to pay a religious visit in England, in which country he principally resided for the next eighteen years. His wife, a valuable woman and true helpmeet, accompanied him. It has been pleasantly said, that when he was about starting, she went into the men's Monthly Meeting at Burlington, where they then resided, and asked the advice of the meeting whether she had better accompany him or not, saying, "I am resigned to go or stay; but I believe I am most resigned to go."

George Dillwyn, a short time before his decease, told a friend who had gone from Philadelphia to visit him, that he had had a heavenly visitation when only four years old. This merciful extension of Divine regard was experienced by him while at meeting in the old Market Street house. He said, that after that visitation he had wandered far and wide, yet he never lost sight of it at any time, and the remembrance of the feelings he had then known remained with him, and was as a rallying point.

His religious services in England were very much

confined to London and its neighborhood. Things were, according to the account given in his letters, very low in our religious Society there; and he says in meetings for discipline, "the guidance of a wisdom superior to human, appears to be but little waited for or attended to, as the rule of action." While there, George was much led into family visits, in which his dear friend and fellow-countryman, Samuel Emlen, frequently joined him. He returned to America in 1791, having visited parts of Holland and France, as well as England and Ireland.

As to personal appearance, George was a handsome man, though corpulent; his complexion in middle age was so ruddy and healthy, that even in England it was thought fine, and rich in color. He was about five feet nine inches in height; his usual dress was drab, although sometimes it almost approached a brown. His voice was in younger life very melodious, and though impaired by age, yet it was agreeable to the close of his life. In matter, he was evangelical — in mode of delivery sententious — and peculiarly solemn and sweet in prayer. Age, which took the color from his cheek, and somewhat of the silver tone from his voice, but added to his heavenly-mindedness, and his religious sensibility.

In 1793, under an impression of duty, he removed with his wife to London, believing that his labors in the ministry for a few years would be principally in the neighborhood of that city. Samuel Emlen, who was there when he arrived, thus writes to his friend, Henry Drinker, of Philadelphia, under date Eighth month 23d, 1793:

"Our beloved George Dillwyn and wife met with a very cordial welcome among Friends in this city. I think George, indeed, honored of his Master, and wisely careful not to rob him of that honor which is only to be ascribed to Him, who is infinite in wisdom, and mighty in power, for promoting the work of righteousness and Truth through such instruments as he chooses. I don't find George has any idea of an *establishment* in London; his amiable Sarah, though allowing England to be a fine country, evinces a strong preference to the land of our nativity. George desires my offering thee his brotherly salutation, and I know from conversation heretofore, that he does love thee." "I sometimes see Dr. Edwards, who offered me a hundred thousand acres of land, saying he is employed by thee, and some others, as a vendor. I told him, it would be very strange, if I, who came over to this country to persuade people to think more of heaven than of earth, should become a purchaser of a *hundred thousand* acres of land!"

While residing in London, George Dillwyn was so often led to administer the word of reproof, that some of his high-minded hearers, whose backslidden or unregenerate state he had sharply spoken to, became much dissatisfied with him. The knowledge of this sometimes caused him deep discouragement, and he often went mourning on his way, in a sense of the degeneracy of many, and the dislike of a few. During one such season of depression, the prospect that it would be right for him to hold an evening meeting in that city opened before his mind. He was so much cast down, that he thought as his Master had led him to utter such hard things, no way would open in the minds of Friends to appoint a meeting for him, and in this tried state he remained for a few days. In the mean time, Thomas Scattergood, who was also then engaged in a religious visit in England, came into the city, and after remaining a short period, felt a concern to appoint an evening meeting. The meeting was held. Thomas had no vocal service therein, but George Dillwyn was largely opened in Gospel power and authority to unfold the Lord's message to the people. When the meeting was about closing, Thomas Scattergood arose, and said, that when he had entered London a few days previously, the language had run through his mind, "What if thou shouldst appoint a meeting for thy elder brother." He said that he had not understood the query, and the remembrance of it was quite taken from him, at the time the concern came upon him to have the people collected for an evening meeting. "I have appointed a meeting," he added, "in which I have had nothing to say, but my elder brother has had the service."

On the 14th day of the Seventh month, 1800, Thomas Scattergood wrote a letter to his friend George Dillwyn, from which we extract a few passages. They were yet both in England. "Thou art, I think, just right with respect to comparing, or bringing us back to youthful days. I was a *diver*, and thou and I have had our dips under the water together, since the day we met in this land. How singular, and yet how comfortable was it, on reading thy lines, to remember afresh the thoughts of my heart respecting thee, within these few days past—they came up somewhat after this manner; for I may assure thee, I have had a very deep plunge: 'There is my friend and brother, George Dillwyn, who appears to be bearing me company, and seems like another Ezekiel; he has prepared his stuff, and has removed; he has had a singular life in this land, much like mine; he has returned again, and though I am separated from wife, and children, etc., yet he appears like one bound as I am. I have seen him as a mark that has been shot at, and the archers have wounded him.' From thoughts like these my mind was brought into near fellowship with thee. Was not this like *diving* under the water, and *touch-*

ing? Can thou recollect that we can see one another under the water, when we cannot speak? I have often wanted to say more to thee, but when with thee have been restrained."

Many very apt illustrations are to be found in the writings and sayings of George Dillwyn, and though not of so poetic a cast of mind as James Simpson, his similies are generally striking. The following extract of a letter from David Sands to Thomas Scattergood embodies one of them. "I have heard of thy late trial in the loss of thy dear daughter, and I believe do sympathize with thee in that and other afflictive dispensations, yet have not the least doubt but all those things that we meet with, and which may seem little else to our taste than the wormwood and gall, are but like the strong winds sent to bring the leaky ship to a safe port. As I remember to have heard dear George Dillwyn say, when in America, to an afflicted Friend, 'Our proper business at such times is to keep the head of the vessel the right way; if we do so, we shall gain by such dispensations.'"

George Dillwyn thus laconically writes to Thomas Scattergood: "Thou and I correspond, in the letter way, like poor day-laborers who have but little to spare to each other. The sparing of that little, however, seems to be saying, 'If I had more thou shouldst be heartily welcome to it.' I may congratulate thee on thy finish at Devonshire house [a family visit], and was pleased with thy retreat into the country, though such little recesses from service often remind me of a speech of the mate of the ship Pigou, one morning to the sailors: 'Come, lads, step down and get your breakfasts as quick as you can, and then you will have nothing to do but to work.'"

In the year 1802, George Dillwyn, believing that his service in England was completed, returned to America, and once more settled at Burlington. He did not travel much in the ministry after this, but was diligent in the attendance of his particular meetings, being seldom absent from either the Monthly, Quarterly, or Yearly Meeting to which he belonged. He was particular in his endeavor to take all the members of his family with him, saying, "He did not find his meetings did him much good, if he could reflect upon having left any person in his service unnecessarily at home." How is it possible for any one who really believes that it is in accordance with the will of the Great Head of the church for his children to meet before him for public worship, to neglect "the assembling of themselves together, as the manner of some is?"

The following anecdote contains a pungent rebuke administered effectually to one, and there may be others to whom it would equally apply. A member of the Society who resided in a village not far from Philadelphia, during a considerable portion of the meridian of his life, evinced little disposition to conform to the testimonies and principles of his profession. Among other things, he was very negligent in the attendance of religious meetings, and on one occasion refused to withdraw a few minutes from his worldly business to sit with his family during the time of a religious visit paid them by two ministering Friends. His son, having been favored with a powerful visitation of Divine love, yielded in measure thereto, and became diligent in going to meetings, walking to the one they belonged to, though at the distance of several miles. One day Joseph Hemphill, a distinguished lawyer of Philadelphia, afterward a judge and member of Congress, came into the store, and, not seeing the young man, inquired of the father where he was. "Gone to meeting," said the father, with a sneer. "Gone to meeting!" replied Joseph. "The more to his credit; for he gets no help from his father, mother, or sister! I tell you what, if I was in your place, if I could not live up to the principles I professed, I would request to be released from membership."

This unexpected rebuke had a powerful effect on the man to whom it was addressed. He said he never had had such a sermon preached to him. He could not get from under the weight of it, and soon found himself most easy to be diligent in his religious duties. At the time of his death he sat head of the meeting he belonged to, and was thought to have become a humble-minded Christian.

George Dillwyn was a watchful, tender, sympathizing friend of those who were young in the ministry, not hastily condemning them because of a misstep in their tribulated way. He remembered his own coming forth in that line; and the difficulties he had met with, caused him to be willing to make full proof of others before he rejected their offerings. It is stated, that when he had spoken a few times in public, a valuable elder, who had come to a hasty conclusion in his case, told George he believed he had mistaken his calling, and requested him to withhold his exercises from the meeting. George meekly replied, if the elder would take the burden upon him, he would be silent. This the Friend was willing to do; and for some time George's voice was not heard in the public assemblies. But while the silenced one was permitted to enjoy quiet peace in submission, the mind of the elder became tried and uneasy; and eventually, under a sense of duty, he called upon George, and told him he could not bear the responsibility of sealing his mouth any longer, and encouraged him to exercise his gift when he felt the Divine call thereto. This is a very instructive anecdote; to elders it is a warning not to be too hasty in judgment,— to young ministers an incitement to leave their cause with their heavenly Father to plead for them, while they endeavor to receive the counsel of their elder friends with meekness and submission.

On his return from Europe, George Dillwyn devoted his leisure more to literary labors for the good of the community, than he had hitherto done. His work, commonly known as "Dillwyn's Reflections," contains many pithy thoughts, well expressed. It also contains some anecdotes, from which a few extracts will be given. He says:

"In conversing with a person of distinction in the community, on the universality of Divine Grace, he related the following anecdote, which I give in nearly his own words. 'When I was a little boy, I went to a school, which assembled by the ringing of a bell; and one morning, on hearing it, I hastened into my father's chamber, to receive a penny or two, which he daily gave me to buy a cake by the way; but found him in a sound sleep. The case was urgent, and as I feared to awake him, I thought I might venture to take my usual stipend from his pocket, and tell him at my return what I had done, not doubting my reason for it would satisfy him. I accordingly took it, but instantly felt it was wrong; and, by the time I reached the head of the stairs, my uneasiness increased to so great a degree, that I could not proceed till I had replaced the money; which having done, I went off quiet and cheerful. Now, sir,' said the relator, 'is this what the Society of Friends allude to, as an universal principle in the heart of man?' I answered, 'Yes.' 'Why, then,' he replied, 'I have been more of a Quaker than I thought myself, from my early days; and the remembrance of this occurrence has proved cautionary to me, on many occasions, in my business and conduct, ever since.'"

Another instance of the restraining influence of Divine Grace narrated, is one in which he himself was concerned; he says:

"When the compiler of these anecdotes was a wild, heedless boy, about seven or eight years old, he had several very corrupt playfellows, and among them was one of an uncommonly daring disposition, who, being paramount in wickedness and profanity, and leading the way into mischief, was envied by the rest; therefore, for them to be as clever as they thought him, it was necessary to curse and swear, without hesitation or fear. In order to which, the compiler, on a certain day, and in a place not easily to be forgotten, attempted to take the Sacred Name into his mouth, and call for damnation to his soul! but he had hardly begun the shocking sentence, when he was seized with a sensation of horror, beyond description. This check to his wicked ambition was effectual, and the temptation to that evil was so completely overcome, that he never afterward dared to indulge it in the smallest degree. It was, indeed, the triumph of mercy over presumption!"

The restraining mercy of the Lord is indeed great! How often have we been preserved from engaging in evil courses by providential hindrances! Sometimes by the voice of His reproofs speaking terror to the soul; sometimes by the persuasions of his love awakening abhorrence of sin. I remember to have heard a son of piously concerned and godly parents say that at a time when he was about engaging in a wrong act, an appearance as of the face of his loved, respected, and honored father came before him, and he could not proceed. Of the saving mercy of the Lord Jesus, the following anecdote, quite abridged in its details, is a striking example.

A youthful member of Philadelphia Monthly Meeting, many years ago, gave way to evil habits until he had become an alien from his father's house. He had taken up his abode in a tavern, and seemed hastening to destruction with rapid strides. The entreaties of his concerned parents, the visible sorrow of their hearts, the secret reproofs of the Holy Spirit, the fear of the "dread after-scene," all seemed to produce no effect upon him. He had taken his own course, he had chosen his own delusion, and little hopes were entertained that he would ever be respectable as a man, much less consistent as a Christian. Yet the long-forbearing mercy of a gracious Saviour toward him was not exhausted. This prodigal, who turned away from his friends, who fled from his father, who seemed to court everlasting destruction, was made a witness of one more gracious, heavenly visitation of saving love. The tavern where he lived was on the Delaware. Late one night he retired to his bed, and while lying on it, as far as he could tell, perfectly awake, and cognizant of all that was going on around him, he heard a voice calling him by name, and bidding him go to the piazza of the house which projected toward the river. He obeyed the mandate, and from the piazza he saw, over the water, what appeared to him a manifestation of the Saviour of the world. Awfully impressed with the sight, the heart of the young man was sensible of remorse and condemnation. He was told that this was the last visitation of mercy he would ever receive, that now there was an open door for his escape from damnation; but that if this opening was not embraced, he was lost forever. He who opened to him his state, bade him go home at once to his father's house. Sensible, at length, that obedience was his only safety, the poor repentant prodigal, in the middle of the night, left the tavern, and went to the door which, in comparative innocence, he had often entered. He took courage to knock, and as he did so, the door opened, and the father, with extended arms, was ready to receive him. He who had given the saving visitation to the son, had been with the father, had aroused him from his bed, and, by the secret inspiration of his Holy Spirit on his mind, had thus brought him to the door to receive his weeping son. Having thus given up to the Lord's visitation, the young man, through faithful obedience to manifested duty, grew in grace, and experienced the work of regeneration carried on in his soul. He became a steady, religious character, was for a long time an overseer of that meeting, and in the hour of death felt himself sustained by the Christian's hope.

George Dillwyn, although often led, in his ministry, to speak at considerable length, yet was remarkable at times for the brevity of his public communications. Some of these were sufficiently startling. One day, while sitting in his select preparative meeting, he broke the silence with this arousing discourse: "Friends, I perceive the cloven foot is getting in among us!" What an incentive for deep heart-searching was this! Well might every minister present have put the question to him or herself, Have I lost my true guide? Am I listening to the voice of the stranger? Has the love of self beguiled me? Do I preach without the life and power that once attended my ministry? Yea, ministers and elders might have united in the heart-raised inquiry, Lord, is it I that have given occasion for this?

George Dillwyn says, "When persons who think they have attained to a stability in religion, speak lightly, or seem to make no account of those little steps of faith and obedience by which the Lord sees meet to lead his flock, and fit them for his fold, it is questionable if they have not missed the right gate, and are trying to get in some other way."

Some individuals are ready to esteem lightly, to speak contemptuously of our testimony to plainness in dress and address. These have either known nothing of those fiery baptisms through which some are made willing to take up the cross to their natural inclinations, and by consistent attire and scriptural language, become as spectacles to men; or having once known and departed in heart from the Truth, they are seeking to persuade themselves that the inward conflicts through which they were led to it, were delusions.

We have heard it related that a young female, perhaps not a member of the Society of Friends, became convinced that it was her religious duty to conform to its testimonies in regard to language and dress. About this time the family were preparing to give a great party, and she believed that on that occasion she must manifest in her conduct her obedience to the will of her Lord and Saviour in this respect. Deep was the trial to her; flesh and blood could but revolt at the mortification self was doomed to experience. While under this exercise of mind, she one morning went into the parlor, the windows of which had not been opened, and there, sitting out of sight of men, she sought for resignation to the Divine requiring, and strength to enable her to perform it. While she was thus engaged, Samuel Emlen, passing along the street she lived on, came opposite the house. A sense of a religious duty to be performed therein suddenly took hold of him. He paused, stepped in the entry, passed on till he reached the door of the darkened parlor. Putting his head inside of it, he exclaimed, "Be thou faithful unto death, and I will give thee a crown of life." Having said this, he returned to the street, and went on his way, having been enabled to administer, through the Lord's holy assistance, the word of strength and consolation to the unseen and unknown mourner. Animated by this providential visitation, the young woman was enabled to pursue the path of duty opened before her.

The following extract from a letter written to one who was passing through the baptisms incident to the transition state between a life of self and a life of self-denial, may illustrate this subject:

"Thou hast suffered from the ridicule of those who would not have thee enter on a religious life, a life of self-denial and the daily cross. Thou hast been tried, I fear, also by the advice of shallow though high professors, who have never submitted to be dipped into those trials and exercises into which the great Head of the Church introduces all those who are truly devoted to him. It is strange how easily some seem to slide out of a gay life into a plain one, out of the obvious rebellions of an unsubjected will, indulging in the vanities of a frivolous mind, into, at least, an appearance of tolerable consistency. They have made changes which have cost others months of anguish and suffering, and yet seem to have known nothing of taking up the cross. Some occupy stations in the church, rightly to qualify for which fiery baptism after fiery baptism must needs be endured, and yet there is but little appearance in them that they have ever experienced that inward burning which can alone purge away the tin and the reprobate silver. They seem to have discovered some bridge of human invention over Jordan, the river of judgment; and it is no wonder to me that they should not be familiar with its depths! Many can talk of the great love and mercy of their heavenly Father, can even vocally rejoice that Christ died for them, who yet know little of those inward, purifying sufferings through which he makes his dear children partakers of that salvation he has purchased for them.

"We suffer tribulation and baptisms, on various accounts, and we cannot always understand how we are to gain spiritually, from that we are enduring. Nevertheless, I believe, however dark the dispensation may seem at the time to us, that every such trial, rightly borne, is of consequence in furthering the work of perfect redemption. The trials we pass through, when obediently bearing the cross, may be necessary for ourselves — may be useful to others. The patience and gentleness with which we bear them, may be an effectual ministry to the unsubdued spirit of some watchful friend; — a ministry owned by the Master, although not even suspected at the moment by us. Beside this, we know not how peculiarly needful all that we endure may be to fit us for some unforeseen service, which our Lord will require at our hands. He may be thus fitting us for a long life of devotion to him, or for an early death. I remember an amiable young friend of mine, who for years had felt inwardly uneasy with respect to his dress, and who, in a season of renewed visitation, after many struggles of mind, took up the cross, and bowed to the requirings of duty. The day he made the change, an elderly female friend not acquainted with the circumstance, called at his house. On entering the door, sensations peculiarly solemn fell on her, and she seemed to partake a little of the deep baptism in which his mind was plunged. Many words did not pass between them, but the few he uttered set forth the depth of anguish which pressed upon him. He said as respected his feelings he could not suffer more, if the skin had been violently torn from his body. He found it no easy matter to make the change — but strengthened by his heavenly Father, he had taken the cup of affliction, and with quiet submission, drunk it to the dregs. Mortified pride submitted; — affection wounded in the house of his friends, found comfort and healing from the Physician of value; — faith grew stronger through this exercise; — obedience became less bitter; and from these inward trials the Christian graces seemed to gain new bloom. His religiously-minded friends sympathized with him, and rejoiced over him. They trusted that this suffering was to qualify him for a useful life; but his Saviour designed it as a preparation for a happy death! A few weeks after this change in his attire, while the freshness and sweetness of his recent humiliation of spirit was still upon him, he became suddenly ill. There were a few days of patiently borne suffering, sustained by a comfortable assurance that for the Saviour's sake, he was accepted in his obedience and dedication — and then he was taken away from all sorrow. The visitation which seemed to this young man but as a powerful incentive to consistency of attire, was indeed the last call of his Almighty Father to obedience, and the resignation of his will. He submitted, and his end was happy;—had he rebelled—how awful might the consequence have been!"

We give a few other anecdotes related in the words of George Dillwyn.

"The following relation was given in a private conversation by a Friend in the ministry from England. Being on his return home from America near to the coast of Ireland, in very hazy weather, he was awaked by an uneasiness of mind, and a strong impression that the ship was in danger. He roused the master, who also lay in the cabin, and requested him to go up and see how things were; but the captain, not liking the disturbance, told the Friend to make himself easy; they would take care enough of him. The Friend tried to compose himself, and refrained from speaking again for some time. The uneasiness, however, continuing, and becoming more urgent, he cried, with great earnestness, 'Captain, thou must get up!' The captain, with some grumbling, at length complied; and, in ascending the companion-way, roused the attention of the helmsman, who, as well as the seamen near the forecastle, were supposed to be dozing. This man, calling to the others, they presently exclaimed, 'Helm hard-a-lee! There's a light ahead!' On immediately sounding, they found themselves in shallow water, and dropped anchor, where, the weather being mild, they remained till the next morning, when, to their great surprise, it appeared they were near the shore, and that if they had continued their course but a few minutes longer, the vessel, at least, would probably have been lost. Such a manifest escape from danger humbled them all, and on the captain mentioning the Friend's uneasiness as the means of their preservation, the mate related a similar intimation to his own mind, by which the vessel he was in was preserved from being suddenly thrown on her beam-ends. 'I think, sir,' said he, 'this emotion of mine was like yours.' 'Ah, man,' said the Friend, 'if thou art so wise as always to heed that, it will guide thee to everlasting happiness!'"

"Another instance is related by a serious person, who, being master of a vessel, was in the harbor of Cape Francois at the time when the blacks revolted, and took arms against the whites. He was leaning on the rail of the quarter-deck, a sorrowful witness of that dreadful scene, when, without any apparent cause, he was suddenly impelled, as by a sense of fear, to quit the rail, and seat himself behind the companion-way for shelter. As he left the rail, the mate took his place, and instantly had his thumb fractured by a musket-ball from the shore, which, had not the master removed, must have entered his body."

"A sea-captain, well known in Philadelphia, being on the point of going on shipboard, felt his mind so impressed with uneasiness, that he could not proceed, and resigned the command. All he could say on the occasion was, that he was not easy to go; and the event proved he was right in attending to the restraint; for the vessel was lost, as is supposed, being never heard of after touching at Batavia."

Many circumstances of a similar character might be collected from the journals of Friends and other sources. One which some of the residents in this city have heard related by a Friend, now deceased, who was acquainted with the person alluded to, is interesting. A man, who was on his way to Europe in a brig, or some craft of small size, one night was aroused from his sleep by a sudden impression of terror, which caused him to spring out of his berth, and, without waiting to dress, hurry up the companion-way. As he reached the top, he saw a dark body rapidly passing; instinctively, as it were, he clasped his arms around it, and found himself suddenly borne to one side. An awful crash instantly followed, the vessel he had been in suddenly disappeared from below him, while a large ship, around the bowsprit of which he was clinging, passed rapidly over it, and swept on in the darkness. He soon made his way to the deck, and was comfortably cared for; but the vessel he had left his home in, and his late companions, were never more seen.

The following quotations from George Dillwyn, are all intended, though in different forms of language, to encourage humility, and discourage pride.

"Humility and love are equally essential to devotion and to happiness." "The root of pride is self-confidence; and they who fancy themselves more humble than others, may be the least so." "Humility of mind is neither arrived at, retained, nor increased, by comparing ourselves with others." "In ascending the mount of rectitude, we are more apt to indulge in reflecting on the past, than in contemplating the future; and so, comparing our attainments rather with those behind than with those before us, we easily, and often, mistake our resting-places for our journey's end."

As a warning to those, who, from any cause, either of personal or mental accomplishments, or because of the supposed more perfect discoveries of Truth to the mind, feel disposed to consider themselves elevated above their neighbors, we will narrate an anecdote.

A ministering Friend residing in England, under a religious concern paid a visit to the meetings in Ireland, in which service he was eminently favored. From place to place, as he travelled, he was furnished with abundance of suitable matter to communicate, and a baptizing power accompanied the Word preached to the tendering the hearts of the hearers, in a remarkable manner. During his visit, he was preserved in a humble state of mind, watchfully attentive to the openings of his Divine Master, and was therefore permitted to return to his home in peace. In his subsequent meditations, however, on his past visit, and the evident Divine influence attending his ministry, spiritual pride crept in; and he was apparently in danger of making total shipwreck of his humility, and thereby losing his hope in Christ.

While in this critical condition, he was instructed by a dream. He thought he was walking on a plain, reflecting on his late visit to Ireland — the wonderful service he had had there — and exulting in his increase of spiritual experience. As he was thus ministering food to his earthly nature, he lifted up his eyes and perceived a person of lofty stature approaching him. Full of presumption, engendered by his late thoughts, he advanced to meet the new-comer, and demanded his name. "My name is Self," said the giant. "Well," added the other, "I will kill thee." He thought in his dream that he immediately commenced the attack, and after a sharp contest, succeeded in beating Self to death. He then renewed his walk, and in addition to his former cause of inward gratulation, he now with much satisfaction thought over his last valorous exploit. While thus engaged, he beheld approaching a figure closely resembling the giant he had just killed, but of more than twice the size. As this majestic person drew near, he was met with the same question which had greeted the other — Who art thou? "I am Self," was the answer. "I thought I had killed thee," said the puffed-up preacher, "but I will do it again." So saying, he vigorously assailed this formidable enemy, and after a very severe and desperate struggle, succeeded in destroying him. Now again he began to meditate on his great deeds; when he saw before him a person, featured as the two others, but of immense stature, his head reaching to the clouds. He approached, and to the demand of his name, answered, "I am Self." Once more a combat commenced; but it was soon apparent that this new giant was coming off victor. The poor crest-fallen dreamer was brought to the ground, and perceived, as he thought, his death inevitable. Then, indeed, he thought of *One*, whose arm of power could bring aid and safety in any difficulty. His heart seemed humble, secret prayer was begotten to the Source of strength, his faith was renewed, and Self vanished. Then ended his dream.

As he pondered over its different parts, the delusion he had been previously under, was made clearly manifest to his mind. In tears and true contrition of heart he looked to the Source of every good and perfect gift, and received therefrom a renewal of that humility and fear, which in the days of his youthful visitations were given to him. Self, which in his first submission to the cross of Christ had been in measure slain — which had subsequently, through unwatchfulness, revived as a mighty giant, after, through Divine Grace, the pollutions of nature had been to a great extent cleansed; which then in a time of renewed visitation had been as it were slain a second time; and again revived by outward flattery, and inward unwatchfulness, into a spiritual monster, whose head reached the clouds — was now once more cast down. He felt in great tribulation; he saw the imminent danger he had been in of plunging himself into everlasting destruction; and with these feelings, and this sense, he dared no longer dwell upon his past labors for the Truth. His eye was now once more to the Lord, and the dream and the interpretation thereof, were to him as merciful warnings never to be forgotten.

George Dillwyn was much interested in the welfare of the Indian natives of this country, and at times felt his mind drawn toward them in that love which persuaded him there was that in them to which the Gospel might be preached. He had divers interesting religious conversations with a deputation of Cherokees who visited the city of Philadelphia in the First month, 1792. These Indians were seven in number, six males and one female. The chief man among them was Nehetooyah, or the "Bloody Fellow," and he appears to have done all the public speaking on their behalf. This being the first opportunity Friends had ever obtained of showing kindness to the members of this distant tribe, they were anxious to treat them with suitable hospitality and attention. On the 29th of the First month, the male part of the delegation, with an interpreter, were, by invitation, at the house of Isaac Zane, and appeared much gratified with examining a terrestrial globe which was shown them, particularly when the place of their own homes was pointed out on it, and the route they had travelled to Philadelphia. After listening to what was told them relative to the shape of the earth and other matters of a kindred nature, Nehetooyah, in a very pathetic tone of voice, gave utterance to a short speech. He first adverted to the great advantages which the white people had over their red brethren in knowledge. He then added an expression of surprise, that notwithstanding the white men knew that the Great Spirit made all, and provided for all his children, they should treat the red men so unfairly. He spoke of the first settlement of the whites, their growth, and how they had driven the Indians from their possessions without compensation. As he had travelled through the country, he had seen the fine houses which the white men had erected on the lands they had taken from the red men; and yet they were not satisfied, but coveted the little the red men still held. He ended with expressing his belief that this could not be consistent with the mind of the Great Spirit.

On Second month 2d, the Indians being again at the house of Isaac Zane, they were met by George Dillwyn, Mary Ridgway, and Jane Watson. On this occasion, these Friends addressed them by way of religious counsel. They spoke on the nature of the Divine Being, the inward workings of his Grace and Good Spirit in the hearts of all to restrain them from doing evil, the dependence of all on him for life, health, and every blessing; and pressed the conclusion, that as all were children of one common Father, they were bound to love one another, and to live in peace. One of them, addressing the Indians, said, "As any one of you would be grieved to observe quarreling and fighting among your children, so our heavenly Father is displeased with whatever interrupts the harmony that should always subsist among his children in the great family of mankind." During the course of the religious conversation, the Indians were told of a red brother named "The Guerre," who had once been a great warrior, but having been convinced of the evil of contention and war, had become a man of peace. He was one who attended the treaty at Lancaster in 1762, and the change in his sentiments being known, he was inquired of as to the cause. Laying a hand on his breast, and looking upward with a reverent expression, he said, "The Great Being has made it known to my heart, that he did not make men for the purpose of killing one another."

When George Dillwyn and his two female friends had fully expressed what was on their minds, the Indians requested time to deliberate on a suitable answer to such important advice as they had heard, and proposed that the Friends should meet them at the same house on the evening of the following day. On that occasion, Second month 3d, Nehetooyah spoke to the following import: "What we have heard from you has opened our eyes and our hearts. We feel very grateful for the concern and love which our brothers and sisters have shown for the red people, and the pains they have taken to bring them more to a knowledge of the Great Spirit above, and to make them acquainted with his will. In all the places we have visited, we never heard anything that opened our hearts so much. We did not believe that any woman could say such wise things as our sisters have said to us. But when we consider that from women came all men, we cannot wonder that they should be as wise as we." He then promised they would carry what they had heard in their hearts, and tell it to the red people in their own country. He said their fathers had told them the white men were wiser than the red men, because they had been able to read the Book which the Great Spirit had given them, and then added, "But we think he takes care of red men, who are his children too. We were told by our fathers to look up to the Great Spirit above when we were in distress, and he would help us."

The next day, Second month 4th, they visited William Waring's school, and had the various changes of the moon and the cause of eclipses explained to them. They were deeply interested, and as they seemed to set a very high estimate on such knowledge, the Friends took occasion to inform them that they considered all such things of less importance than goodness of heart.

On the evening of the 8th, George Dillwyn and others being present, the Indians were asked if they had ever heard of William Penn, or brother Onas, as the northern Indians called him. They replied they had not, but they thought it likely their fathers might have done so. The principle of the Society of Friends in respect to war was more fully unfolded to them; and they were informed that its consistent members would not undertake to defend themselves; and that this was so far from generally provoking abuse, that they had been often permitted, during the late war, to pass through both armies without molestation. One of Nehetoʻyah's speeches during this evening was this:

"The life of all men is given by the Great Spirit, and life to every one is allowed but for a short time. There are many ways by which it may be taken from us when the Great Spirit pleases, without our killing one another. This killing, I believe, would all cease if people would all love each other, and live according to the mind of the Great Spirit."

During George Dillwyn's last sojourn in England, he became closely attached, as a father in the Truth, to Susanna Horne, a young woman then just coming forth in the ministry. In the year 1812, she came to this country on a religious visit, and George had near unity with her in her ministerial labors among us. A few weeks after Susanna had sailed from this land, George Dillwyn rose, at the close of a meeting for worship in Burlington, and, in much brokenness and humility, said, "As many Friends are interested in Susanna Horne, I may tell them she has arrived safely in England." This annunciation was startling to all; and the weak in faith were no doubt full of fears, lest the slowly revolving weeks should not bring its confirmation. But time proved that George had been enabled to follow her in spirit even to her port, and was made sensible, although at three thousand miles' distance, of her landing.

Many somewhat similar circumstances are narrated. One is told of Martha Routh, who being from home attending her Quarterly Meeting, became very much agitated under a revelation to her mind that a nephew, whom she was bringing up as a son, was drowned. The accident took place at Manchester, some miles from Warrington, where the Quarterly Meeting was held. Martha gives the details in a letter, from which we take the following: "A Friend coming into our women's meeting with some papers for us to sign, said he thought it might not be improper just to mention that our friend, Robert Valentine, who had intended to proceed forward, was, on further consideration, most easy to return to Manchester. No sooner had he spoken, than a very unusual sadness, like a dart, struck through my whole frame, so that it was with difficulty I sat till the meeting was done, and then could not refrain from telling my aunt something had fallen out at Manchester since we left it yesterday, which is the cause of Robert's going back. She tried to put it from me, believing it was only a turn in his own mind, that he did not feel quite clear of us. But the intelligence in my own mind waxed louder and louder, so that before we were well out of the meeting-place, the voice said plainly, 'Thy nephew is dead!' I then told my aunt again, who, seeing me very sorrowful, said, 'My dear, do not afflict thyself so, but have faith and patience till inquiry can be made.' I said, 'My dear aunt, I do not afflict myself, but am distressed, and not without cause.' I then looked inward to see if he was removed by any kind of accident in the warehouse; but the answer was, 'No; he is sunk in deep water.' I then turned into a Friend's house, and sat in as much stillness as I could, but in great agony of spirit, which the Friend perceiving, inquired if anything was amiss. I told her my nephew was dead, and the way it had been permitted. She seemed much astonished, for she knew him well; but was willing to hope it was not so, and tried to comfort me; but I could receive none till another intimation was sounded in the ear of my soul: 'Be not overmuch troubled; he is taken from the evil to come, and is entered into rest and peace.' Nature then got some relief by tears, which were soon renewed by my dear husband's coming in, who was then told of the event, and was deeply afflicted therewith.

"We got home that evening in a carriage, and found the remains of our adopted son laid out, a fair corpse, except a little settling of blood in his face, being found, face downward, in what is called the whirlpool, near the usual place of bathing. Our before-mentioned Friend, and many others that were standing around him, I trust felt such a time of solemnity as will not easily be forgotten, when Robert was drawn forth in testimony, in which he had to express, from Divine authority, 'Sorrow not, my Friends, for I feel an evidence that it is well with the young man!'"

Joseph Priestley, the Unitarian preacher, and experimental chemist, who belonged to a school of philosophers who believe nothing they do not comprehend, hearing of this incident, applied to William Rathbone, of Liverpool, to inquire of Martha Routh herself, whether it were true. William, intending to ask the question, came to a meeting where Martha was, who rose with the text, "If they believe not Moses and the prophets, neither would they be persuaded, though one rose from the dead." In commenting upon these words, she was so sharp on the incredulous, unbelieving spirit of the world, that William was ashamed to speak to her on the subject.

Our late honest, plain-spoken Friend, George Withy, related the following anecdote while in this country. On a certain time, as he was travelling alone in Wales, where he was paying a religious visit, he felt a sudden impression that it would be right in him to turn round and go directly home. It was about midday, or shortly after, for he had attended a meeting in the morning, and was on his way to another, to be held in the afternoon. On receiving this apparent direction to forsake the work to which he had previously felt bound, he paused, and endeavored to weigh the matter in his own mind, looking for the pointings of Truth. The result of his secret breathing for right guidance was a strong impression of duty, to "Go home, and that quickly." He obeyed, and by travelling all night, reached his residence in the morning. He found that at the time the call to return home was felt by him, a niece of his was drowned — and as his wife had a family of children to care for, his presence and assistance on the occasion, seemed indispensable.

Of a similar character is the following incident, which is given as narrated in a letter bearing date some years since.

"A married man* in the younger walks of life, who had long been under the preparing hand of the Lord, for service in his church, believed it right to give up to accompany a minister in an extensive religious engagement. This was no small trial to him. He had a comfortable home, a lovely wife, several sons, and one daughter. He however bowed his neck to the cross — gave up to the requiring of duty, and with the consent and approbation of his Monthly Meeting set forward on the journey. During the visit his mouth was opened in the ministry to the comfort of his friends. As he and his companion were, one day, about entering a meeting-house, a letter was handed to him, which he saw was from home. Instantly a sense of sorrow seized him, and he felt that afflicting tidings

* Our late friend Samuel Bettle.

were contained in that letter. After a severe inward struggle, he believed it would be right in him to go into the meeting-house without breaking the seal. He did so, and notwithstanding the feeling of sorrow, he was enabled to get under religious exercise, and was strengthened to labor vocally with the people. His duty toward them over, his mind was turned in much love and solicitude toward his family at home. His wife was first brought into view, and in the opening of Truth, he saw her at home, and well. One by one his children seemed to come before his spiritual vision with the assurance that they were all in health, until he came to the last, his only daughter. His spiritual eye could not discern her in the family circle, and as he sadly mused, this language was spoken to his inward ear: 'She is dead.' The evidence which accompanied the words was so strong, that he could not doubt the truth of the opening, and the anguish of his mind was great. The meeting closed; and yet he dared not open the letter, for he felt what was in it, and was afraid to trust himself to read it in company. When he entered the carriage with his companion, and a valuable female minister, they queried what ailed him? He told them from his feelings he was sure his daughter was deceased. His companions were not willing to believe the opening on his mind, and endeavored to encourage him to think it was not true.

Nothing however shook his faith, and when they reached the place where they were to dine, he retired to a private room and opened his letter. It was but a confirmation of that which he by faith already knew. With tears he read the account of the dear child's sickness and death, and then summoning up fortitude, he passed into the parlor, threw the letter into the female minister's lap, and once more retired."

George Dillwyn had been unusually exempt from bodily pain, even in advanced age, but on the 3d of the Second month, 1820, when on his way to meeting, the ground being covered with sleet, he fell and fractured the hip bone. The attendant pain being very distressing, and every exertion failing to afford relief, a state of deep suffering ensued; his exercised mind was tempted, tried, and afflicted, as he expressed, beyond what he had ever before known, yet his concern was that he might be enabled to wait in deep abasement until light should arise upon his dwelling. Thus he passed nearly five months of great bodily suffering, and seasons of close mental conflict, through all which the Christian character shone with brightness. "I find there is a comfort over which disease has no power," was his remark on one occasion. Again, "Now I am prepared to adopt the language — Lo, the winter is past, the rain is over and gone, the flowers appear on the earth, the time of the singing of birds is come, and the voice of the turtle is heard in our land."

Patiently awaiting the coming of his dear Master's summons, he was released from his suffering tabernacle on the 23d of the Sixth month, following, in the eighty-third year of his age.

ARTHUR HOWELL.

ARTHUR HOWELL, the son of Joseph and Hannah Howell, was born in Philadelphia, Eighth month 20th, 1748. Although he was naturally of a quick, lively turn of mind, by obedience to the inward teachings of Truth he early knew his own will brought into subjection, and continuing faithful to his Heavenly Teacher, he came forth in the ministry in his minority.

He was acknowledged as a minister by his Monthly Meeting, in the Ninth month, 1779, when but twenty-one years of age. He was a frequent visitor at neighboring Monthly and Quarterly meetings, and meetings for discipline, and often had minutes from his Friends to visit those at a greater distance.

Various circumstances had indicated that he was often gifted with clear discernment in spiritual things, and that his Master at times favored him with prophetic foresight. The following incident illustrating this is in accordance with anecdotes told of many other faithful servants of the Lord Jesus Christ. An English woman Friend who was in this land on a religious visit, apprehending the time of release drew near, went, accompanied by Arthur, on board a vessel just ready to sail for her native country, to feel if she would be easy to take her passage in it. Arthur became distressed and agitated, and drawing a circle with chalk on the deck, said, "I can see, as plainly as I can see that ring, that this is neither the time, nor the vessel." The Friend did not take the passage, and the vessel sailing was never afterward heard of.

In 1793, when the yellow fever prevailed in Philadelphia in so alarming a manner that great numbers of the inhabitants fled from the city, Arthur Howell deemed it his place to remain, rendering such aid as was in his power to his afflicted fellow-citizens. One day, about the middle of the Ninth month, a colored man, named Benny, called on him, soliciting occupation in sawing and preparing the winter's wood.

The next morning one of his children, noticing he seemed very serious as he descended from his chamber, anxiously queried if he were ill? "No," he answered, "but Benny is dead." His son asked how he could say so, as the man had been at their house only the evening before. Arthur reiterated his conviction of the colored man's death, and taking his son with him, started for his residence. Where Dock Street now is, in those days was an open stream, and in a small hut on its banks, near Second Street, Benny had been living. As they passed along, meeting some acquaintances, Arthur Howell called to them, informed them of the death, and asked them to accompany him to the house. On forcing open the door, Benny was found within, dead. This was one of the last cases of death from the prevailing fever that year.

In the First month, 1794, Arthur Howell visited the families of Friends belonging to Haddonfield Monthly Meeting, and in the Fifth month, 1795, attended the Yearly Meeting held in the city of New York, and the Yearly Meeting at Rhode Island. During the visit to New York, as he was walking one morning along a street, he felt a strong impulse to go into a house he was passing. The pointing of duty was so clear, that although he supposed himself a perfect stranger to the inmates, he was made willing to obey;—he stopped at the door, found it the residence of an acquaintance from Philadelphia, whose wife, a minister, was confined to her chamber, sick in body, and deeply discouraged in mind. At Arthur's request he was admitted by her bedside, and was soon dipped into spiritual sympathy with her. In the arisings of life, his mouth was opened, and he had a powerful and consolatory testimony to deliver to her, which reaching her spirit in the land of her captivity, was made, through the Lord's blessing, the instrument of awakening her hope, and quickening her faith. She was comforted, and he being relieved from concern on her account, passed peacefully on to their Yearly Meeting.

On one occasion a company of young women who had come from a distance to Philadelphia, and who were anxious to see whatever was interesting and curious in it, concluded to step into Friends' Market Street meeting-house. At the head of the women's gallery sat a ministering Friend from England, whose person and attire peculiarly attracted the attention of one of the strangers, who could not cease looking at her. Perhaps something of the work of grace might have been traced by the gazer in the outward attire, and in the deep solemnity which sat sweetly on the countenance of the Friend. Some longings after spiritual good were awakened in the mind of the young woman, secretly giving birth to the wish, which she found herself saying over and over inwardly, "I wish *I* was like that lady! I wish *I* was like that lady!" While thus engaged, a man of full habit of body and of a medium height, rose in the gallery, and, in an energetic manner and sounding voice, spake out, "Leave off wishing and desiring, and seek for thyself!" "How does that gentleman know what I am thinking about?" said the young woman to herself. Serious thoughtfulness was increased in her. She felt drawn earnestly to seek after the Truth, and, through the mercy of God in Christ Jesus, found it to her rejoicing. The young woman became a useful member of the religious Society of Friends; the brief preacher was Arthur Howell.

How fearful is it for any one to be found resisting the calls of the Lord, refusing obedience to manifested duty. He waiteth long and is kind, but he will visit in righteous judgment the backsliding and rebellious. As Arthur Howell was passing through the markethouse one day, he saw a woman Friend standing with her back toward him. He did not know her, but under a sense of duty he came to her, and, placing a hand on each arm, said, "What art thou doing, standing with thy arms akimbo in the market? Go and preach the Gospel!" This woman had long felt an impression of duty to appear in the ministry, but she would not submit to the call of her Divine Master. Depression of mind followed, and still she refused obedience. The warning given her by Arthur was suffered to pass unimproved. After many loud calls and invitations, her mind became agitated, unsettled, and at last insane. She was deranged many years; and this arose, according to her own confession, from her want of submitting to the commands of Him who, as our Father in heaven, the Giver of every temporal and spiritual blessing, has a right to demand obedience from every soul which he has created.

Many unlooked-for warnings did Arthur give. Once passing along a street in Philadelphia, he suddenly addressed a person who was passing: "Young man, if thou enterest into that thou art going about, it will be thy utter ruin!" The young man was at that moment planning a speculation into which he was about entering. The salutation he thus received was accepted by him as a word of warning; he gave up his speculation, and soon saw that if he had engaged in it, temporal ruin would have been the consequence.

One First-day morning, after his own meeting was over, Arthur felt a sudden but strong impression of duty to attend the Quarterly Meeting which was to be held at Salem, New Jersey, the next day. At the time we are writing of, the Quarterly Meeting of Ministers and Elders of that Quarterly Meeting was held on Seventh-day, two meetings for worship were held on First-day, the meeting for business on Second-day, a youths' meeting at Salem on Third-day, and a youths' meeting at Pilesgrove on Fourth-day. As Arthur endeavored to weigh the concern, he felt most easy to attempt to fulfil it, notwithstanding it seemed late to engage in it. His old friend, Benedict Dorsey agreed to accompany him, and they set off for Salem. It was very late at night before they reached the house of a

Friend who resided near that place, where they purposed to find shelter. The family had all retired to their chambers; but being aroused, they quickly gave the Friends a hearty welcome, and ere long a warm supper.

The next morning, after breakfast, Arthur was inclined to walk, and while passing along, he saw many Friends collected about a house. A concern now came upon him, to go in among them. He obeyed his feelings, and after he had saluted them, silence almost immediately fell upon the group. After a time of deep exercise, Arthur began to address the owner of the house, and his wife, with whom he was unacquainted, and of whose private history he had had no hint. He told them from the impressions on his mind he did believe they were endeavoring to force their daughter, who was present at the interview, to marry contrary to her inclination. He added, if they should succeed in their endeavors, it would be the daughter's ruin, temporally and eternally. So much Divine power and unction accompanied the ministry, as to baptize the company into tears; and some of them — we have the testimony of an eye-witness — went to Quarterly Meeting that morning, with eyes bearing witness of recent strong emotion. This remarkable communication had a prevailing effect — the match was broken off — and the young woman was afterward happily married.

In the First month, 1798, Arthur Howell was set at liberty by his Monthly Meeting to visit Friends in the middle and western parts of Pennsylvania; in the Eleventh month, 1799, to attend meetings in New Jersey, and some other parts of Philadelphia Yearly Meeting; in the Tenth month, 1800, in company with Anne Mifflin and Ruth Richardson, to visit Friends in Philadelphia Quarterly Meeting, and elsewhere; and in the Second month, 1801, to perform a general visit to Friends of New Jersey.

On one occasion, after a meeting in New Jersey, he felt himself drawn to approach a carriage, which, having received its passengers, was about being driven away. Looking in, he beheld a woman, and addressed her in the following words: "Thou hast a work to do. Do it! and if they knock thee down, get up and go at it again." The woman Friend thus addressed, came forth in the ministry, in which she labored to an advanced age.

One bright summer morning, Arthur Howell felt an impression that some service was required of him out of the city, but where, or what, was hidden from him. He mentioned his feelings to some members of his family, and was encouraged by them to prepare himself to start; the idea suggesting itself to them that his concern would prove to be for Merion meeting, which was held that day. His horse was accordingly attached to the family chair, or chaise, which was one of those old-fashioned, roomy vehicles, with one seat, on which you could stow comfortably about as many persons as in a modern two-seated carriage. Arthur took a seat in it, accompanied by his son Israel, and a young man, named William Mott. At Arthur's direction they drove to Fourth Street, turned northward up it, and as the young men would occasionally inquire, "Which way?" he continued replying in the words, "Drive on." Thus they proceeded, Arthur yet in the dark as to where his service might be; but still his watchword to the young men was "Drive on," "Drive on," till they reached the house of his journeyman, John Nutts, who lived in Germantown, directly opposite Friends' meeting-house. Stopping the horse, they alighted, and as they did so, saw a funeral approaching. The carriages were driven into the yard by Friends' burial-ground, and Arthur, feeling now a clear manifestation of duty, followed after, accompanied by his two young men. Soon a fire was kindled within his heart, and a word was put into his mouth. "Blessed are the dead which die in the Lord from henceforth: Yea, saith the spirit, that they may rest from their labors, and their works do follow them." This was his text; and in his communication he set forth the blessedness of redeemed souls set at liberty from the shackles of mortality, in energetic language, and spoke as though this had been the happy experience of the individual, whether man or woman, he had no information, whose body was then being consigned to the earth. When this service was over, Arthur returned in peace to his home.

The next day, when his journeyman, Nutts, came into the city, he inquired of Arthur if he knew that people said he was a prophet? Arthur demanded what he meant. John, by way of reply, informed him, that the person whose funeral he had attended the day before was a woman who resided on the Logan estate. Her nephew, who was under her care, having died, some malicious person had spread abroad a report that she had caused the death of the child in order to inherit his property. The aunt was so affected at hearing this wicked charge, that her spirits sank, her health became impaired, she declined in strength, and at last died of a broken heart. During her season of sickness and sorrow, she had learned to look to the Lord for comfort, and, in full faith in the verity of the openings of his Holy Spirit on her mind, she had declared, when near her close, that the Lord would, in token of her innocence, send one of his ministers to preach at her funeral.

Arthur Howell was remarkably nice in his habits. He was neat in his person, and loved to have everything about him in order and clean. In his leather store, if the removal of hides, or other causes, brought dust on the floor, he would take a brush and sweep it out. His friend, Nicholas Waln, while passing by his place of business one day, seeing him busily occupied in this way, called out, "There are sweepers in high life as well as in low ones, Arthur."

In his public ministry, Arthur Howell was peculiar. His voice was loud, and as he only gave utterance to a few syllables with each breath, his communications appeared somewhat abrupt. In this particular he resembled our late Friend Thomas Shillitoe. He was peculiarly led to attend the funerals of Friends, and not many took place in the city among his acquaintance that he neglected.

The last minute he obtained for religious service from his Monthly Meeting was one in the Ninth month, 1812, setting him at liberty to visit the Western Quarterly Meeting and Baltimore Yearly Meeting.

He was now growing in years, and evidently believed that the time of his release from earthly cares and troubles drew nigh. He settled all his outward affairs that could be settled; and many little incidents remembered after his departure, gave his friends the undoubted assurance that he saw his end approaching, and was making himself ready. He was, as he himself expressed to one of his sons, much weaned from the world.

On the 24th of First month, 1816, he arose as usual, but soon complained of indisposition. On the afternoon of the next day, he appeared extremely ill, and much oppressed. This oppression continued to increase, and he expressed a desire to be allowed to remain perfectly quiet, without being interrupted by the administration of medicine or of any kind of nourishment. One of his sons asked him how he felt as respected his future prospects. He replied, calmly, "There is nothing in my way." His physician, Samuel P. Griffitts, added, "That crowns all." His illness increasing, he rapidly failed in strength, but continued perfectly sensible to the close, which took place early on the morning of the 26th, he being in the sixty-eighth year of his age.

Having been enabled in various ways to administer to the spiritual and temporal wants of others, his heavenly Father richly supplied his needs, and blessed him with a quiet and peaceful close. Oh, how holy the faith of those who, having proved that the Lord Jesus is gracious through the many trials of an obedient and dedicated life, can rest in quiet, unfaltering confidence upon his saving mercy in the hour of death! Thus died Arthur Howell. He had lived beloved by his intimates, respected by the community in which he dwelt. His funeral was largely attended by the members of the religious Society he belonged to, and by a very large concourse of his fellow-citizens, who gathered without ostentation or parade, in the deep feeling of a public loss.

WILLIAM JACKSON.

AMONG those members of the Society of Friends in Ireland who, about 1720, had their minds turned to the consideration of removing to America, was Isaac Jackson. He had a family of children growing up around him, and his thoughts were often upon them and their future settlement in life. He did not wish to take them to a new country, even though it offered many advantages over those they could hope for where they were, unless it should be according to the will of his heavenly Father. Both he and his wife had this subject much on their minds, being deeply exercised that they might know what their duty in this matter was. While Isaac was still undecided, and his mind full of earnest thought, he was favored with a remarkable dream, which he believed was providential, and which had the effect of convincing him that his removal to America was in the ordering, and would be with the approbation of Him who still leads his humble, dependent children, even in temporals, in the paths wherein they should go. The dream is thus described in the record made of this circumstance by one of Isaac's descendants:

" While Isaac and his wife were under exercise and concern of mind about so weighty an undertaking, and desirous that best Wisdom should direct, Isaac had a dream or vision to this import: That having landed with his family in America, he travelled a considerable distance back into the country, until he came to a valley, through which ran a pretty stream of water. The prospect and situation of the place seemed pleasant — a hill rising on the north, and a fine spring issuing near its foot; and in his dream he thought that there he and his family must settle, though [it was] then a wilderness and unimproved."

This dream seemed accompanied by a Divine unction, which satisfied him that it was right for him to remove to America, and in 1725 he came over to Pennsylvania. Soon after his arrival, he went into the country to seek for a place wherein he and his family might settle. In the course of his travel he came to the house of Jeremiah Starr, a Friend, who, in 1720, had settled in the wilderness in that part of Chester County known now as Londongrove Township. During conversation at this Friend's house, Isaac related his dream; and when he had described the beautiful spring, the uprising hill behind it, the lovely valley spreading out before it — which even the forest which clothed it could not hide — he was told that a spot just such as he described was near by. In the words of the account from which we have already quoted, "He soon went to see it, which, to his admiration, so closely resembled what he had a foresight of, that it was cause of gratitude and humble thankfulness."

He purchased the spot, and there, in Harmony Valley, his descendants reside at this present day. The valley spreads out now in beautiful greenness, and the pure water of that spring continues as refreshing as in the day when it bubbled out in the shade of the primeval forest.

The labor of Isaac Jackson, and his son William, a young man about twenty years old at the time of their removal to Pennsylvania, soon caused the hidden beauties of the spot they had chosen, to become apparent to the most careless passer-by. A portion of the valley was quickly stripped of its timber, and grass and grain soon covered the earth with verdure — the noble spring was opened out to day, and its waters sparkled in the bright sunlight, as the old overhanging trees were felled. A dwelling in which, although elegance was wanting, yet content found a resting-place, was speedily erected, and beneath its sheltering roof the father and mother, although possessing little

WILLIAM JACKSON.

wealth, except their lovely farm, lived in peace, enjoying all necessary comforts. This Isaac Jackson was a grandfather of the William Jackson mentioned below.

William Jackson, the youngest son of William and Catharine Jackson, was born in Londongrove Township, Chester County, on the 14th of Seventh month, 1746. His honest-hearted parents endeavored to bring him up in the nurture and admonition of the Lord, restraining him from evil, and leading him, as ability was received from above, into the way of Truth. In after life he felt and expressed his thankfulness for the care bestowed upon him by his parents, and referred to the beneficial effects resulting from their labors.

Toward the close of the Ninth month, 1754, Samuel Fothergill, who had come to America on a religious visit, and John Churchman, who had been to England on a similar errand, arrived in the Delaware River. John Churchman passed directly to his home at East Nottingham, and after a month or two, Samuel Fothergill came out through Chester County, being on his way to attend some of the meetings in the southern and western parts of Philadelphia Yearly Meeting. He, with John Churchman, held an appointed meeting somewhere near the dwelling of the elder William Jackson, and his young son William, then eight years old, ran to the place along with others of the family who were going. The house in which the meeting was held was probably crowded, for William, in describing the occurrence, said, "They pushed me in, that they might not lose me, and being where I saw the strangers, their solemn appearance and communications made lasting impressions." Samuel Fothergill in the course of his ministry dwelt much on the Saviour, and his miraculous birth, and the heart of the young child was open to receive the truth as it is in Jesus. The ministry of that day relative to the Lord Jesus, his conception and birth, "fixed," William said, "the belief immovably in my mind;—which shows the necessity of making right impressions on children's minds early."

As William Jackson continued faithful to the inward manifestations of the Lord's directing, illuminating grace, he grew in the knowledge of the Truth to the stature of a young man in Christ Jesus. A gift in the ministry of the Gospel of life and salvation was committed to him, and his public exercises being weighty and savory, were acceptable to his friends. It was about the year 1775 that he first appeared as a minister. In that same year he accompanied that father in the Truth, John Churchman, in his last journey on religious service.

The following memorandum, found in William

Jackson's handwriting, bearing date Second month, 1775, has doubtless reference to the exercises he was passing through to fit him for the ministry. "Having for some months in the beginning of this winter felt the refining hand to work mightily upon me, and believing it to be for some good end, a prayer was often formed in my heart: 'Thou knowest, O Lord, for what end thou thus dealest with me; grant me, therefore, patience, and to my soul a place of quiet, that I may wait to know the end.'" From other notes made by him about this time, it appears that he had many baptisms to pass through in view of the awful work to which he believed himself called.

His ministry was sound in doctrine, and his delivery was clear and forcible. The matter was good, and the manner characterized by simplicity and solemnity. He was recommended as a minister in the Second month, 1776, and was soon engaged to travel abroad in the work of the ministry.

In 1778 he married Hannah, daughter of Thomas and Hannah Seaman, of Westbury, Long Island, to which place he removed, residing there about two years.

Of his Gospel labors while a member of New York Yearly Meeting, we find no account preserved. He returned to Pennsylvania in 1790, and a certificate for himself and wife was accepted by New Garden

Monthly Meeting in that year. At the time of her removal from Long Island, Hannah Jackson stood in the station of elder. She had been carefully and religiously trained in early life, and, through the blessing of the Lord's Holy Spirit, and humble obedience on her part, the watchful care bestowed on her had not been lost. The memorial issued concerning her and her husband says, that her father, "being concerned to train up his children in the nurture and admonition of the Lord, in the frequent reading of the Holy Scriptures and the writings of our primitive Friends, in the diligent attendance of religious meetings, and the practice of frequently sitting together in silence to wait for the renewal of strength, her mind was prepared to embrace the early visitations of Truth; and by yielding obedience to the gradual unfoldings of the Divine counsel, she became qualified for usefulness in the church, and was, at an early period of life, appointed to the station of elder. In this situation, the integrity of her life, and the sweetness of her spirit, brought her into near unity with her Friends; but a further dispensation being allotted her, she passed through various humiliating exercises, and was thereby prepared to engage in the important work of the ministry."

Having received a gift in the ministry of the Gospel, and, under the fresh puttings forth and qualifying influence of the Holy Spirit, having made full proof of her calling, she was, in the Sixth month, 1792, recommended as a minister by New Garden Monthly Meeting. The comforts which William now experienced in his happy home did not prevent him from the faithful performance of his religious duties. He continued earnestly endeavoring to fulfil all the requirings of his blessed Saviour, whose providential mercies had crowned his life with blessings. His Gospel labors for several succeeding years appear to have been extensive in Philadelphia, New York, and New England Yearly Meetings, but no particular description of his services has come under notice. From the account received, it appears he was enabled to move under the puttings forth of the Lord's Spirit, and was favored with his holy help from day to day. In the simplicity of the Truth, and by plain, honest integrity, he advocated the cause of his blessed Master, and was enabled to adorn, by a circumspect life and conversation, the doctrine which he delivered to others.

His Master now called for further dedication at his hands, and in the Second month, 1802, he opened to the Friends of his Monthly Meeting a prospect of a religious visit to Friends in Great Britain and Ireland, which had for some years rested on his mind. Much unity was expressed by his Friends with this concern, and his Monthly and Quarterly Meetings, and the

Yearly Meeting of Ministers and Elders liberated him for that service.

After an unpleasant voyage, during which he suffered much from sickness, on the 27th of Eighth month, the ship Mars, on which he was a passenger, reached her place in the dock at Liverpool, and soon after James Cropper and James Ryely came on board. William says, "It did my heart good to see the faces of Friends; my heart filled my eyes." James Cropper kindly invited William to go to his house, which invitation was accepted. He was kindly welcomed by his host's wife, and William says "her cordial reception, attentive, tender care, and good nursing, made it a comfortable retreat. [It was] a satisfactory home during my stay in this great town."

We extract the following from a letter to his wife, written a few days after his landing.

"Last Fourth-day evening came dear Richard Jordan to my lodging. Grateful [the being together] was to us both. Next day [we were] at meeting. Oh! it was a most precious season to me, as [it was] also to him, when on the bended knees of both soul and body, he had to petition the Father on my behalf. In truth, I could say as holy Paul did at a certain time, 'God that comforteth those that are cast down, comforted us by the coming of Titus.' So have I been comforted by the coming of dear Richard! We have been comforted in one another, and in the Lord Jesus Christ."

Doubtless at that meeting Richard was favored, as he often was, with a powerful manifestation of Divine Grace, in the exercise of his gift. There are those now living who can remember divers occasions wherein meetings have been baptized under his ministry, into such a holy, such an awful solemnity, that it seemed as if all present felt, and were tendered. On some such occasions, with such weight and authority did he utter the Gospel promises, that they appeared to come with fresh power, and as new offers of mercy, then first made to poor sinners from the Fountain of love. The fathers and mothers in the Truth, as well as the babes and sucklings, at such times were animated and made glad, through the extendings of Divine Grace.*

On the 12th day of the Twelfth month, 1797, in the authority of Truth — in the power and prevalence of Gospel love, Richard Jordan thus preached the Word at the North Meeting-house in this city, and old and young, the learned and unlearned in the school of Christ, felt the precious influence. When he sat down, Samuel Emlen, that venerable minister of the Gospel — that prophet and seer — that true-hearted lover of the Lord Jesus Christ, animated by the participations

---

* A journal of the life and labors of this eminent minister of the Gospel has been published. See also Friends' Library, vol. xiii.

of the spiritual food which had been blessed by the Master, and distributed by the servant, rose and exclaimed, "I have been made to rejoice in the Lord, this day, for the offers of his salvation."

In the course of this visit William Jackson rode to Peter Price's, near Neath, in Wales. He says: "Having been much unwell the evening and night before, this was a hard day's work, thirty-two miles. Here I had to tarry for some days."

Of this friend, Peter Price, with whom William Jackson was comfortably resting for a few days, the following interesting circumstance is given in a letter from a Friend who travelled in England on a religious visit some years since.

"We came from thence into Glamorganshire, to the house of our dear worthy friend, Hannah Price. She is a minister, and in her eighty-sixth year. Her son Joseph is an elder. They are altogether a lovely family, and reminded me of the 'household of Narcissus,' and of 'Grandmother Lois.' The family relate a very remarkable circumstance which took place with Peter Price, their father, Hannah Price's husband. He was the son of a very rigid Roman Catholic widow, and at the age of fifteen, he and a sister were both taken ill of a fever. The sister died, and was buried. He too, as the family thought, was dead, but the doctor said there were symptoms about him which seemed to indicate some glimmerings of life; and although the family several times prepared to lay him out, yet the doctor would still say he would rather they would defer his interment; and in that way they kept him for thirty days! On the night before his revival, his mother felt impressed with the wish to place a small loaf of baker's bread near him, and in the morning when she came into his chamber, he was up, and the small loaf was gone. He afterward manifested very little uneasiness, except hunger; and when he alluded to his sister, they told him that she had been taken to her uncle's, for the doctor had desired them not to tell him of her death. 'Ah!' said he, 'she is not there, for I saw her in heaven!'

"He could not be persuaded to tell them what he had seen while he lay in that state, only that he had seen heaven and hell. He said it was too awful for him to describe. When arrived at manhood, he went over to America, but when the war commenced, he felt that he must not fight, and so returned to England. Soon after he became acquainted with Friends, joined the Society, and was always a very serious and exemplary character. He told his family that he intended to leave in writing, what he had seen, while he lay in that state of seeming death; but he was taken so suddenly ill, that it was not in his power to write. When he was expiring, the room was so filled with melody, that his family thought their servants were singing a hymn, and sent to see, but there was no such thing, and the sweet melody continued, to the utter astonishment of all in the chamber; so that such a saint might well leave a family of faith behind him."

We have not the means of following William Jackson through the various religious engagements of his after life. He appears to have kept no journal, and no letters of his writing after his return from Europe have come to hand. He visited many meetings within our own, and the Yearly Meetings of Virginia and Maryland, and in 1824, attended the Yearly Meetings of New York and New England. "In these various engagements, his edifying ministry and solid, circumspect deportment obtained the cordial approbation of Friends, and rendered his memory precious to many of those among whom he travelled. When at home, he was exemplary in the diligent and timely attendance of religious meetings. His appearances there in the ministry were not very frequent, but carried with them the seal and evidence of Truth. As he bore a faithful testimony in his own practice in favor of plainness in dress and the furniture of his house, so he was frequently concerned to recommend it to others, being often deeply pained with the departure of many among us from primitive simplicity. The ancient testimony of the Society to live within the bounds of our circumstances, and to avoid engaging in hazardous enterprises to the disturbance of our own tranquillity and the endangering of the property of others, lay very near to his heart, often advising his friends, and particularly those who were just setting out in life, to make their wants few, and thus avoid the danger of being driven to doubtful or improper expedients to supply them."

William and Hannah had, in their old age, two girls living with them, who were wont to accompany them to meeting, leaving the house to take care of itself during their absence. On one Fifth-day, a young man going late to meeting, saw that the roof of William's dwelling was on fire. He hurried to the meeting-house, and, opening the door, said, "William Jackson's house is on fire!" The meeting rose in a body, and while the men ran down to the dwelling, the women followed as fast as they conveniently could. William and his wife were too aged to be hurried; he must get his horse, and get his beloved Hannah behind him, before he could start, and that took time. They found that the activity of their loving friends had succeeded in arresting the flames, and after a time spent in clearly ascertaining that the fire was all extinguished, the whole body of Friends returned the half-mile to the meeting-house, and, taking their seats, held their usual meeting. The members of some families who had been left at home that day wondered much what could have detained Friends at meeting an hour later than usual.

Some time before his decease he found himself diseased, and suffered much at seasons; yet he was sometimes able to attend his own meeting, and was favored to minister in Gospel authority therein. At one time seeing a number of young people at the meeting, his heart seemed to yearn over them in a peculiar manner, and he repeated the patriarch Jacob's benediction: "God, before whom my fathers Abraham and Isaac did walk, the God which fed me all my life long unto this day — the angel which redeemed me from all evil, bless the lads." The solemnity with which this was uttered, made a deep impression on many of those in attendance.

During his decline he made many remarks showing the soundness of his Christian principles, and his love for the simplicity of the Truth. He told those about him of a legacy which a Friend had left his children. The legacy was to this effect:

> "Let your wants be few,
> Then a little will do."

In commenting on it, he said he found it true.

Being asked if he had any pain, he answered, "No; 'but the end of all things is at hand:' yet hope is an anchor to the soul, both sure and steadfast. I often feel more [desire] than I can express, that the youth may walk in truth and righteousness."

In speaking of an aged friend who had been removed from the trials of time, he said, " 'The righteous perisheth, and no man layeth it to heart, and merciful men are taken away, none considering that the righteous is taken away from the evil to come.' We know not the value of our friends until we lose them." He afterward added : " I plainly see that if ever Friends are a true Society again, they must come through suffering into primitive simplicity, as in former days. Though the present generation may think themselves wiser than our forefathers, yet they cannot experience the same joy in the Holy Ghost, which they did, unless they practise their abstinence." He then expressed a deep concern for some of his connections, and his desire that they might know the truth in themselves, as it is in Jesus. And especially the parents, for their dear children's sake, and bearing in mind, "all must die." His mind had evidently been travailing on behalf of some who he feared were in danger of infidelity, and he added, "Holy men of old, spake and wrote as they were moved by the Holy Ghost. What was written aforetime, was written for our learning, that we, through patience and comfort of the Scripture might have hope. As he spake by the mouth of his holy prophets, which have been since the world began."

A Friend bidding him farewell, William, in allusion to their taking leave again of each other, sweetly said, "I expect every time to be the last. Death has no sting, neither the grave any terror. I shall soon be cold. Dust thou art, and unto dust shalt thou return."

He at one time said, that his mother's advice to him was, not to talk too much, nor to laugh too much, but to take his father for an example, and walk as he did. He then referred to his father's dying direction relative to a plain coffin, and said that the mechanic who made it had expressed his desire that every person were like the deceased.

Hannah Jackson, who had been enabled to wait on and minister to the comfort of her beloved husband during most of his illness, toward the close of his life, began to fail rapidly, and deceased Twelfth month 25th, 1833, aged about eighty-five years. The bereaved husband, by the remains of his beloved companion, was enabled to say, "Peace — peace be to him that is far off, and to him that is near. Peace to the Israel of God!" and that he believed that she had witnessed this through life.

On one occasion, speaking of faith and hope in God, William Jackson said, "I may say they have been my great stay through life, even from my youth up; or, in other words, they were my guide and stay in youth, my strength in manhood, and now, in my old age, a support to me — a staff for me to lean on." Toward his close, he expressed his anxiety for the spread of simplicity and plainness in his own immediate neighborhood, where he had lived for nearly ninety years, and which he was about to leave, expressing a hope that his neighbors might yet be united in simplicity and true holiness, meeting together with one accord and under the influence of one Spirit.

At another time he alluded to the necessity of endeavoring always to keep a sound mind. Then, after being silent awhile, he added, "The time is *near* when those who wish to walk in the Truth as it is in Jesus, will meet with great trials."

He continued alive to the best interests of others to the close. One day, hearing those about him speak of a young man who had given evidence of a change of heart, having become concerned to dress more simply, and who had spoken in meeting, the account fairly animated this lover of the Lord Jesus and sincere laborer for the Truth. Thus, with his spiritual faculties alive, and the love of God sweetly flowing within him, he waited patiently till his close came. The Lord Jesus, whom he had loved and served in his measure through his long life, was near to support him through the valley and shadow of death, and to give him the victory over the last enemy. In the hope and faith of the Gospel, he quietly and peacefully resigned his spirit to him who gave it, on the 10th of First month, 1834, in the eighty-eighth year of his age.

Of him and his beloved Hannah it may truly be said, they were lovely and pleasant in their lives, and in death were not long divided.

PETER YARNALL.

ON the 17th day of the Fifth month, 1772, at Springfield, Pennsylvania, a group of mourning children was gathered around the death-bed of Mordecai Yarnall. All the children of that ancient minister of the Gospel were with him except his two sons, Mordecai and Peter, who, in the wildness of youth and the wickedness of an unsubjected will, had departed from the advice of their father — had disregarded his wholesome admonitions, his Christian counsel, his secret and public prayers for them — and had both of them joined the army. Their conduct, with other causes of grief, was depressing the spirit of the good old man, and bringing down his gray hairs with sorrow to the grave. The life of the dying man had been one of early dedication to the Lord's service, and, though encompassed with outward trials and afflictions, he was not forsaken now. Two of the lambs committed to him, to train and lead forward to the heavenly fold, had widely and sorrowfully wandered; but he had endeavored to do what he could for them, and, no doubt, felt that assurance of the Lord's merciful visitations to their souls, which brought him hope for them even now they were as prodigals, far — far from the mansion of spiritual plenty and peace.

Mordecai Yarnall had been, early in life, called to the ministry, and was fervent and faithful therein. His labors were abundant in America, different parts of which he often visited; and he paid a short but very acceptable visit to Friends in England in 1757 and 1758. While on his way thither, the vessel he was in was taken by the French, and he was carried a captive among a people of strange language. He was, however, soon released, and permitted to cross the Channel to his allotted field of labor. While Mordecai was endeavoring to fulfill his duty in England, Samuel Fothergill, sympathizing with the bereaved wife in America, wrote a letter to Mary Yarnall, of which we give an extract: "I early felt with thee, and for thee, when he was suffered to fall into the hands of unreasonable men; but He whom thy dear husband served, set bounds to their wrath, and vouchsafed a speedy deliverance. And why may we not suppose the Lord of the harvest perfectly wise, in now and then lighting a candle in these lands where darkness prevails? It is, doubtless, consistent with his sovereignty and goodness who would bless the utmost borders of his ample empire, and make the place of his feet glorious." . . . "I remember, and at this time it is fresh with me, that in my honorable father's absence — he being in your land — the humbling, converting Hand effectually prevailed with me, to embrace the day of his visitation. And my heart is anxious that you, the beloved offspring of the Lord's servant, may be enriched with the same blessing, and that you may give up your names to be inserted in the roll of the Lord's servants, which is the Lamb's book of Life. For this his prayers ascend, who, having proved the service of the Most High, has found it to be freedom and perfect liberty. May a holy union of spirit unite the whole together, that you may availingly follow after those things which make for your peace; and may innocent hands be put up to the Almighty for a beloved father's return to you in safety, and with sheaves in his bosom."*

Peter Yarnall was bound apprentice to a Friend in Philadelphia, who was a tanner and currier; but his master soon after declining business, the youth was placed with another Friend following the same occupation, within the limits of Uwchlan Monthly Meeting. As Peter grew up toward manhood, his fine talents, liberal education, pleasant manners, and great

---

* This letter, with others of that highly gifted minister of Christ, is published in the "Memoirs of the Life of Samuel Fothergill." See, also, Friends' Library, vol. ix.

powers of mimicry made him a favorite with the young. Pride took deep hold of him, and although, when about eighteen years of age, he was deemed religiously thoughtful, yet the serious feelings were not of long duration. He was proud; he could not, or would not bear reproof, or aught that seemed disparaging to his dignity. Exasperated by treatment which he had received at the hands of his master, he suddenly left his employ, went to New York or its neighborhood, and there enlisted as a soldier. Exulting in his freedom from his former yoke, he soon wrote to his father, explaining where he was, but manifesting no desire to be released from his military servitude. It was not long, however, before he found that the freedom he now possessed was slavery itself compared to his former mild restraints. But pride was in the way of an immediate acknowledgment of error.

The heart-afflicted father, when he knew the situation of Peter, came into Philadelphia, and sought to interest his friends there, in behalf of his high-minded, misguided boy. That meek disciple, John Pemberton, who honored Mordecai Yarnall through all the period of his adversity, who loved him truly in these his days of affliction — for the father's sake, and for the Lord Jesus Christ's sake, became earnestly watchful to promote the welfare of the son. While Mordecai was in the city — bowed down under sorrow of heart, he attended the Market Street meeting, and therein spoke this language: "Many are the afflictions of the righteous, but the Lord delivereth him out of them all." His own time of release drew near. As sickness wasted his strength, all his children but Mordecai and Peter were with him to receive his blessing, and minister to his comfort. A short time before his death, in a sense of the Lord's unfailing mercies, he thus addressed those around him:

"I believe it to be my duty, as it was a command given to Israel of old, [diligently to teach his children,] to tell of the loving-kindness of God to my soul, during my pilgrimage on earth; that, through the various changes it has been my lot to meet with here, I have ever had a refuge to flee to. And though I have sometimes had to think how nearly I have been tried, even in great tribulation, when in the hands of the enemy, and separated from the near and dear connections in life — yet I had faith to believe, that the same Divine hand which had been with me, and led me safely through the peril of deep waters, would still continue with me to the end; and my confidence was so firmly fixed in him, that he never suffered me once to fail. I always thought I should not want; and have now reason to believe I never shall. He that hath been my Alpha, will be my Omega.

"And my desire is, that you, my dear children, may

steadfastly place your trust and confidence in that same Power which has preserved me;—that the days of your youth may be devoted to his service. Though many may be the close trials that you will have to meet with, in passing along through this world, I have to say for your encouragement, that he will never forsake them that trust in him. He that hath delivered out of six troubles, will not leave in the seventh. Therefore, let not your dependence be on anything which this world can afford; but in Him alone; and He that is the guide of your youth, will become a staff for you to lean upon in your advanced age."

Thus was this ancient laborer sustained in faith at the approach of death, and thus he could comfort others with the same consolation, wherewith his God, in trials and distresses, had comforted him. He died in peace;—and by his bedside, as the spirit departed, and by the open grave which had received the clay tabernacle wherein he had dwelt, there was felt that calming presence of his Divine Master, sealing the assurance on the minds of those assembled, that he had escaped from all sorrow, and had entered into perfect rest.

Peter Yarnall soon grew weary of his position in the army. Before the death of his father he wrote two letters to John Pemberton, expressing his regret for the course he had taken, and asking that the influence of Friends might be used to obtain his release. John Pemberton took no direct notice of these letters, but through the agency of a Friend in New York, took some steps to obtain the discharge of both Mordecai and Peter from the army. After the death of his father, Peter again wrote to John Pemberton, who replied to him in an honest, plain-dealing letter, which was preserved by Peter through all his subsequent deviations from the paths of righteousness, in his wanderings by sea and land. One passage in the letter is as follows: "I wish thy mind may become so humbled, and thy spirit contrited, that thou may experience greater degrees of light and favor, after having passed through the righteous judgments of the Lord, because thou hast transgressed his holy laws, and run counter to the convictions of his grace. I much wish to see some *one*, and indeed *all* the offspring of thy worthy father, tread in his steps, and become ornaments of our holy profession." *

Soon after receiving this letter, Peter Yarnall obtained, through the efforts of John Pemberton, a discharge from the army.

Although Peter had not submitted to Divine grace,

---

* John Pemberton and his elder brothers Israel and James, were prominent and influential members of civil and religious society, and during the American Revolution, suffered much for their conscientious testimony against war. A Life of the former has been published. See Friends' Library, vol vi.

so as to qualify him to walk in the way of holiness, with fear and Christian circumspection, yet a sense of gratitude to his benefactor led him to take his advice. He went at his recommendation to live with Stacy Potts, at Trenton, with whom he remained until he was twenty-one years of age, when he removed to Germantown, and worked as a journeyman tanner. He followed that business, however, for a very short time: being encouraged to study medicine, he obtained a situation in the Pennsylvania Hospital. Here he found time, even in the midst of his medical pursuits, to peruse the writings of our early Friends, and some of his visitors entertained strong hope that his mind was becoming more seriously and thoughtfully engaged for his own everlasting good. These hopes were premature. The war of the Revolution coming on, and the American army being scantily supplied with medical men, an opportunity was opened for young students of medicine, to obtain employment, experience, and preferment. Peter Yarnall was anxious for all these, and his vague admiration for the principles of peace, truth, and righteousness, exercised little restraint on his actions. He entered the army as a surgeon's mate, early in 1776, and in the summer of that year was stationed at Fort Washington, on the Hudson. Being now thrown among irreligious men, he gave full play to his evil propensities, and was in the habit of gross wickedness, particularly of profane swearing.

Although Peter was now, to justify his own course, disposed to condemn Friends and their principles, yet the remembrance of John Pemberton's labors of love on his account, and of the affability and kindness with which Samuel Emlen still continued to greet him when they met, exercised at times a salutary restraint on his tongue, and, as he acknowledged, prevented him from abusing the Society, as he would otherwise have done. We will not follow him in his various posts of labor, but briefly state that in the Seventh month, 1778, being in poor health, he obtained a discharge from the army. He now prosecuted his medical studies, and obtained a diploma, dated the 10th of Second month, 1779. The next day he embarked on board the Delaware, Captain Barry, sailing under a letter of marque, and bound to the West Indies, to seize on all English trading vessels they might meet. They were successful in this robbery, and had prize money, the price of blood and of outrage, to distribute. What character could be found less resembling that of Mordecai Yarnall, meek, humble, and hopeful, as he approached the grave, than his son at this period of his life? The father had believed in, and preached Christ Jesus, as the Saviour and sanctifier of men — the Prince of Peace, full of mercy toward all — and had been engaged, for his dear Master's sake, to press on men the necessity of holiness, of living in love, of doing unto others as they would have others do unto them. The son, actively engaged in robbery, in legalized murder, in doing deeds of wickedness, speaking words of profanity, and in enticing others by example into acts of evil. But the mercy of the Most High was not yet exhausted toward him; a saving visitation was yet to come upon his poor soul.

During the continuance of the war, as Peter Yarnall was riding up the valley of the Schuylkill, on a First-day morning, he found a number of persons collected round a house, and on inquiring the cause, was informed that it was a place of worship, and the minister had not come to preach for them according to engagement. Peter, perhaps, was dressed in black; at least, from his dress, the company supposed him to be a preacher, and on his being questioned if he was not, he did not disclaim the office. He was then invited to address them that day. Having a great share of self-confidence, and a retentive memory, he did not hesitate to accept the offer; — and this wicked man, this profane swearer, this scoffer at religion, undertook to preach of repentance, of purity, of peace! So pleased were the hearers with his eloquent language, and good sentiments, that they pressed him to become a stated minister for them. They detected not the hollowness of the language uttered, which came from the intellect and memory, unseasoned with spiritual unction, unaccompanied with the baptizing power of the true ministry of the Gospel of life and salvation. Where the hearers are rightly brought to wait on the great Minister of the sanctuary, Christ Jesus, the everlasting Teacher of his own people, they will be burdened by that which is offered as ministry without life and power, let the counterfeit be ever so perfect, let the outside appearance be ever so conformable to the truth.

An interesting anecdote illustrating this, is told by our ancient Friend, Richard Davies. He was in the city of London on a First-day, and being unwell, could not go to the morning meeting. Indeed, he was so weak as scarcely to have strength to rise out of bed. Notwithstanding his condition, when the time for the afternoon meeting came, he believed it would be his duty to attend that held at the "Bull and Mouth." The Friend, with whom he lodged, thought him unable to accomplish his prospect, but Richard said he would go as far as he could. The Friend accompanied him, and they reached the house, but not until after the meeting had gathered. Richard thus describes what followed: "As we went through the passage to go in, I heard a voice that I was satisfied was not the voice of a true shepherd, the meeting being already gathered, and many people there. When I went up to the gallery, one was preaching of perfection, who said, 'Be ye perfect, as your heavenly Father is perfect,' etc. I stayed to hear him but a very little while, till I stood up and judged him, and told the people that the kingdom of God stood not in words, but in power, righteousness, and holiness. Then the man went in a rage out of the meeting, and a considerable company followed him. . . . We heard afterward, there was a wager laid, that this man, who was a Jesuit, would preach in the Quakers' meeting, and that he should not be discovered; and had he gone without reproof, they would say, that a Jesuit preached in the Quakers' meeting, and that they could not discern him. . . . We have cause to bless the Lord for his goodness to his people, that gives them a discerning spirit to judge between good and evil, and between those that serve God in truth and righteousness, and all deceitful hypocrites, who are to be judged and condemned by the word of his power."

After his privateering career was over, Peter Yarnall settled down to his profession, attending the practice of the Pennsylvania Hospital, in physic and surgery, during one year; and was then appointed apothecary to the institution; the duties of which station he discharged with the strictest attention and fidelity.

At this period, while on an excursion with some young persons toward Virginia, Peter was taken ill near the Susquehanna River, and being unable to proceed with them, was there left. Here, while death seemed to stare him in the face, the sins of his past life came up before him, and profitable impressions were made upon him, which were not afterward entirely effaced. Nevertheless, on the return of health, it does not appear that any marked change for the better was immediately apparent, and this visitation also of the love of God to his soul, seemed as though it would pass away, like the early dew or the morning cloud, leaving no trace.

On the 11th day of the Fourth month, 1780, Mordecai Yarnall's last wife was buried at Springfield; after which a public meeting was held. Among those gathered on that solemn occasion, was her stepson, Peter, clothed in his uniform as a surgeon in the army. There were other wild young men present, and among the rest, Timothy Matlack, Jr. Samuel Emlen in that meeting was clothed with an earnest concern for the eternal well-being of some of those assembled. He quoted the passage from Jeremiah, "Weep ye not for the dead, neither bemoan him: but weep sore for him that goeth away: for he shall return no more, nor see his native country.' He also rehearsed the words of Ezra, "Then I proclaimed a fast there, at the river of

Ahava, that we might afflict ourselves before our God, to seek of him a right way for us, and for our little ones, and for all our substance. For I was ashamed to require of the king a band of soldiers and horsemen to help us against the enemy in the way, because we had spoken unto the king, saying, The hand of our God is upon all them for good that seek him; but his power and his wrath is against all them that forsake him."

Clothed upon with Gospel authority and power, Samuel addressed those present, dividing the word given to him with prophetic discernment and heart-tendering power. Various were the states he addressed, and his heart was turned with love and ardent solicitude toward the wayward son of his old friend and father in the truth, Mordecai Yarnall, who was yet apparently wandering in the path of sinful indulgence, which leads down to the chambers of death. He said he had often been led to labor with one present, in public and in private, with no beneficial effect; that now there was a renewed visitation of mercy to the soul of that sinner, and if the present offers of grace were not accepted, no others would be made; but, in his sins and transgression, the wanderer from the father's fold would *soon* be cut off!

This testimony reached the heart of the young man, and he felt that part of it which was for him. Nevertheless, that very afternoon, being with a company of young men, most of whom were his relations, he was led to display his power of mimicry and of memory, by repeating the discourse of Samuel Emlen, and imitating his gestures and tones. As he delivered the sermon, whenever a passage occurred which he thought suitable for any of the young men, he would tell them so. At last he came to the awful warning to one of a fresh and a last visitation of Divine mercy. As he said, "Now this is for none of you, it is for myself," his gayety of manner departed, and he became much affected. The day closed, and Peter returned to the city. He entered on his usual avocations, but he had that working within him that gave him no rest until he submitted his neck to the yoke of Christ, and withdrew from his evil associates, walked consistently and circumspectly among men, and made public acknowledgment of the evil of his youthful career.

One of the young men who was present, and to whom we are indebted for recording the above affecting incident, added to his account of it, "The next time I saw him he had on a plain coat."

He felt the truth of Quaker doctrines and testimonies, and he felt the obligation resting upon him to maintain them; yet being called on to give testimony at a court-martial a few weeks after the funeral, he could not then bear the cross of using the plain language. Soon, however, submitting to the inward operation of the baptism of fire and of the Holy Ghost, he became prepared in this particular to perform his duty. We are told, that having to deliver a message to an officer, he felt that the time of dedication had come, and that he must speak as a Quaker. It was a grievous and sore trial to him, and during his walk to the officer's dwelling, poor nature seemed ready to rebel; yet he was favored with strength to submit to the plainly-felt requiring of Truth. When he reached the house, he knocked, and the door was opened by the person he wished to see. Peter addressed him, and surprise sealing up the officer's lips, he did not immediately reply. Thus having taken up the cross prepared for him by his Divine Master, he was strengthened to bear it with patience, and the change wrought in his general deportment was rapid and permanent. Conflicts of spirit were his portion; for he had much to repent of, much to be forgiven, the habits of years to overcome, the pollutions of sin to be burned up. He became diligent in the attendance of meetings for worship, and soon, in the midst of fiery baptisms of spirit, he received a call to enter on the ministry of the Gospel, which awfully affected him in a sense of his utter unworthiness. In the Ninth month, scarcely four months from the time of the memorable meeting at Springfield, he opened his mouth in public testimony in the Market Street meeting-house. An awful sense of his long rebellion was no doubt upon him; a fervent fear lest he should not prove faithful in this last visitation of mercy no doubt affected him, as he declared, "Whosoever shall be ashamed of me, and of my words, of him shall the Son of man be ashamed, when he shall come in his own glory, and in his Father's, and of the holy angels."

When Peter had received his share of the prize-money obtained by privateering, he had invested it by purchasing a tract of land in the State of New Jersey. Now he dared not partake of the spoils of that unrighteous robbery, and therefore relinquished all benefit from the property, seeking with earnest diligence for some opening to restore it to its rightful owners.

Among those who entered the American army during the Revolution, was Robert Hatton, son of Susanna Lightfoot. Unmindful of the sorrow of his deeply-tried mother, turning aside from the counsel of his careful and concerned stepfather, he took up the murderous weapons and engaged in the war. But long before the war was over, he withdrew from all participation in military scenes, being brought into deep repentance for the course he had pursued. In such a state of mind, he was prepared to rejoice over the change effected in his friend, Peter Yarnall, and a correspondence ensued between them. In a letter from Robert, dated Uwchlan, Eleventh month 14th, 1780, he says, " May we hold on, by taking good heed to that Light which doth reprove for evil. Herein we shall find a hammer and a fire to break and to consume that which is contrary to the Divine will. May thou and I hold on in well-doing, steadily looking to our Guide, who has been with us in many dangers, and who will lead us along in the way that is cast up for the ransomed to walk in, even the redeemed of our God, who is willing to be gracious unto the returning prodigals. This I know by his gracious visitation to my poor soul, who has been, what if I should say, thy brother-companion in vanity. But I hope and trust we may become brother-companions in righteousness, even to the exaltation of the pure Truth here on earth more than ever we did to dishonor it."

Having forsaken his sins, and taken all the steps in his power to make remuneration to those he had wronged, Peter felt that the time had come to condemn before the church his evil conduct. He no doubt remembered the declaration, " Whoso confesseth and forsaketh [his sins] shall find mercy." In the Twelfth month of the same year, 1780, he offered the following acknowledgment to Uwchlan Monthly Meeting, which had disowned him:

" DEAR FRIENDS, — Notwithstanding I was educated, and for some time made profession with the religious Society of Friends, yet, for want of a strict attention to the teachings of Divine Grace, I so far deviated as to deny, in my life and conversation, the principles of the blessed Truth, absconded from my master, with whom I was placed as an apprentice to learn a trade, and enlisted myself as a soldier in the British army; for which misconduct a testimony was publicly read against me some years since. Although frequent visitations of Divine love were extended, I continued in a long course of vanity and dissipation. At the commencement of the present unhappy war, I took an oath of allegiance to one of the contending powers, and, actuated by heat and malice, frequently engaged in a task which was conducive to destroy men's lives, contrary to the pure principle of Jesus, who gave his cheek to the smiter, his hair to those that plucked it out, and hid not his face from shame and spitting. Thus was I pursuing one scene of licentiousness and cruelty after another, and soaring above the Witness which frequently convicted me of sin. Being in some measure sensible of the reproach brought on Truth by such repeated transgressions, I do hereby sincerely condemn the same, hoping, through repentance and amendment of life, to be preserved from future snares and entanglements,

"I remain your loving Friend,

PETER YARNALL."

Uwchlan Monthly Meeting received this acknowledgment, and sent a certificate for Peter to the Southern District Monthly Meeting in Philadelphia. But the poor penitent was not satisfied with this public confession: he prepared another, addressed to the meeting in the city he now belonged to.

"I, some time since, delivered a paper of acknowledgment to the Monthly Meeting of Friends at Uwchlan, where I formerly had a right of membership — yet, as part of my conduct was more generally known in this city, and is not particularly mentioned in my offering to that meeting, I have been under weighty exercise, and my mind drawn to a further declaration, for the clearing of Truth from the iniquity of my conduct in engaging in the station of a surgeon on board a privateer. In the course of that employment, I became a party in seizing by violence the property of others, and a sharer therein, contrary to the law of righteousness, which directs to do unto all men as we would they should do unto us. I hereby sincerely condemn the same, fully intending to make restitution to such whom I have thus injured, as far as I may be abilitated."

Peter Yarnall continued in obedience to what he considered the requirings of his Divine Master, to minister in the assemblies of his people. His particular friend, William Savery, was also just coming forward in similar acts of dedication. At a meeting in the Market Street house, both of them having spoken, Nicholas Waln stood up and quoted the text, "Put me, I pray thee, into one of the priest's offices, that I may eat a piece of bread." His comments on this were close, aiming at such as were endeavoring to live on the priest's office, in other words, preaching for hire. The two young ministers, jealous over themselves, and fearful of acting out of the unity of Truth, and giving uneasiness to the church, supposed that the remarks of Nicholas were intended for them. On comparing sentiments they concluded to call on Nicholas, and learn the truth from himself. They did so, and received from their elder brother in the ministry the assurance that he had unity with their labors, and that in his communication, he had no reference to them. Some time after they learned that a young man who had come to Philadelphia to prepare himself by study to preach for hire, was at the meeting, and his judgment was so enlightened as to the freedom of Gospel ministry, by the communication delivered by Nicholas, that he abandoned his design, and returned to his home. Thus the word preached did not return void, but it accomplished that for which it was given.

We have it on record that John Salkeld once, while sitting in a meeting for worship, suddenly struck the floor with his cane, and exclaimed, "Resist the devil this once, and he will not trouble thee again." The singularity of this proceeding, drew on John caution and reproof from his friends, who, while loving and honoring him for the powerful gift committed to him by his Master, were watchful to repress his eccentricities. John, in reply, said, he believed what he had at that time done and said, was by direction of Him who had called him to the work of the ministry. Some time after the delivery of this sermon, a man with whom he met, inquired of him if he remembered the occurrence. The reply was, he did, and had cause to do so, because of the reproofs he had received for it. The man expressed his belief that the singular manner in which John had been led, had been designed for his benefit, and stated that it had under Providence been the means of preventing him from committing suicide. In explanation, he said, that having been in a low, melancholy state of mind, for some time, he had fully determined to destroy his life, and thus leave the world in which all was gloomy and dark to him. On the morning of the day on which the occurrence above referred to, took place, he had taken a rope with him into a neighboring woods to effect his dreadful purpose. While there, he felt a sudden inclination to attend the meeting, and postpone his self-destruction, until that was over. He entered the house, and while meditating on his gloomy earthly prospects, and his intended mode of escape, the raps of the cane on the floor attracted his attention, and the short discourse that followed came with life-quickening power to his soul. He saw that his purpose to destroy himself, was formed at the instigation of Satan; he felt that if he resisted it, there yet was mercy for him — and strengthened and encouraged he turned away from this temptation, and found relief. The impulse to destroy his life being resisted, had passed away, and he had since found the prediction realized, for in that way the devil did not trouble him again.

The following anecdote of a similar character is instructive.

While the late David Sands was one day travelling in Ireland, he felt an impression of duty to appoint a meeting at a place where he was. It was in a district thinly inhabited — the night was stormy, and there was little probability that many persons could be got together. As his companions urged these objections, David said, "If there are but few, the great and good Shepherd has promised to be with us, and I shall feel clear in having done what appears to be my duty." Steps were immediately taken to have a meeting, and notice being spread as circumstances permitted, more persons came to it, than could have been expected. The opportunity was a favored one; a solemn covering spread over the meeting, and David Sands was clothed with ability that night to preach the Gospel with power and authority. He commenced his testimony with these words, "Resist the devil, and he will flee from you. Turn unto Him who is able and willing to save. Although your sins be as scarlet, He will make them white in the blood of the Lamb. He is still waiting to be gracious, and though you have strayed far from the fold, He will lead you as unto pleasant pastures, where streams of living water flow forevermore." With deep earnestness the preacher dwelt on the Lord's unfailing goodness, and invited the listeners to come to the Fountain of mercy for help and salvation. He then added, "I am bound to express my feeling and impression, (though I know not for whom it is intended,) that I believe there are those present who have been so far led astray by the enemy of their soul's salvation as to be ready to take their own life." The meeting closed solemnly, and after it had broken, a well-dressed man, apparently in great distress of mind, came to David Sands, and said, "Your message is to me. I now have the instruments of death in my pocket. I have become weary of life, and have no resolution to withstand the tempter, so as to face the cruel blasts of adversity, and had determined this night to commit the fatal deed. Yet I felt the awful responsibility; and having heard of this meeting, and knowing that Friends often sat in silence, I believed that I should be enabled to become calm and composed before the awful close of life. But now I have abundant reason to bless God, in that he has made you the instrument of saving my life, as also my immortal soul; which, but for this interposition, would have rushed unbidden into the presence of an insulted God." There stood the penitent — the loaded pistols still in his pocket, with which he had intended to end his life — his sorrow still upon him, and yet grateful emotions stirring within him to God the Father of all soul-saving mercies, and to David Sands, the instrument made use of for his good! This remarkable providence had an abiding influence upon his future life.

About the time of the change in Peter Yarnall, his brother Mordecai, who had absconded and joined the army while a minor, also came under religious convictions, and submitted himself to bear the cross of the Lord Jesus. He thus wrote to his brother, under date of First month 1st, 1781:

"My Dear Brother, . . . Let me say to thee, hold fast that which thou hast experienced to be Truth. May the God of Truth not spare nor pity thee nor me, until he has purified our hearts by his powerful judgments, mixed with infinite mercy and adorable love! And may the God of our father be our God forever!

"Give my kind love to John Pemberton, who has been our father's friend, and almost unspeakably *our friend;* and ungratefully have I returned his tender love and care over me.

"With true and tender regard, I remain thy affectionate brother, Mordecai Yarnall."

In the Second month, 1781, Peter Yarnall having appeared in supplication in the Market Street meeting-house, George Churchman, who was present, felt fearful that the youthful minister had extended his petitions somewhat beyond what was best. On returning toward his home, this experienced elder believed it would be right to drop a tender caution and hint to his young friend, and therefore wrote him a letter. He expresses therein his sympathy for Peter, his desires for his preservation, and also his feeling that there was a savor of life about the supplication which had been offered. He then tenderly hints he had thought it might have been better to have closed it sooner, adding:

"[I feel] great tenderness, yet withal a care that thou, in thy infant state, may be preserved from getting out of or swimming beyond thy depth in the stream with which thy acquaintance and experience have been but short,. although thy mind has been mercifully turned, I hope, toward the way everlasting.

"I have apprehended some danger has attended, and may attend young hands, without great care, in regard of repetitions; public prayer in a congregation being a very awful thing, and He to whom it is addressed being the Author of infinite purity. I believe there is no need of discouragement; but if the mind is sincerely devoted to the merciful Father, to seek for preservation out of every danger of forward stepping, superfluous expressions, and fleshly mixtures, there will be Divine assistance afforded to contrited souls, so that experience and strength will, from time to time, be enlarged, and a gradual growth witnessed in a state which is sound, healthy, and safe. That this may truly be thy state is the sincere desire of thy well-wishing friend, GEORGE CHURCHMAN."

Peter Yarnall having given up the wages of iniquity — the gain he obtained in his privateering robbery — and having no patrimonial estate to resort to for a maintenance, was now anxious to find some place where he might successfully enter into practice as a physician. There appeared to be an opening in Concord and its neighborhood for him, and there he settled in the spring or early in the summer of 1781, although he seems to have spent some time there during the previous winter.

It need be no cause of wonder if some persons were slow to receive the ministry of Peter Yarnall. Yet the fear of those who were anxiously regarding him wore off as he continued humbly watchful, waiting on his Divine Master for strength, and seeking in patient faithfulness to do his will. In the summer of 1782 he was acknowledged as a minister by his friends at Concord, and about the same time married Hannah, daughter of Benjamin Sharpless, of Middletown.

Continuing faithful to apprehended duty, he soon felt drawn in Gospel love to visit Friends in other places, and, with the unity of his Monthly Meeting, in the year 1782, he visited the Quarterly Meeting of Fairfax. In 1783, besides religious labors within the limits of his own Yearly Meeting, he visited parts of New York and New England. He was engaged in various labors of love in 1784, and in 1785 he removed to Yorktown, Va., where he resided for about six years.

Often, very often must the remembrance of the sins of his youth been brought to the recollection of Peter Yarnall, with mingled emotions of anguish for their enormity, and of humble thankfulness to that Almighty Saviour, whose mercy had given him free pardon for the past, and whose grace sustained him against present temptations.

Samuel Fothergill could say long after he had been a faithful minister of the Lord Jesus, in recollecting a certain sin of his youth, that it was "a sword which seemed as though it would never depart wholly from his house or heart."

Being now an acknowledged minister among Friends, and frequently engaged in Gospel labors for the good of others, Peter Yarnall found it needful to watch against his natural eloquence, and the fervor of his own spirit, in the Lord's cause. How difficult it is for eloquent men, and those of ready utterance, to be restrained within the true limits in their ministerial exercises! And more particularly so, if popularity and applause follow them. Sometimes such ministers, without having entirely strangled the gift, have grown faster than the Truth would warrant, have shot into great branches, when as yet the root was small, and thus have endangered themselves to be overturned with the first high wind of temptation. The records of our Society need not be traced very far back to find illustrations of this. Popular preachers are always in danger of craving popular applause — of expanding in words without a corresponding depth of inward exercise and feeling. Two of this class, whose popularity was evinced by their being followed from meeting to meeting by a multitude of those who loved to hear good sentiments eloquently expressed — words well-fitted together — being at a meeting in Philadelphia, at the time of a Yearly Meeting, held many years ago, both spoke for an hour each. After these were over, our plain-spoken Friend, James Simpson, remarked, that he had been thinking of those who pinned their faith on popular preachers. "They seemed to him to resemble the children of Israel, who danced round the golden calf that Aaron had made for them."

In 1791, Peter Yarnall settled within the limits of Horsham Monthly Meeting, Montgomery County, Pennsylvania, and during the fall of that year held many public meetings in the neighborhood, having frequently on these occasions the company of James

Simpson. These meetings were largely attended, and the testimonies delivered powerful and edifying.

Peter Yarnall, in exercising his gift in the ministry, was wont to be very slow in delivery, when he first began to speak. Soon, however, his manner became animated, his articulation rapid, and as the whole energy of his soul seemed to breathe forth for the good of others, and the Divine blessing was with him, his labors were powerfully awakening, particularly to the young, who were wandering afar from the fold of peace. For such his soul yearned, with earnest longings to gather them back to the Lord Jesus Christ, to bring the prodigals from feeding on the swine-husks of self-indulgence, to partaking of the fatted calf of Divine acceptance. Oh, how he could tell of mercy to prodigals! — an allusion thereto seemed to call up the deepest energies of his feelings. He had not forgotten, when, being himself far off from his Father's house, yet looking there — longing for acceptance, if it might be as a hired servant — the Father himself had beheld him — had drawn nigh to him — had caused his rags to be taken from him — clothed him with the best robe — made him welcome as a son beloved, and caused the household to rejoice over him, as one that having been dead, was alive again — having been lost, was now found.

His style of expression was elevated, his manner

emphatic, and he had a peculiar ease and felicity in expressing his thoughts. When he arose and commenced speaking, he stood nearly perfectly still, but as his delivery gained strength and force, as his earnest exercises began to find fitting language, his whole body seemed to partake of the ardency of his feelings.

We are told that being on a visit in New Jersey, in the year 1791, the exercise of his mind was very great, so that before rising to address the assembly, the perspiration started as freely from him as from a mower in the harvest-field. This was in part occasioned by the close and searching testimony given him to deliver. As he stood up he said — and we can well imagine the deep solemnity and awe which covered him as the words came slowly forth — "It is a cloudy time, both inwardly and outwardly. Clouds of thick darkness have spread themselves." From this he proceeded to lay open the deficiencies of those present in a "powerful and searching manner," so as to draw the acknowledgment from some, "This is going to the bottom of things." Such was Peter Yarnall's usual manner. Loving, affectionate, courteous, yet faithful to his Lord's bidding, and careful to sew no pillows under armholes.

In 1793, Peter Yarnall paid a religious visit to New England, in the course of which he attended a meeting at East Hampton, that had been appointed there at eleven o'clock, of which he says: "We found the time was not altogether suited to the convenience of the people; yet I hope it was a good meeting. A proposal was made to us to hold a meeting in the evening, and, not feeling my mind wholly relieved, I felt willing to encourage it; and we accordingly had another meeting there at seven o'clock, which, I believe, was the largest meeting we had on the east end of the island; and although I was silent therein, my mind was much relieved through secret, hidden exercise. I heard no complaint respecting it, and the people appeared very affectionate."

This secret, hidden exercise, this prostration of soul before the Lord, and silent prayer to and communion with him, which constitute true worship, have at times wrought upon those who were strangers to this inward operation of the Spirit, in meetings where not a word was spoken, as effectually as could have been done by any vocal utterances. The following incidents are illustrations of this remark.

It is related that an individual residing near Richard Jordan had heard of his powerful preaching, and felt a great desire to hear him. He attended a Friends' meeting on a First-day; but Richard, though present, was silent. He did so again and again, and still no ministry was heard. Concluding that Richard must preach at the week-day meetings, he tried them with no better success; but at last he began to feel what these meetings were for; his heart was opened to perceive the beauty and excellency of silent waiting and inward spiritual worship, and then the seals were taken from the lips of the minister. "This," said William Williams, "was Richard Jordan's way of making a convert."

Richard Jordan used to relate an interesting account of a man of note in England who was convinced of the Truth, in an opportunity wherein not a word was spoken. The man was a captain in the navy, and was in expectation of receiving an admiral's commission. He had fallen in company with Richard Jordan and some other Friends, and on their sitting down to talk a solemn silence came over them; during which, the inward power and effectual ministration of Truth so reached his soul, that he burst into tears; the doctrines of the Gospel were unfolded to him in their fulness, and he laid down all his weapons of war.

After Peter Yarnall's return from his eastern journey, he was frequently engaged in Gospel labors about home. He also visited New York Yearly Meeting, and the families of several Monthly Meetings, including that of Philadelphia.

On the 11th of Fourth month, 1795, his wife, Hannah, was removed from him, and in less than three weeks after that event, while wounded affection was mourning in the fresh grief of recent bereavement, he laid a prospect of further religious service to the north before his sympathizing Friends. After much labor in New York and New Jersey, in the Eleventh month of the same year, he started on a visit to the South, accompanied by his friend, James Emlen. James was a useful and baptized elder, a firm though an affectionate and tenderly concerned parent, a self-denying Christian, a meek-spirited, humble-minded man. Through the strengthening influences of Divine Grace, and a constant watchfulness unto prayer, he had obtained great command over his passions, so that the evenness of his temper amid the trials of life was very remarkable. Having attended the Yearly Meeting in Philadelphia in 1798, James Emlen took the yellow fever and died, being able to say, just before his departure, that he felt in "such a calm, quiet frame of mind, he did not stand in need of any human consolation."

They returned from this journey about the close of summer, and in the following Second month, (1797,) Peter Yarnall was married to Hannah Thornton, a Friend in the ministry, residing at Byberry, where he now settled, and where he continued to reside during the short period allotted him on earth. He had accumulated but little of this world's goods, for although very much esteemed as a physician, his dedication to his Master's cause took him away so frequently, and kept him so long from his medical practice, that his emolument derived from thence was small. The memorial issued concerning him says, " Much of his time was given up in travelling abroad to promote truth and righteousness among mankind." He had a belief that his day for labor would not long be lengthened out, and in a letter written during his last visit to the Eastern States, he said he had been under a close apprehension, "I should never have it in my power to be here more."

In his personal appearance Peter Yarnall was tall, yet, being well-proportioned and graceful in his motions, it was not at once strikingly apparent. His features were prominent, and his countenance earnestly lighted up when pleading with prodigals — when setting forth the inexhaustible store of mercy laid up in Christ Jesus for the penitent and obedient. His powers of conversation were good, and he very often felt freedom, in innocent cheerfulness, to take a prominent part in social intercourse with his friends. Having passed through many scenes, having acute perception and an astonishing power of memory, he was, on such occasions, full of matter, and his company was very attractive to the young. But at times, even in the midst of the free conversation of those he loved, a solemn awe would steal over him, his interest in what was going on around him would instantly cease, and he would seem to feel himself in as complete solitude as though no mortal beheld him. As a physician, he was considered skillful, and being of a tender, sympathizing spirit, he was much beloved by his patients.

We draw near the close of this faithful, dedicated servant of the Lord. He had a dream a short time before his last illness, the import of which was, that he and his early associate and long-cherished friend and fellow-laborer in the Gospel, William Savery, were enclosed together in a place of safety, out of the reach of everything that could hurt them or interrupt their joy and peace.

On the 14th of Second month, 1798, he was taken sick; that afternoon he told his wife this dream, and afterward said, "Heaven is a glorious place, into which I have no doubt of an entrance, if I should be removed at this time. I acknowledge it is awful to think of appearing before the bar of the just Judge; but on looking at it, I feel my mind centred in an uninterrupted quiet." On the 18th: "I have been sensible of many infirmities; but I believe I have an evidence that my gracious Master has blotted out my transgressions." Again: "The Lord Jesus, my Saviour, is near, whatever becomes of this poor body. I hope my gracious Master will grant me patience to wait his time." "Oh, the goodness of the blessed

Jesus!" Addressing a friend, he said, "I have blessed the Lord many a time, for that he brought my poor soul acquainted with true *silence*." The night before his close, being asked how he was, he replied: "In the Lord's keeping." He died on the 20th of Second month, 1798, in the forty-fifth year of his age. His sun went down in brightness, and in a few years his friend, William Savery, having been kept by the Lord's power on earth, followed him to the regions of everlasting safety and blessedness.

ANTHONY BENEZET.

ONE of the memorable and honorable Friends of Philadelphia, at the time of the American Revolution, was dear, quaint, humorous, straightforward, kind-hearted, Anthony Benezet. An indefatigable laborer for the good of others, he even restricted his hours of sleep, saying, in allusion to the usual period allotted for rest, "he could not reconcile a habit of such slothful indulgence with the activity of Christian fervor." He was quick-witted, and apt at repartee, and his witticisms were generally instructive and playful. Benevolent to all — ever ready to furnish from his own store supplies for the needs of others, and moderate in his desires, he never acquired much property. Nay, restricted by the narrow bounds of his own wants and wishes, he felt inclined to doubt whether the accumulation of a great estate was consistent with the self-denying religion of the cross.

If born to the inheritance of a large fortune, we know not how far Anthony's view of wealth might have been modified; nor how differently he might have acted if large possessions had been suddenly left him. We know, however, his actions were beautifully consistent with his theory; and though the opinions of men are liable under peculiar temptations to change, we trust he was too well grounded in Christian principle, to have altered much in theory or practice.

The testimony of Anthony Benezet against the love of riches had a deep root; yet he knew that it was natural for young men to aim at that wealth which gave them influence and respectability in civil society. He saw no remedy for the evil, but Christian principle, constraining to Christian moderation.

We have said that Anthony Benezet was an active, industrious man. He had no sympathy with that spirit which seems ever on the watch to evade bodily labor — to withdraw from exertion and toil. Some individuals, loving ease, and luxuriating in inactivity, have plead in excuse a conscientious dislike to hard work. Such a plea would have stirred up Anthony Benezet's zeal, and would have called down on the avower of it, his earnest rebuke. He believed that man was created for labor — that independent of pecuniary emolument, he was bound to work for his own bodily and mental benefit, and to be liberal in his exertions for the good of others. His own heart expanded toward all; he was willing to help, to labor for, and by every means in his power administer to the true comfort of those around him. Thus he knew he should best accomplish his duty as a man — thus best fulfill the law of Christ.

But though earnest and active, he was not a man to do things in a hurry. He loved to see persons, while industriously attending to their occupations in this world, giving evidence that heavenly things had the pre-eminence in their affections, and in the direction of their movements.

One day, while walking the streets of Philadelphia, he saw a man approaching him rapidly, who was habitually *in haste*. In reply to Anthony's call to stop, the man, as he hurried by, said, "I am now in haste, and will speak with you when we next see each other." Quick as thought the arrow of reproof was fitted to Anthony's keen bow of wit — "Dost thou think thou wilt ever find time to die?" The arrow was not shot at a venture; it reached the conscience of him to whom it was addressed — and he afterward strongly expressed his obligation for the admonition.

One of the principal occupations of Anthony Benezet's life, was that of a schoolmaster. In a letter, the original of which he kept, as was his custom, sending a fair copy to his correspondent, we find him saying, he had been so long engaged at that occupation, as to be then instructing the grandchildren of his first pupils.

As a teacher, he was kind and affable — ever ready to remove difficulties out of the way of the learners, and to encourage and promote with them the freedom of an affectionate intercourse.

He wrote and compiled many books. There was sound sense — there was enlarged humanity — in all his literary productions. He lacked not strength of argument; he gave expression to fervid bursts of feeling. But in his compositions little of clear connected outline was discernible. They seemed like masses of good thoughts, susceptible feelings, enlarged views, strong arguments, heaped together, as they happened to arise in a discursive mind.

Anthony Benezet could not descend to use compliments to flatter the pride of a fellow-man, a poor worm of the dust, whose only hope of eternal happiness depended on that humility which compliments and flatterers were fitted to destroy. His earnest expression of good-will and kind feeling, however, were generally acceptable to strangers, even to those most used to receive fulsome adulation, and those highly wrought phrases, which say much, and mean little. He frequently visited Count de Luzerne, the ambassador from France, to enlighten him on the subject of Abolition. A reciprocal interest was awakened in each other, and when the Count was about returning to his own country, Anthony thought it right to call and take a parting farewell. Many persons were gathered on the same errand, and Anthony retreated out of sight, where, unobserved, he listened to the compliments poured forth on the Count. When several had retired, he came forward, and thus addressed his friend: "Thou knowest I cannot use the compliments which the company have expressed — but I wish thee the favor of heaven, and a safe return to thy country." "Oh! Mr. Benezet," said the Count, warmly embracing him, "you have exceeded them all!"

That he knew how to give a reproof very delicately, the following anecdote shows. Having called on one of his former scholars then recently married, he was ushered into a room where he found her in full dress for a ball. He was surprised, and, in a plaintive voice, exclaimed, "My dear S——, I should not have recognized my amiable pupil, but that thy well-known features and excellent qualities are not to be hidden by so grotesque and lamentable a disguise!"

The usual gentleness and equanimity of his temper would sometimes be stirred to vehement zeal when he found those abounding in riches manifesting a covetous disposition. He was wont to say, "The highest act of charity in the world was to bear with such unreasonableness of mankind."

His heart was naturally open and generous; he

would give the coat from his back, or the blankets from his bed, to relieve the sufferings of others. His benevolence sprang from the fulness of feeling which made it a relief to him to give.

Anthony is said to have been at times truly eloquent in his appeals on behalf of the rights of the oppressed. At one time a proposition was before the Yearly Meeting to make some new movement against slavery. Some opposition was made, when he arose, weeping, and, in broken accents, exclaimed, "Ethiopia shall soon stretch out her hands unto God!" These words, with the feeling that accompanied them, silenced all opposers, and the proposition was adopted.

Ever active for the good of others, Anthony Benezet passed on his way, blessing the world by his exertions and by his example. On his death-bed, he exclaimed, "I am dying, and feel ashamed to meet the face of my Maker; I have done so little in his cause!" "Alack! alack! we are poor creatures; I can take no merit for anything I have done. There is mostly something underneath that is selfish, which will not bear sifting." "I could wish to live a little longer, that I might bring down self!" To his wife, Joyce, to whom he had been a faithful and loving husband for forty-eight years, he said, "We have lived long in love and peace."

Many tears of real sorrow were shed when it was

known through the city of Philadelphia that Anthony Benezet was removed from the sphere of his charities on earth to the resting-place of the righteous. Many were the testimonies to his worth which came forth from persons of every rank and station in society.

Rebecca Jones thus wrote from England: "The removal of that little, valiant man, Anthony Benezet, will be a sensible chasm; but I remember from whom he derived his qualifications, and that the Divine Fountain is inexhaustible. I feel as I should on the occasion, and for dear Joyce, who is not far from the same peaceable mansion."

Henry Drinker, writing to John Pemberton, says:

"I expect thou wilt have heard before this reaches thee, of the removal of our beloved friend and brother, Anthony Benezet, who peacefully passed away, full of years and full of honor, to a better inheritance. Where shall we find another Anthony Benezet — a man so uniformly and steadily engaged in promoting the real good and true happiness of his fellow-man? It was thus he was engaged, early and late. That the just man's life is a shining light has, I think, been verified in the example of this pious man, whose love and good-will was of that enlarged kind that all ranks and descriptions of men were the objects of his Christian regard and notice."

We are called to good works; yet our own deeds,

even those which seem most the product of genuine benevolence, will not purchase a place for us in the kingdom of heaven. Anthony Benezet had been long an open-hearted benefactor of mankind, yet in his last illness he was kept by his Divine Master in a state of mind remarkably stripped of all dependence on former experiences and former faithfulness. The works of mercy he had been enabled to perform gave him no satisfaction in review, and, in poverty of spirit, he lay, trusting alone in the Lord Jesus Christ for salvation.

During this season, James Thornton paid him a visit, and, in relation thereto afterward, said, "On entering the room, he had never been more deeply impressed with a sense of spiritual poverty than at that time." He was permitted to enter into sympathy with the dying man, who, in a sense of inward want, was, in humility and self-abasement, drawing near the hour of his departure. At the time of the funeral, James Thornton again entered the house; but, oh, the change! "It felt to him as if it were divinely perfumed — something so like the opening of heaven and a sense of the Divine presence as he had at no other time experienced!" Those good works and almsdeeds which, through the aid of the Lord's Holy Spirit, he had been enabled faithfully to perform, had been accepted of his Master, and were even as a sweet-smelling savor poured forth. The Lord's gracious acceptance of his past labors, withheld from the perceptions of the dying man, lest being trusted in, it might hinder his heavenly progress, was now made manifest to the spiritually-minded in an extraordinary degree.

He died Fifth month 3d, 1784, aged seventy-one years.

Perhaps it may be safe to assume, that all portions of the human race, who are not disabled by some peculiar providence of God, are called to industrious habits, and to cultivate a social disposition, fulfilling the duties they owe to their kindred and friends, as fellow-partakers of infirmity.

We are not all endowed with the same natural and spiritual qualifications; we do not all fill the same position in life, neither have we the same outward means of contributing to the wants and necessities of others. But let each one wait to know his own calling, and therein abide.

JACOB LINDLEY.

JACOB LINDLEY was born in the year 1744, and was by nature affable in manners, excitable in feeling, and energetic in action. Although often pointed in rebuke, he did not willingly hurt the feelings of any, and seldom took offence at the remarks or reproofs of others. Men of strong minds and determined characters are often — perhaps generally — characterized by a disposition which leads them harshly to reprove, and causes them easily to take offence at the reproofs or actions of others. Jacob Lindley would, doubtless, have been no exception to this rule, if he had not come under the regulating, heart-softening influence of the Spirit of the Lord Jesus Christ. He knew the Spirit of the Saviour was a Spirit of love, because he felt it clothing him with charity and kind feelings toward those whose actions he was bound publicly to condemn. He labored to keep his excitable temperament under control, and to manifest the reality of that religion of whose heart-cleansing, love-inspiring influence he was at times drawn to speak unto others. He knew that if he were allowing himself to indulge in angry thoughts, harsh feelings, and overbearing manners and remarks, it would matter little how much or how eloquently he might plead for love and meekness, or how truly he might speak in praise of the gentleness of Christ.

Having received a gift in the ministry, and being faithful in its exercise, he grew in grace, and was qualified by his Lord and Saviour for much usefulness in the church.

He was a powerful minister of the Gospel, and an earnest advocate for the rights of humanity. He was large in person, and before his death became quite corpulent. With a voice of great power and compass, he was wont, when under impressions of religious duty, to sound forth an alarming cry to sinners, to call them to repentance and amendment of life. Often has he warmed cold hearts and shaken the strongholds of prejudice in them, as with the earnestness of hearty feeling, and in the authority of Truth, he has pleaded the cause of the oppressed, the enslaved, the suffering, the neglected African. Such was he in the meridian of life; such was he to the close of his days.

He came forth in the ministry during the commotions which immediately preceded the American Revolution; and in those times of trial he was led to caution all classes, but especially the young, against allowing themselves to be caught with the spirit of war. It is, indeed, very difficult for those living in a community which thinks itself wronged, not to partake, more or less, of the resentful spirit which prevails about them. We may, in the abstract, think war sinful — may deem that the weapons of the Christian are love, meekness, and forgiveness of wrong — and yet when we partake of public or receive private injuries, we shall find it hard to retain or to regain true love for those who have injured us. Jacob Lindley saw clearly into the evil principle from which war arises, and he had a powerful testimony to bear against it. He knew the horrors of the field of battle, he knew the human sufferings that attend the wounds of the musket-ball and the bayonet and sword, and he knew, however much the love of liberty and the necessity of protecting their rights might be insisted on by those engaged in it, yet that war, in its origin and its progress, its glories and its triumphs, was rooted in sin, and was sustained by the pride and corruption of man. His Friends, in the memorial issued concerning him, state their belief that his labors against war "were productive of salutary effects."

Jacob Lindley was fond of telling anecdotes, especially if a religious impression could be made with them. On one occasion, he narrated the following occurrence. A man who resided in his neighborhood, one day undertook to burn an old greasy hub of a wheel, in order to get the iron that was on it. He watched the flames curling in great beauty round the old wood, licking up the grease and tar, and all other impurities; and the impression was made on his mind, that thus would the Holy Spirit consume all the impurities of his nature, if he would submit to its operations. This reflection was raised in his mind by Him, who, in love, seeketh that all His rational creatures should turn, repent, and live. The heart of this hub-burner was effectually touched, and this accident was as the turning point of his life. He became a religious man. "Oh!" exclaimed Jacob, after relating the circumstance—"Oh! that there were some more old hubs to burn."

Jacob Lindley, when a young man, was present at a meeting of Friends, where a proposition was considered, which he and his companion believed ought to have been adopted. But a member of the meeting who did not seem prepared with arguments against it, yet expressing that he had "scruples;" the meeting in deference to those unexplained scruples, laid by the subject for the present. After the meeting was over, Jacob and companion being at a Friend's house, and thinking themselves alone, began to discuss what had taken place, expressing their earnest disapprobation of the result, and treating the "scruples" of the Friend with little respect. While thus freely expressing themselves, Elizabeth Coale, a very small woman, though an able minister of Baltimore Yearly Meeting, rose up in a corner where she had been sitting unobserved, and thus addressed the startled faultfinders: "Young men, I know in the *gross* weight of *millers* a scruple is of little account; but in the balance of the sanctuary, a scruple is a scruple!"

Jacob could not but feel the clear-witted rebuke. He knew, and must have acknowledged it as a general truth, that it is not the magnitude of wordy reasonings, which should lead religious meetings into action; and that it is far more safe to wait on, and to suffer the restraints of secret feelings of uneasiness, which may not have as yet shaped themselves into logical arguments. The expression of uneasiness, from the lips of one who is an earnest seeker after the mind of the Spirit, is in truth, as good and sufficient a reason as that person could offer. Sometimes it so happens, that a reason, with undeniable arguments to sustain it, does exist, and yet cannot well be brought forward. On such occasions, how much better would it be, simply to offer the true Quaker plea of "uneasiness" — of "a scruple" — rather than to look out for other arguments against the measure we disapprove, which, when we have uttered them, may be weighed in the scales of critical opponents, and found wanting.

When Jacob in after-life related this anecdote, he used pleasantly to remark, that he never entered into free expression on the character, opinions, or actions of others, without looking around him to see if there was not "a little Betty in the corner."

An amusing anecdote is related of Jacob Lindley, who, when riding on horseback one day not far from his own residence, was overtaken by a shower, and took shelter under the sheds belonging to the New Garden meeting-house. Here the grave-yard was open before him, and his mind soon became busy in recalling to recollection the many worthy Friends and faithful ministers of the gospel buried there, who, having served the Lord in their generation, had died in peace. His feelings became warm, and at the top of his powerful voice, he broke out in the words of Addison:

> "How are thy servants blest, O Lord!
> How sure is their defence!
> Eternal Wisdom is their guide,
> Their help Omnipotence."

Such a voice as his, echoed far and wide. A neighbor who was passing along the road at the time, hearing the words uttered in such a tone, proceeding apparently from the grave-yard, and perceiving no one, he deemed it was something unearthly, and putting spurs to his horse, fled from the place with fear and precipitation. Jacob, hearing the clatter of the horse's hoofs, as the man galloped off, immediately comprehended the cause, and to appease the man's alarm, he shouted after him. In his earnestness he did not let his voice fall, and the man's fears were aggravated by hearing himself called by that voice. His spurs did not cease their office, until he had gone a considerable distance from the spot whence such sounds proceeded.

We have an account left by William Savery, in his Journal, of a journey performed by himself and several other Friends, to attend a treaty with Indians, to be held at Sandusky. Jacob Lindley, who was one of the company, also kept a journal, which has been preserved. He left his home on the 28th of Fourth month, 1793, and joined his fellow-travellers in Philadelphia. Feeling a religious concern to see President Washington, with whose approbation Friends were going to the treaty, Jacob Lindley spoke on the subject to William Savery, "and found he was under a like impression." He says, "James Pemberton, William Savery, John Elliott, and myself, went about nine o'clock; met with a favorable reception, and had a full opportunity to relieve our minds: which we thought tended to his [the President's] satisfaction, as well as ours."

This treaty had for its object the establishment of peace with the Northwestern tribes. The Six Nations besought the President to send as agents "men of honesty, not proud land-jobbers, but men who loved and desired peace," and also suggested that the agents should be attended by a Friend. This request of the Indians does not appear to have been known to the Friends at the time they first opened their concern.

On Seventh-day, the 4th of Fifth month, they left New York for Albany, in the sloop Schenectady, Captain Lansing, with a favorable wind; but soon after the wind changed, and a storm came on, which obliged them to cast anchor. The fury of the wind increasing, the vessel dragged her anchor, and was almost driven on shore, so that the captain was glad to retrace his path, and get once more to the wharf from whence he had sailed. This gave the Friends an opportunity to attend the usual First-day meetings in the city of New York. A concern came on William Savery to hold a public meeting in the evening for Friends and others, and notice was given to that effect, at the close of the afternoon meeting. The meeting was to commence at seven o'clock, and was gathering when Friends received notice from Captain Lansing to come on board the vessel. The concern to hold the meeting continued pressing on their minds — public notice had been given — and people were assembling — but if they did not go immediately to the vessel, they did not know that the captain would wait for them. The trial was great to the Friends, but religious duty was paramount. Jacob says, "William and I agreed, let the consequences be what they might, we would attend the meeting. We did so, and a favored time it was. About nine o'clock, several Friends, merchants of the city, accompanied us to the vessel, where the passengers and captain were in a heat; but *we kept down*, and it blew over. Captain Lansing told me afterward with seriousness, he did believe the storm was permitted in order to give us time for meeting."

While Jacob Lindley and his friends were crossing Oneida Lake by night on this journey, a storm suddenly arose, and they were in great apparent danger. The water being shoal, and the shore rocky, they durst not attempt to run in, but by break of day they succeeded in getting their boat into the safer waters of the Oneida River. Jacob says, on this occasion, "I underwent a close and searching baptism, not only respecting the present embassy, but all the actions of my life, for eternity appeared very near."

Jacob could doubtless amid all his inward cogitations trust in the Lord for succor, knowing that it was in obedience to what he believed to be his religious duty, that he was then in apparent danger. The feeling of being in his proper place, would take away from the fear of death. Very different were his feelings from those of our dear Friend, Anthony Benezet, who being at one time persuaded to go down to the Capes of the Delaware, without having any call of duty, or necessary business there to attend to, was caught in a violent storm. As he looked at the sea and saw the storm raging, and looked on the vessel and perceived the sickness and distress of the passengers, the sense of impending danger drove him to consider where he was, and why he was there, and forced from him the inward ejaculation! "What business have I here?"

Doubtless the same kind of feeling has been experienced by many when brought into trial and trouble. The sense of having run into them without being sent has added bitterness to sorrow, and fearfulness to danger. On the contrary, the feeling that it was obedience to the Lord's will which has brought on the Christian the trial, the difficulty, the suffering, the danger, will have a tendency to sustain him under them, and to enable him to believe that all things will work his furtherance in good.

In prison-houses, at the whipping-post, at the scaffold, on the bed of death, the sense of the Lord's approving presence has made many to rejoice and bless his name that they had been created — that they were then and there suffering according to his will. What to our ancient worthy Friend, Anthony Patrickson, was the affliction of the body when he could exclaim, "The Lord hath given me assurance of that blessed inheritance that never will have end!" * Strong was the faith, holy was the hope, and glorious the assurance that animated Margaret Molleson, when, according to the Lord's will, she was about to depart from her earthly tabernacle. To her physician, who tried to encourage her to believe that she should recover, and who told her not to fear, she said, "Fear! I have no cause! My Advocate is with the Father, and my peace is made; I am feeding at a table none of you perceiveth. My eternal joy is already begun!" †

So abiding was the holy feeling of the Lord's approbation with Mary Dyer, for a few days before her execution, so joyful the flow of peace that poured through her soul, that as she ascended the ladder to suffer, she could, as a living testimony to her Saviour's grace and mercy, declare, "I have been in Paradise these several days!" ‡ She was there in the Lord's will — she was suffering for his Truth — the strength of earthly ties was dissolving, and through his mercy she was made spiritually to partake of the river of the water of life, and to know a holy communion with him.

---

* Piety Promoted, vol. i., p. 341.   † Ibid., p. 69.

‡ Sewel's History of the People called Quakers, vol. i. (stereotype ed.) p. 300.

Continuing their journey, on the 11th of Sixth month, Jacob Lindley and his Friends were at Detroit, and called to see Isaac Williams, a noted Indian trader. He narrated many instances of the cruelty of the Indians, and stated that they were at that time more haughty and insolent than they had been. He expressed his doubts of the company ever returning from Sandusky, unless the United States commissioners should yield to all the Indians demanded. This appeared, also, to be the sentiment of others, and the information tended to drive Friends to look to the Lord for safety in this their season of trial and danger. The Indians around them were often intoxicated, and in that condition they manifested much ferocity. In considering all he heard and all he saw, Jacob Lindley remarks, "It evidently appears a serious business, and little, if anything, short of offering up life by those who attend it."

The Friends arrived safely at Sandusky in the Seventh month, and spent several weeks in the company of the Indians and United States officers at that point. While there, as well as at other places on their journey, they held meetings for Divine worship, which were attended by some of the Indians and also by the whites; and on some occasions they had opportunities of a more private character with individuals.

On the 27th of the Seventh month, the Friends had

a close, solid conversation with some of the officers in the army on the subject of slavery, war, swearing, and debauchery. Jacob makes the following remarks relative to this opportunity: "When men are closely pinched, I find their nearest way to get rid of a difficulty is a denial of the Scriptures, to turn deists, and explain away the weighty parts of the moral law."

It is not wonderful that men who are living in the indulgence of the fleshly appetites, should desire to disbelieve the truth of that religion which calls for purity of heart, for purity of life, for a constant walking in fear and reverence before God. They know how far they are from fulfilling its moral requisitions, and they know (if the Christian religion is true) the dreadful penalty they must pay for the sin-pleasing pleasures they now indulge in. "How," exclaimed the noted infidel, Carlile, to Wilberforce, who had a Bible in his hands, "how can you suppose I can like that book? for if it be true, I am undone forever!"

We have it recorded that a late literary character was, in younger life, in the habit of conversing with a fellow-infidel against Christianity and its evidences. They were living in sin, and a sin-condemning religion was not wide enough and easy enough to suit their inclinations. After a time, this man, touched by the power of Divine Grace, repented of his sin, and found, in the Gospel of Christ Jesus, the very religion which a soul anxious for the favor of God, for true peace in life, and for a sustaining hope in death, needed.

Having been brought to repentance, he was anxious to do away, as far as he could, the effect of the evil influence he exerted in the days of his wilful estrangement from the path of purity and peace. Many of his infidel conversations had been carried on in the presence of a religious but uneducated man. Fearful lest some seeds of skepticism might have been sown in his mind, and taken root there, he sought him out to express his concern. The man replied, that their remarks had produced no impression upon him. "No impression! Why, you must have known we had read and thought on these things much more than you had any opportunity of doing." The man, though illiterate as to this world's knowledge, was wise in a higher wisdom, and he made this sensible reply: "Oh, yes; but I knew your manner of living! I knew to maintain such a course of conduct, you found it necessary to renounce Christianity."

The Indians, with whom it was proposed to make a treaty, showed no disposition to come to terms, excepting on the condition that all the whites settled beyond the Ohio should retire to the east of that river, which should thenceforward be the boundary between them and the United States. After a period of nearly two months spent in fruitless attempts at negotiation, it became evident that a treaty could not be concluded, and on the 17th of Eighth month the Friends and some of the commissioners started homeward. Jacob says, "My mind felt sorrowful in reflecting on the important subjects of our journey. On turning my mind to consider if we had omitted anything we might have done, or that might be done, nothing appeared to give uneasiness. I therefore rested satisfied in leaving it to the Lord, who judgeth righteously, and with joy turned my mind homeward, willing to leave a settlement so greatly dissipated with every species of iniquity, that they appear to live almost without law, morality, or religion."

In the Ninth month, 1793, Jacob Lindley proceeded to Philadelphia to attend the Yearly Meeting. The yellow fever was raging with fearful violence in that city, but the knowledge of this did not release our valiant warrior in the Lamb's army from the belief that it was his duty to attend at that time. During the sittings of the meeting, his mind, with that of many others, was lifted up above fear, so that he could rejoice in the Lord, and joy in the God of his salvation.

In 1797 the yellow fever again prevailed to an alarming extent in Philadelphia, and many of its inhabitants fled for safety to the surrounding country. In the Ninth month, Jacob Lindley, in writing to his brother and sister, J. and A. Dawes, who lived in that city, thus expressed the emotions of his mind at this solemn period:

"My inmost feelings have often been exercised, and my spirit has been drawn in near sympathy toward you, with others of my beloved friends resident in the long highly-favored, sumptuous metropolis, since the awakening sound of this second awful trumpet has reached my ears. But what shall we say? Is it not a dispensation from that unerring Hand who doeth all things right? At whose sovereign beck ten thousand times ten thousand ministering angels wait the execution of his almighty decree? His bowels of compassionate mercy endure forever. When a proud and rebellious people are humbled to hear the rod and him who hath appointed it, then I assuredly believe, the Sun of righteousness will arise, with healing in his wings, and turn the sound and shadow of death into a glorious morning; when the stars shall sing together, and the sons of God shout for joy.

"The sacred declaration was, that the Lord of hosts would be sanctified in righteousness and exalted in judgment. Truly great and marvellous are his works, who shall not fear him? saith my soul. How suddenly hath that great and populous city, almost equally the envy and admiration of kingdoms and nations, become a terror to its own inhabitants! How contrasted the prospect must appear in the southern parts, especially where the throng of busy merchants resorted, and the adventurous mariners disburdened their deeply-laden vessels — now, the yellow flag and other ensigns of sickness and mortality!

"I need not expatiate upon these obvious occurrences to those who, doubtless, have more deeply pondered the affecting subject, and I trust have experienced, proportionate to the trials of the day, the fulfilling of that Scripture testimony, 'Thou wilt keep him in perfect peace, whose mind is stayed on thee, because he trusteth in thee.' The name of the Lord, which is his power, remains unalterably a strong tower and refuge for the righteous. I thought I never more fully experienced the weight and force of a sentence or two divinely fraught with consolation to the church of Christ, and I believe to every baptized member, than when in Philadelphia in the Ninth month, 1793: 'Thou shalt be far from oppression, for thou shalt not fear; and from terror, for it shall not come near thee.' May your minds be supported and rightly directed in this truly alarming crisis, has been my request on your behalf; whether to stay or to go I cannot undertake to determine. I humbly hope the Shepherd of Israel will availingly care for you, direct and keep you as under the hollow of his hand, until his indignation be overpast. . . .

"I trust the sure and strong foundation [of our attachment] is that love which is only derived from our Father which is in heaven.

"I deeply feel for that important, essential branch of our Christian testimony which relates to the public worship of Almighty God. May his unsearchable wisdom, his sustaining arm, preserve the ark of the testimony from falling before the Philistines.

"The prospect looks very solemn in contemplating

the attendance of our approaching annual solemnity. Only this remains: times and seasons are in the hands of Him who can do great things — things that we look not for — in a short time."

A number of Friends having settled in Canada, many of whom were from the limits of Exeter Monthly Meeting, the meetings established there were considered as belonging to Philadelphia Yearly Meeting. In 1797, at the time when the yellow fever was raging in Philadelphia, a committee was appointed by the Yearly Meeting to visit the Friends in Canada. Of this committee Jacob Lindley was one, and amid many discomforts, arising from the wilderness character of the country at that time, the journey was performed. They had many comfortable meetings in Canada, and doubtless returned well satisfied that the visit had been in the Divine appointment.

On one occasion, when camping out for the night during this journey, an incident occurred which, however trying at the moment, was not without instruction. When preparing to kindle a fire, everything being covered with snow, it was very difficult to find suitable wood. At last a fire was struck, and there seemed little doubt but with care it might be enlarged so as to make them comparatively comfortable. While the little fire was slowly increasing, Jacob Lindley, finding in the woods a log which he thought might aid them in getting warmth for the night, had placed it on his shoulders, and brought it where his companions were. A little proud of his success in obtaining such a treasure, and perhaps of his strength in carrying it without assistance, he threw it on the ground, exclaiming, "See what a man can do!" Alas for his pride and their comfort! The log fell upon the burning wood, and utterly extinguished it. In vain they tried to rekindle it; every effort proved ineffectual, and they passed an uncomfortable night.

Jacob Lindley was not the first man, who, by endeavoring to give great aid and assistance to a cause, has been the very means of ruining it. Some who have come forward with an air of importance, which plainly said, "See what a man can do," have put out every spark of life by their untimely aid. Every effort to benefit the church, performed in the spirit that feels like taking credit for what is being done, will fail to make the fire of Truth greater, if it does not seriously deaden its burning.

Jacob was noted for his genuine kindness, as well as warmth of feeling. A respectable mechanic once, during the lifetime of his first wife, alluding to the hospitality which characterized them, said, "Their house is in one respect like the kingdom of heaven, no profession or complexion being excluded."

JACOB LINDLEY.

Jacob Lindley lost his first wife, Hannah, in 1798. She had gone to attend the Yearly Meeting in Philadelphia that year, and soon after her return, being taken with the prevailing fever, she was called to receive the reward of a life of dedication to her heavenly Father's will. She was a minister of the Gospel.

His second marriage was with Ruth Anna Rutter, also a minister. Ruth died in 1810. Jacob still continued zealously to labor for the good of others, and for the salvation of his own soul. The poor Africans continued to claim his tenderest sympathy, and to call forth his most energetic labors. He thus wrote: "Oh! surely I may say, I shudder, and my tears involuntarily steal from my eyes, for my poor, oppressed, afflicted, tormented, black brethren — hunted — frightened to see a white man — torn from every source of comfort that is worth living for in this stage of being. The tears — the groans — the sighs of these, have surely ascended to the ears of the Lord of Sabaoth, and as a thick cloud are awfully suspended over this land. I tenderly, and tremblingly feel for the poor masters, involved in the difficulty. I am awfully awakened into fear, for our poor country — with the language, 'I gave her time and place to repent; but she repented not!'"

On the afternoon of the 12th day of the Sixth month, 1814, while at home at Burlington, Sarah

Dillwyn observed her husband, George Dillwyn, sitting with such a peculiar and awful expression of countenance, as to create an alarm in her affectionate heart. She immediately approached him, and in the kind carefulness of love, inquired what was the matter. In answering her question, he said, he was very sorry she had disturbed him, for he had at that time been visited by Jacob Lindley's spirit! That day Jacob Lindley, in usual health, had attended his own meeting at New Garden, in Chester County, more than fifty miles from Burlington. In the meeting he was engaged in a living, powerful testimony, wherein he intimated his conviction, that there were those present who would not see the light of another day, and added, "perhaps it may be myself!" That afternoon, by a sudden jolt he was thrown from his vehicle into the road, and fell upon his head. Being a heavy man, his neck was dislocated, and his spirit was thereby suddenly released from the shackles of mortality. He was in his seventieth year.

ELI YARNALL.

ELI YARNALL was one who from early youth was much devoted to the Lord Jesus, and prepared by his Holy Spirit to exercise a gift in the ministry, which he was enabled to do to the comfort and strength of the church militant. He was born about the beginning of 1753. During his youth, being favored with the visitations of Divine Grace, he gladly accepted them, submitted his own will to the will of his God, became inwardly acquainted with the motions and leadings of the Spirit, and was made a partaker of that blessed liberty and freedom which is under the yoke of Christ. Being faithful to the manifestations received, he grew in godliness, and the blessing of the Almighty, in spiritual gifts and graces, descended upon him.

In the beginning of the year 1779, when he was about twenty-six years of age, and while the various exercises which were preparing him for the work of the ministry were heavy upon him, he received notice of an appointment from the commissioners of Chester County as collector of the taxes in the district he resided in. Besides the taxes at that time assessed—most of which must go to the support of war — there were to be collected fines for not taking the test oath or affirmation. Of course Eli Yarnall could not conscientiously do aught under the commission, which had, no doubt, been conferred upon him with an evil intent.

On considering the subject, it seemed to him best, in refusing to act, to furnish the commissioners with his reasons for so doing, and he accordingly addressed a letter to them. In this letter he says: "Ye may read, that it was said of old, by way of comparison, 'The fig-tree said unto them, Should I forsake my sweetness and my good fruit, and go to be promoted over the trees?' In like manner, I say unto you, shall I forsake that spirit of calmness, tenderness, and humility that breathes peace on earth and good-will toward all men, with which I am, through mercy, measurably favored, and accept of that power offered by you, and exercise the same by tyrannizing over the consciences of my brethren, violently distressing and spoiling their goods? Nay, surely, I dare not do it, let my sufferings in consequence thereof be never so great. I make no doubt but ye have been informed, that we cannot, consistently with our religious principles, have any hand in setting up or pulling down governments. Part of this, that is called a tax, is a fine for not taking a test of fidelity to one government and abjuration of the other, which would immediately make us parties."

The letter is throughout well written, and sets forth the blessed, peaceable nature of the Christian religion, and the contradiction manifested by its professed believers in their oppressing tender consciences and spoiling the goods of their brethren, whose only fault lay in their endeavors to be faithful to what they deemed the commands of their God. Soon after, Eli Yarnall was called on to exhibit Christian patience in suffering. For his refusal to collect these taxes, he was fined by the commissioners, and on the 7th of Seventh month, 1779, a valuable horse was taken from him to satisfy that fine. This was but the beginning of this kind of trial, for he had afterward to witness various parts of his property seized, because he could not muster as a militia man, and because he was as much opposed in conscience to paying another to fight for him as to fighting himself.

During these trials he appeared in the ministry, to the relief of his long-exercised mind, and to the satisfaction and edification of · his friends. Toward the close of this year, he received a letter from John Pemberton, encouraging him and other Friends in that neighborhood, who were suffering because of their testimony to the peaceable nature of the Gospel of Christ, to bear all with patience and resignation. In replying to this letter, Eli thus writes: "Thy exhortation to patience and resignation I hope will be duly regarded, most of us being mercifully preserved in measure possessors of that happy attainment. Our greatest concern, some of us can truly say, is to stand faithful, and approve ourselves worthy to suffer on the behalf of Christ. I have a comfortable hope that our patient sufferings will add to the furtherance of the Gospel, and in due time be a means of inclining the hearts of others to seek after the pearl of great price, to purchase which, many of us seem willing to part with all, if it be the Divine will."

About that time many suffered much, principally because those who had espoused the cause of the republic, regarded Friends' testimony against war as an indication of attachment to the royal cause. This was not a sure criterion. The doctrines and principles of the Society were well fitted to make its members good citizens under all governments, yet it can scarcely be denied by any close observer, but that the whole tenor of its influences is in favor of that freedom of thought and action that brings all classes to a common level, and which is most in accordance with republican equality and equal rights. The body of Friends, therefore, if they could have dared to have harbored a desire in the matter, would have been best pleased to live under a republic; but some, considering the mode adopted by the republicans, in asserting and fighting for their rights, to be wrong, and remembering how peaceably and comfortably they had lived under the king, would have been willing to have slipped back from the state of persecution and privation they were then in to the peace and plenty of their former condition.

At one period in the war a number of peaceable Friends were dragged from the comforts of their homes, and carried prisoners to Lancaster. Some for no other charge than for attending their Yearly Meeting in Philadelphia while the English had that city in possession, and for refusing to take the test. During their confinement, that true-hearted Christian and bold, unflinching advocate for the Truth, Abraham Gibbons, having gone from his residence at Lampeter to Lancaster to see them, thought it right to call on an officer of rank then in that place, to see if anything could be done to obtain their release.

The officer demeaned himself haughtily when Abraham was introduced to his presence, and when he heard the application on behalf of the innocent men who were suffering in prison, he broke out in words of the following import: "You talk of innocent men!

I will ask you, whether you yourself have not a choice which of the contending powers shall get the victory? For my part, I believe every man has a choice, and that you also must have one." Abraham had a courage which danger could not daunt, and, believing it was his duty to speak the truth plainly, he boldly said: "Thou hast asked me a close question, and my words may involve my liberty, but I shall give thee a candid answer. When I take into view the conduct of the Americans, and consider how Friends have to suffer under your treatment of them, I sometimes wish that the British might get the better of you; but these wishes and feelings I am liable to as a man. When I gain the state I wish to live in, and which I believe it to be my duty to attain as a Christian, if the turning of my hand would give either party the victory, I would not do it." The officer was affected at the answer, which, perhaps, opened to him a view of a state he had never before thought of. His harshness of manner disappeared, and at that time, and ever afterward, he treated Abraham Gibbons with distinguishing courtesy and respect.

Another meek-spirited man, whom duty made bold and unflinching in this time of trial, was Warner Mifflin, who having been appointed with some others to present a memorial to General Washington, from the Yearly Meeting of Philadelphia, passed across the battle-field at Germantown, among the wounded and dying. In the course of conversation with the General, Warner frankly told him, and no doubt the scene he had just witnessed, gave energy to his expressions, "I am opposed to the Revolution, and to all changes in government which occasion war and bloodshed." Some years after, while Washington was President of the United States, Warner again visited him on an errand of mercy. The President, in reference to their former conversation, asked him on what principle he had been opposed to the Revolution. "On the same principle," said Warner, "that I should be opposed to a change in this government. All that ever was gained by revolutions, is not an adequate compensation to the poor mangled soldier, for the loss of life or limb." Washington paused awhile to consider the position assumed by the philanthropist, and then said, to him, "I honor your sentiments; there is more in *that* than mankind have generally considered."

We have seen in the above anecdotes the beneficial influence of speaking the truth in love, without fear or flattery; we will relate an incident occurring during the same period, showing the powerful effect of Christian meekness, which, without verbal reproof, reached to the conscience, and subdued the wicked spirit of a backsliding clergyman, who had become a partizan officer.

A company of armed republicans from New Jersey, crossed the river Delaware into Bucks County, Pennsylvania, intent on plundering all the tories they could find. They considered all Friends in that class, because they were opposed to war — and this predatory excursion could only be considered as an intention of robbing them, there being many residing in that neighborhood. The leader of this company had been a Baptist clergyman, who had evidently once known something that would have taught him better than to rob the innocent and unresisting.

William Blakey, a minister of the Society of Friends, residing at Middletown, was well known by repute, as a friend of peace, and as the fearless opponent of war. It was to his house therefore that this renegade clergyman first led his troops, and commanded them to seize all the horses and wagons, and load upon them as much of the grain as they would contain. William Blakey stood by, a patient, unresisting, uncomplaining beholder of the spoil of his produce, the robbery of his stock. He felt the supporting presence of his Divine Master with him, and he sought for the spirit of supplication wherein he might not only be enabled to ask strength for himself, but to say, " Father, forgive them, for they know not what they do." The officer was evidently much disconcerted at the quiet, Christian submission of him he was wronging. He could see no fear nor anger manifested — he could hear no petitions, nor invective, but he saw in William courage, crowned with a Christian spirit, and an evident sense of God's overruling providence, sustaining and supporting amid all. He tried for a time what a domineering, insulting behaviour would effect, evidently wishing to provoke the sufferer to make some sharp or angry rebuke, which might justify him to himself for that which he was doing. Perhaps he wished to proceed to still greater acts of outrage, which he could not do, unless he could feel, or imagine, some provocation.

As William continued calmly to look on the labors of the men, the officer at last became silent, and evidently agitated in mind. He came at last to William, and with a faltering tongue, tremulous with emotion, asked him, if he ever prayed. This question was put to one, who, in his quiet resignation to his heavenly Father's will, was living in prayer — and he could answer with a modest assurance, that he had at times been favored with access to the throne of grace; and that he had, on the present occasion, been endeavoring to feel after the spirit of supplication. "Do you ever pray for any one but yourself?" William replied in the affirmative, and his interrogator then said, "I wish you would pray for me. I would not endure the wretchedness I now feel, for all you are worth!" By this time the men had secured as much of the grain as the wagons and horses could carry, and were ready to depart, but the officer commanded them to return it all whence they had taken it; and after some serious conversation with William, they all rode off, having done him no injury.

On the 26th day of the Eleventh month, 1783, Eli Yarnall was married to Priscilla Walker, who proved a valuable companion, being a nearly united spiritual sympathizer with him in his journey Zionward. They married, in some sense, as though they married not. For though their love to each other was strong and fervent, yet their love to their Divine Master was above all. In a little more than four weeks after their marriage he left her, his dearest earthly treasure, and went to pay a religious visit to Friends in Maryland and Virginia. The day of his leaving home to enter on his journey, she wrote thus in her diary: "The Lord of heaven who pointed us out for each other, I have a hope, and most ardent desire indeed, will in his time safely conduct us to each other's arms again. Remember, O Lord, him who hath now left his most endeared connections, to obey thee. Be pleased to be his companion, and conduct him safe to the bosom of her, who for his sake, believing it to be thy will, hath left the hospitable house of her father, wherein thy love has often descended as the dew of Hermon."

On the next day she writes of "being most affectionately engaged in sympathy with my darling, who, from all others I have chosen, humbly beseeching Almighty God to enable us to walk hand in hand through every trying dispensation, and though outwardly separated, that we may be present in spirit, feeling that that which joined us together for thy glory, is now separating us for thy praise. Oh, thou most gracious and everlasting Father and fountain of goodness, preserve us in the hollow of thy hand, that so we may not stray so far as to have a single wish contrary to thy will!" Her constant state of close union with her distant husband is noted in her diary, in which she records her thanks to the Lord, who permitted her to feel him in spirit with her as she lay down to rest, and when she awoke in the morning, saying, "Thou withholdest him not from assisting me to sing forth thy evening hymn and morning praise." Other striking instances from her diary might be quoted to show how closely she felt bound to her husband in Christian love and fellowship of spirit.

Eli, who although not a frequent minister, was yet one of the most powerful and favored of his day, felt the aid of her spirit in his Gospel labor, and after her death thus wrote of her: "Through the increase of that union which makes male and female one in Christ Jesus, she proved a great strength and confirmation to me in the exercise of the small gift bestowed upon me Such was the sympathetic travail of her spirit when with me in meetings, that when I have had anything to say, she was generally favored with a sense of the very time wherein I have felt the motion of the Spirit to appear; and also when I have been at neighboring meetings, and she remained at home attending to her lawful concerns, she hath been made a partaker with me in seasons of favor, and a sharer also in more stripped and trying opportunities; which being the Lord's doing, was marvellous in my eyes, and cause of great humiliation and gratitude. I believe few, if any, ever performed the duties of a wife to a husband with more loyalty and upright affection, being desirous of contributing toward my present and eternal happiness to the utmost of her power. An affectionate mother and kind mistress, watching over and encouraging her family, as well as reproving and restraining from things of an evil tendency those under her care. She was a lover and promoter of retirement in the family, some of which opportunities were eminently favored with the overshadowing of Divine goodness and mercy."

At the commencement of her last illness, in 1795, she said she was preserved even from the desire of knowing what way the Lord designed to dispose of her. At times she spoke of the love and mercy of the Lord manifested to her in the overshadowing of his presence while alone in her chamber, saying her sense of his fatherly tenderness was so great, she had no language to set it forth, being at times dumb with admiration of his goodness.

After many sweet and comforting seasons, and dropping many encouraging expressions, on the 10th of Sixth month, in the year just mentioned, she took an affectionate farewell of her family, and quietly and trustfully departed. Eli says, "At which awful season, my mind being gathered into stillness, the language of the apostle was comfortably revived, 'There is, therefore, now no condemnation to them which are in Christ Jesus.' A firm belief that she was enrolled among that blessed and happy number tended much to alleviate my affliction on account of the loss of so valuable and much beloved a companion and a helpmeet indeed, whose sympathizing spirit hath been instrumental to strengthen and console my mind under many adverse and trying allotments. Concerning her, I have been enabled to adopt the sentiment of Job, 'The Lord gave, and the Lord hath taken away; blessed be the name of the Lord.'"

At the burial, Eli was strengthened in the renewed feeling of the Lord's mercy, and in the assurance that it is in righteousness he afflicts the children of men, to bear a close testimony, commenting on the text,

"Affliction cometh not forth of the dust, neither doth trouble spring out of the ground."

Eli Yarnall continued faithfully obedient to the requirings of his almighty Caretaker and Saviour, and day by day grew in spiritual stature, till he stood as a father in the Truth. He was not frequent in the ministry in his latter years, but was a good example of fervent inward exercise and travail of soul for the arisings of life among those assembled. His spirit was often tendered in silent meetings, and, under a sense of Divine love and regard, tears of grateful thanksgiving would at times flow from him.

An interesting anecdote relating to his Gospel services, and illustrating the true fellowship which exists among those who are rightly called into the solemn work of the ministry, is as follows:

James Simpson, though endowed by his Divine Master with a remarkably baptizing gift in the ministry, was often greatly depressed. On one occasion, after attending a meeting, in the course of a religious visit at Springfield, Delaware County, Pennsylvania, he experienced a season of great discouragement and desertion. Thinking himself unfit for the ministry of the Gospel, and for the service he was then engaged in, he pressed upon his companion the necessity of returning home. To this the Friend objected, saying, that they had appointed a meeting at Providence for the next day, and must attend it. James replied that he thought he could not go to it, and plead to return home. After an afternoon and night of distressing conflict of mind, James arose unrelieved, and bent on leaving the neighborhood at once. His companion, unwilling to take this course, invited him to sit down, and they would try to wait on the Lord for direction and consolation in this time of trial. They had not sat long when James, with a bright countenance and cheerful voice, announced his readiness to attend the meeting, telling his friend, "My Master has been here, and said to me, 'Go, and I will send my servant, Eli Yarnall, and he shall come and pray for thee.'"

On that morning, Eli Yarnall, who lived several miles from Providence, was ploughing one of his fields, when he felt a strong impression to go at once to Providence meeting-house. He wondered at this, as it was not the usual meeting-day there, and he had not heard of the appointed meeting. But the call was clear, and he obeyed it. His wife was also surprised, remarking, "It was not meeting-day there, and she could not think what he was going for." He, however went, but did not reach the house until the people had gone into it. Taking his seat in the gallery, the mind of Eli Yarnall was soon brought under religious concern, and he felt it his duty to break the silence by prayer, in which he interceded for his beloved friend, James Simpson, that his faith might be strengthened, and help vouchsafed of the Lord to enable him to prosecute his religious services to the edification of the Church and his own peace and comfort.

James soon afterward arose in a living and awakening Gospel testimony, which had a powerful effect upon the audience, many being greatly affected and contrited into tears.

Toward the close of his life, Eli Yarnall married Thomasine Roberts, a daughter of John Roberts. In his intercourse with his family and in the world, his conduct was marked with Christian circumspection and watchfulness. He was upright in his dealings, honest toward man and toward God, prompt in the fulfillment of his duties, and cheerfully dedicated to attend to all the services the religious Society he belonged to required of him.

In the Seventh month, 1812, being taken unwell, he had a sense that death was drawing near. In the Eighth month, to one visiting him he said, "My dear friend, I believe I am going the way of all flesh. My pain is often very great; but my mind, under the prospect of approaching dissolution, enjoys entire resignation. Indeed, the quiet and peaceful serenity with which I have from day to day since my confinement been favored, even when under excruciating pain, is cause of much thankfulness and admiration." On one occasion, after supplication for preservation, he addressed his two sons, reminding them of visitations immediately and instrumentally, which had been mercifully granted to them. He sought to encourage them to walk in obedience to the Lord's requirings, and to make their Saviour their friend, that he might be their strength and support in after life. Soon afterward he broke forth into a strain of praise and thanksgiving to the Father of mercies for the blessed present assurance of his love, and that the work of his soul's salvation was perfected, and his peace made with his God forever. "'Glory to God in the highest, and on earth, peace, good will to men.' Often before now I have been made sensible of the universality of the love of our heavenly Father, and now I feel it to flow toward all men. If I die now, give my dear love to all my friends, and tell them I die in peace and unity with all faithful Friends."

At another time he said, "My dependence is on the Lord Almighty, whose blessed will be done. I can say in truth, Come, Lord; thy servant is ready. I have not now to suffer the pangs of guilt." Two days after, he said his mind was at peace with God and man, and then added, "The sting of death is sin, and that is taken away." Relieved from severe pain, full of gratitude to his Almighty Helper, he went rejoicing through the dark valley and shadow of death, fully assured that he who sustained him in faith and hope here would crown him with glory hereafter. On the 25th day of the Eighth month, 1812, hope was lost in certainty, and faith in fruition. He was in his sixtieth year.

SARAH HARRISON.

SARAH HARRISON was a daughter of Rowland Richards, and was born about the year 1748, in what is now Delaware County, Pennsylvania. She was naturally cheerful, and animated, and in the days of her youth suffered herself to give way to vanity and frivolity, which afterward caused her much suffering and mental conflict. She says:

"In my youthful days, I gave way to things that proved a snare to me, and caused me many sorrowful days and nights, yea, months and years, before I witnessed reconciliation with my God; and I now stand as a monument of his mercy. All unrighteousness is sin; and the wages of sin is death. This I know by sorrowful experience; for it brought death upon the innocent life of God in my heart, and made me a long wilderness travel. I too lightly esteemed the early visitations of God to my soul, until I became somewhat like the deaf adder that would not hear the voice of the charmer, though he charmed ever so sweetly."

"But in these my young years, when I was flying away as upon the wings of vanity, the Lord was pleased to meet with me in a narrow place, where I saw there was no way for me to escape his righteous judgments, either here or hereafter. I was led deeply and awfully to consider the woful consequence of my sins being brought to judgment after death, where there is no remedy; and I was made willing to bear his indignation, because I knew I had sinned against him many a time, though in what the world calls little things; yet I was convinced they were great enough to exclude me from the Divine presence forever, if I did not repent, and endeavor to walk more circumspectly. I can with thankfulness say, that the awful impressions that were then made on my mind, have never been erased. No; they were too deep for any blast of temptation to blow away."

The natural mind is, and ever will be, in enmity to the cross of Christ, and many young persons have experienced baptisms of an awful character before they have been brought to surrender their own will to the Divine will. Some, after having submitted, again rebel, and thus bring on themselves trials and sufferings, deeper and heavier than those which they had previously encountered.

A valued minister, now deceased, in speaking of the trials he passed through, in becoming a plain and consistent Quaker, stated the following facts. He had, under a conviction of duty, and through an obedience springing out of many fiery baptisms, become plain. But after a time, the cross appearing too great to be borne, he once more changed his attire, and in opposition to the dictates of conscience turned back to the world. It was not long that he could with any comfort pursue the old road he had once more taken. Reproofs were inwardly administered to him by the Holy Spirit, until he was thoroughly aroused to his awful condition. He saw the path of duty before him, but he saw no forgiveness for the past acts of rebellion, particularly for his wilful turning back from what he knew to be right. He had been a youth of uncommon vivacity, constitutionally cheerful, and seeing the bright side of things — now all was changed. He lost his animation, the fear of eternal death and everlasting punishment took hold of him, and for five long years he was traveling in the deeps where no ray of light seemed to reach him. During these years, he said, "I never smiled." Divine Goodness at last extended a saving hand to him — he felt his backsliding pardoned, and in due time a true Christian cheerfulness was given to his heart, and once more vivacity, tempered by the fear of the Lord, sat smiling on his face.

Sarah Richards, about the twentieth year of her

age, was married to Thomas Harrison, and became a resident in the city of Philadelphia. She fulfilled with faithfulness and activity the duties of her new sphere of life, was managing and neat as a housekeeper — warm-hearted and kind to friends and neighbors, hospitable to strangers, charitable to the poor, and ever ready to perform services of kindness to all. The Lord, her almighty Caretaker, did not permit her to pass along without trials. Several of her children died in infancy, and she was dipped into various baptisms to qualify her for the ministry of the Gospel, to which service her Lord had appointed her. During the time of the Revolutionary war she first spoke in the meetings of Friends, and was acknowledged as a minister in 1781.

In his Journal, Thomas Scattergood makes this entry: Third month 5th, 1783 — "Spent some time with Sarah Harrison with unusual openness, in comparing our getting along in a religious sense."

Sarah Harrison had been acknowledged as a minister a short time before Thomas Scattergood was; and a precious feeling of Gospel fellowship subsisted between them, until death.

The following anecdote respecting Joseph Lukens and Sarah Harrison, is interesting, as setting forth the truth of the openings of the Divine gift. Joseph Lukens, who resided at Horsham, came to Philadelphia, on the 16th of the Ninth month, 1784, and attended the High Street Meeting, where he had a lively and acceptable testimony. Toward the close of the meeting, Sarah Harrison, under the constrainings of religious duty, rose up and spoke to this import: "There is one present, who will not have the opportunity of again thus meeting with Friends." After saying that this made it necessary that such an one should improve the present, to prepare for the final change — she, in the warm feeling of Gospel fellowship, bade the individual she was addressing, "farewell in the Lord." This short communication was delivered with great solemnity, and Joseph Lukens had an inward assurance, that he was the individual referred to. In the afternoon he attended a sitting of the Meeting for Sufferings, and before night went out of the city, part of the way toward his residence. The next morning he again started, but was taken sick before reaching home. In obedience to the warning given, he endeavored to prepare for leaving his earthly business and Friends — and as his illness gradually increased on him, he took leave in a solemn and weighty manner of his wife and children. He passed from this scene of conflict and sorrow, on the 27th of the same month, aged fifty-five years.

On the 28th of the First month, 1785, Sarah Harrison was set at liberty to pay a religious visit to the families of her own Monthly Meeting. This arduous work, to prepare the poor servant for which many previous baptisms seems needful, is often very beneficial to the church. If the minister is rightly qualified to dip into the states of the visited, he may be enabled in Divine authority not only to deliver words of consolation, counsel, entreaty, and warning, but to bring them home where they are needed, with a "Thou art the man." It is related, that during the last war with England, a woman Friend being on a religious visit in the northern part of New York State, held a meeting to which a small number of persons came, among whom was General Brown, the commander of the American army in that neighborhood. The Friend found her mind exercised on behalf of those assembled, and was led to speak to them one by one, looking at the person she was speaking to. The General, who had been brought up a Friend, did not like such close work, and as he watched her turning from one to the other, as they sat around the room, laying open their states, and administering the needful advice and warning, he became very uneasy. He doubtless had sufficient reasons, as he deemed them, for desiring not to be singled out, and have his sins brought home to him publicly. He sat until she began to speak to the one next to him, when he suddenly rose and left the meeting.

Thomas Carrington, of Pennsylvania, a simple-hearted Friend, but honest minister of the Gospel, being in England about the time of the American Revolution, paid religious visits to the keepers of the ale-houses in Bristol. In one of them he found that the head of the house was dissipated, but his wife was a religious woman, who was endeavoring, as far as it lay in her power, to counteract the evil influence of their situation on the minds of her children. One of her sons, then about thirteen years of age, had fallen into bad habits, and was very far from the path of Christian rectitude. This lad had no intention of being preached to, and understanding when Thomas Carrington would, in all probability, be at his father's house, he absented himself. After a time, supposing the Friends to have departed, he ventured home. He entered the parlor, where, to his surprise, he found them still remaining, although on their feet ready to go. His mother was in sadness of heart speaking to the Friends about him, and lamenting over him with tears. Thomas Carrington feeling his mind filled with Gospel love toward the youth, looked at him with a solid countenance, expressive of deep religious concern, and then addressed a few words to him, withal laying his hand on his head. The future career of this youth was at that time, in the openings of the Lord's blessed Spirit, made known to the minister, who turning to the mother, bade her be comforted, saying her son would be a comfort to her old days — that he would become a member of the Society of Friends — a minister of the Gospel — and that in that capacity he would be led to visit the continent of North America. All this, the pious mother lived to see realized. That son was George Withy, and she did not decease until after his visit to America was accomplished, when she was gathered to her heavenly Father's house in peace, being about ninety years of age.

About the close of 1803, Elizabeth Foulke, a minister of Philadelphia Monthly Meeting, under a religious concern to visit certain individuals, who had been disowned from the Society of Friends, opened the subject to her meeting, and received permission to perform the service, and the expression of much unity therewith. She knew of no one to accompany her; but after the meeting, Peter Andrews, from sympathy, offered to go. He did so to two or three families, when finding he had nothing to do with the service, he told her, that his free-will offering was not accepted, and that he could go no further. In her distress, she looked round her for help, and wrote to James Simpson, stating her condition, and quoting to him the passage, "Come over into Macedonia and help us." James had no inclination to engage in that to which he was not called, but in giving his refusal, he said he had, in a dream or vision, seen a woman Friend, who, he was persuaded, was designed to accompany her in this service. Soon after Martha Routh came to Philadelphia, and felt the concern laid immediately upon her. The Monthly Meeting approved of her joining Elizabeth, and their labor appears to have been remarkably blessed. Several, being reached through their ministry, were brought back to the fold, and of these some became ministers of the Gospel.

Isaac Jacobs, a minister belonging to Uwchlan Meeting, having been, through the winter of 1784-5, engaged in visiting meetings in the Southern States, thus wrote from Petersburg, Virginia, to Sarah Harrison, under date of Third month 12th, 1787: "Now dear Sarah, I address myself to thee, and may inform thee that there is a field of labor for those who are entered into the public vineyard. We found the spring of the ministry at a low ebb in some places, meetings rather on the decline, and some almost ready to be laid down. I am thankful to find that there is a seed preserved in every place, and though small, yet I found my mind united to that little, so that I could say it was enough to reward for my poor labor in leaving my connections at home. In places where things seemed the least, there appeared marks of the love and gracious regard of the holy Shepherd, in turning some from the barren wilderness of an empty profession, to seek him and become of his flock. This I trust some are, who have come in by convincement. . . . We seem to be on our way home, and can say for thy encouragement, (apprehending that thou art rather diffident at times,) that in most places there is an openness among Friends and other sober-minded people to receive Friends among them with a great deal of goodwill. Our esteemed Friends, Edith Sharpless and Sarah Talbot, having been through many places where we have been, have left a pleasant savor; and in divers places not among Friends, their services, I believe, will redound to the credit of Truth."

The mind of Sarah Harrison had been drawn to the South, but the time for the performance of her visit had not yet come. Isaac Jacobs appears, by this letter, to have entered into feeling on this subject with her.

The following message from her friend, Samuel Emlen, then in Dublin, contained in a letter written 22d of Seventh month, 1785, expressing his sympathy with her in her exercises, must also have been as a cordial to her mind, and strengthening to her faith in this time of trial. He says: "I desire my affectionate salutation given to Sarah Harrison and husband. Tell her, though she has received no written testimony of my continued brotherly regard, yet she is, as a Christian pilgrim in the path of tribulation and varied exercise, largely interested in my sympathy and truest well-wishings. I trust she knows in whom she has believed, even in whom it is said, 'There is none holy as the Lord, neither is there any Rock like our God, May she then, with a perfect submission and a righteous confidence, at all times give up to the heavenly vision, and not furnish occasion for the reprehensive expostulation, 'O thou of little faith, wherefore didst thou doubt?'"

In the Fifth month, 1786, Sarah Harrison left her home, accompanied by her friend, Mary England, to attend the Yearly Meeting of Virginia, after her return from which her mind was impressed with a sense that further religious labor in the Southern States was required of her. In the latter part of the same year she was liberated by her Monthly Meeting to attend all the meetings of Friends in Virginia and many of those further south.

In the course of this visit she attended North Carolina Yearly Meeting, in the Tenth month, 1787, where she remarks, "The subject of holding mankind as slaves came weightily before the meeting, and a committee was appointed to visit such as have slaves, and if they continue to disregard the wholesome advice of the body, Monthly Meetings were directed to disunite them."

In the early part of the year 1788, she spent several weeks in Charleston, S. C., where she wrote as follows: "Great has been the oppression we have felt here; the Gospel truths we have had to deliver being so repugnant to the disposition of the minds of most of the inhabitants, who, like many others, love ease, and do not want their false rests disturbed. They say much against slave-holding; all we have conversed with agree that it is not right to hold their fellow-creatures in bondage, and wish they were all free, declaring that they are only a burden to them. But when anything is said to promote their freedom, they soon turn and say they are not fit for freedom, because they are such poor, helpless creatures. But, oh, that God may be pleased to hasten the coming of that day when the eyes of them that see shall not be dim, and the ears of them that hear shall hearken to His in-speaking voice!"

On the 27th of the Third month, Sarah Harrison again wrote: "Yesterday I was at a small meeting in Charleston, when the states of those present were laid open before them, I trust in a clear light, though not with enticing words of man's wisdom. I often think I am one of the most stammering speech of any that ever were sent forth on such an errand. May he that promised to be with the mouth of Moses, be with me at all times, especially when engaged in his cause, and teach me what I shall say, is the desire of my heart; that so his great name may be exalted, and self may be abased in me. Although the Lord has been pleased at times to lead me through the valley and shadow of death, yet there have been times when I could sing praises to his name, and extol him that rideth upon the heavens."

Much religious labor was performed by Sarah Harrison and her companions during this journey with those members of our Society who then held slaves. Going from house to house, clothed with meekness, yet in the power and authority of the Lord's Holy Spirit, their labors were blessed with unexpected success.

Many individuals, particularly in Virginia, were much contrited under the Divine power attending her ministry, and, from a heartfelt conviction of duty, bore a righteous testimony against slave-holding by manumitting all their slaves. Within the limits of one Monthly Meeting in that State, the Friends had the satisfaction of seeing nearly fifty of their fellow-beings released from bondage in their presence. Toward the conclusion of their journey, Sarah Harrison remarks: "I can with gratitude say, I believe the arm of God's salvation has been made bare for our preservation thus far."

They reached Philadelphia in the Eighth month, 1788, having been nearly a year engaged in this arduous service. The annals of our Society furnish no similar record of such successful labor in the cause of the oppressed.

While engaged in her labors in the South, Sarah Harrison received an encouraging letter from her adopted daughter, and affectionate sympathizing companion, Sarah Dickenson, who, a short time previously, had been united in marriage, to a sweet-spirited Friend, Charles Williams. Sarah Williams had passed through many outward trials, and inward baptisms, in early life, and had appeared in the ministry, when a very child in years. Under date of Fourth month 19th, 1788, she wrote:

"Being informed by thy dear husband of an opportunity for conveying letters to thee, I thought I felt a freedom once more [to address thee], as a testimony of my unshaken love and sympathy for thee; and more especially as my mind was peculiarly impressed, upon receiving such intelligence, with a sacred and blessed promise uttered by the lip of Truth, that every one who had left father, mother, houses, and children, for his sake, should receive in this life an hundred-fold, and in that to come, life everlasting: the remembrance of which I thought was sufficient to bear up *such* through every proving dispensation, allotted in this state of pilgrimage.

"Yea, my dear mother, permit me to say, that I

believe it has not been for nought that thou hast been called into that desolate part of the vineyard; for the Master, it seems to me, is about to visit the highways and hedges, and to draw, as it were, the heathen by his powerful love to come in and sup with him."

While in Baltimore, in a subsequent visit to the families of Friends in that place, in 1789, Sarah Harrison received intelligence of the death of Sarah Williams, which occurred on the 18th of the Seventh month, at the early age of twenty-four years. It was a great shock to Sarah Harrison, yet, she says, "The language occurred, 'Weep not for me, but weep for yourselves, and for your children.' Dear Sarah has been the subject of my thoughts almost every day, for several weeks, while we have been visiting families; and often in the course of my testimonies, I have had to mention her zeal for the honor of Truth, at so early a period of her life, though she labored under many difficulties and discouragements. Many trying circumstances of her life were brought to my remembrance, as well as her growth and experience in the work of religion, and at what age her mouth was opened in meetings. She was recommended to the meeting of ministers and elders at about the age of eighteen years. And now methinks I hear a voice, saying, 'Blessed are the dead which die in the Lord, from henceforth; yea, saith the Spirit, that they may rest from their labors, and their works do follow them.'"

Such was the testimony of Sarah Williams's adopted mother — and a deep feeling of lamentation for her loss was experienced by the church, while its members could but feel, that their departed sister, though young in years, had been enabled to work out her portion of labor in the Master's vineyard, and had been taken as at noon to receive her penny of everlasting peace.

While absent on this journey, the tender feelings of Sarah Harrison experienced another shock in the removal, by death, of her son Thomas. When information reached the poor, heart-stricken mother, she found that there was One who could heal her. She felt his Holy Spirit near her, and was enabled in true submission to the Lord's will, to bow down in supplication, that herself and husband might be preserved in a state of perfect resignation, so that they might be enabled to say, "The Lord gave, and the Lord hath taken away; blessed be the name of the Lord."

She was enabled to feel that those of her children, seven in number, who had been taken from her by death in their early years, had been gathered in mercy among the saints in light. She knew that for them, there was no cause to sorrow, and in the strength which the Lord alone can give, she felt that she would rather that all should be taken in the innocency of youth, than that one should grow up a servant of sin.

It is the duty of all of us to strive after resignation to the loss of friends and connections, when it is the will of our heavenly Father to gather them from us. He knows when it is best to remove them, and it behoves us earnestly to seek for resignation to his will. The following anecdote in relation to this subject conveys much instruction. A religious woman had a son apparently near to the gates of death. She believed he would be taken, and felt it would be right to resign him, but her maternal feelings overpowering her religious sense of right, she refused to do so, and continued to petition, that her son's life might be spared. It appeared that her requests, unsanctified by resignation, were granted in judgment, not in mercy. The child recovered, and grew up to be the thorn and sorrow of her life — the bitterness of anguish, and of shame to her! Why should we mourn and weep for the loss of friends who have been gathered in mercy, and safely housed, as we humbly trust, in one of the many mansions in glory? Here, had they been continued, it would have been in probation, with a possibility of losing the crown in the end; there, they are forever at rest — forever settled in unending happiness. Our late Friend, Thomas Kite, while on his death-bed expressed the sentiment, that to be removed when in the prime of usefulness, from the church, was desirable. He alluded to one who had fallen away in his old age, and stating that this individual had in early manhood a very severe illness, added, "Had he been taken then, all Israel would have mourned for him!"

In 1792, Sarah Harrison was liberated by her friends to pay a religious visit to Great Britain and Ireland, a prospect of which had for some time previously weightily impressed her mind. She sailed for Liverpool on the 15th of the Seventh month, in company with Mary Ridgway and Jane Watson, who, after having accomplished a visit in Gospel love to the churches in America, were returning to their native land. Samuel Emlen, who had also been set at liberty for religious labor in Europe, was a fellow-passenger.

In the course of this visit Sarah Harrison felt a great care not to minister to itching ears, but would rather travel on in silence and sorrow than speak, unless under the clear requiring of duty. Her feelings were much in unison with those of Richard Jordan on this subject, as thus expressed by him in a letter written from England to his wife in 1802:

"Alas! what can we do, when He who hath the keys of David is pleased to shut? Who can dare attempt to open? . . . I fully believe that attempts of this sort is the reason of so much lifeless ministry prevailing in the world, (even among *us* as well as other people,) which I believe seldom (rightly) either opens the understanding or convinces the judgment. Many seem to get on very easy, as if custom had made it so, and it may be so to them, but, verily, I cannot learn how they come at it; for when I am apprehensive that I have missed it in this respect, the affliction and anguish of my soul are beyond description. It is only by the breath of life from God that man becomes a living soul, and it is only by the renewing of it in our souls that we are enabled to offer acceptable offerings unto Him. . . . I cannot bear the thought of being numbered among those that encompass themselves 'with sparks of their own kindling,' whose portion is (if they persist) to lie down in sorrow. . . . When I have been favored with patience to wait, through deep suffering, for the lifting up of that that smote the rock in the wilderness by the hand of Moses — blessed be his name — he hath been pleased to smite it again and again, and cause living water to gush out, and many more souls with mine to drink as into the everlasting fountain, to our mutual refreshment and humble rejoicing in the renewed offers of his salvation."

It is very important that ministers should be strengthened to refuse the demand of the itching ears for words, when nothing is committed to them to deliver; and equally so, that they deliver faithfully what is given them, even though it may be disagreeable truths to those to whom it is addressed. The following account contains a very instructive moral. An honest, simple-hearted minister of the Gospel, belonging to Philadelphia Yearly Meeting, had been liberated by his Friends to pay a religious visit, and no doubt was often exercised in secret prayer that he might perform it safely, and return with peace of mind as the reward of faithful obedience. Just before the time came for him to leave home to commence his proposed labor, he dreamed as follows: He thought that he had already started on his journey, and was carrying a white bag with him. Around him many people were collected, all anxious for a portion of the contents of the bag, but each one desiring to choose for himself what he would have. His heart was stirred up with earnest zeal, and, in Scripture diction, he emphatically declared, "As the Lord liveth, and as your souls live, I will not give you aught, save that which cometh to hand." The remembrance of the dream remained with the Friend on his journey, and he thought it proved of good service to him.

In many places which she visited abroad, Sarah Harrison was often under much discouragement of mind, but she was at times comforted and animated to pursue her religious engagements by the messages sent her by her valued co-laborers in the ministry and other sympathizing friends.

Samuel Emlen thus addressed her in the language of encouragement, in a letter dated London, Tenth month 12th, 1793.

"My belief is that the Lord will bless the faithful in his work, and prosper it in their hands. Be not, therefore, improperly discouraged, although at times thou may be ready to exclaim, 'Who hath believed our report? or to whom is the arm of the Lord revealed?' If we are really and sincerely devoted to Divine appointment, there is cause reverently to hope that we shall, at least, 'deliver our own souls' from that condemnation which the unfaithful and negligent are incurring, to their own abundant loss and grievous disappointment. I feel that I yet love thee as a coworker unto the kingdom of God; for thou art, and often hast been, a comfort to my best life.

"I am thy cordial, well-wishing friend,
SAMUEL EMLEN."

In scenes of trial and apparent desertion, the sympathy of those rightly qualified to feel is often blessed to the revival of a little grain of holy hope. The letters received by Sarah Harrison gave her evidence that her Friends at a distance felt with her and for her, and so did her closely united companion, Sarah Benson and others, where her lot was cast. A Friend in the ministry, while travelling on the Continent of

Europe, being under deep depression of spirit, was suddenly comforted with an assurance inwardly given him that Mary Dudley was at that time engaged in supplication on his behalf. So strong was the impression that he noted down the time, and when afterward in England, he learned that at that very time Mary Dudley had felt constrained to kneel down in a public meeting, and vocally to approach the throne of mercy and grace on his behalf.

Sarah Harrison was several years in Europe, visiting Friends' meetings in the limits of London and Dublin Yearly Meetings, and also travelling on the Continent, where the unsettled state of the country subjected her to many trials and difficulties in the prosecution of her labors of love, being, on one occasion, held prisoner for several days, by the French authorities, on suspicion of being an English spy.

After her return home, her health became much broken, so that she seldom got out, except to her own meetings.

Her last illness was very short. She died the 29th of Twelfth month, 1812, in much calmness and quietude, her last words being, "Lord Jesus, receive my spirit." She was in the seventy-sixth year of her age.

JOHN PARKER.

JOHN PARKER was born in Wilmington, in the State of Delaware, in the year 1748. He was by birth a member of the Society of Friends, and we may believe that he experienced some beneficial restraints from his connection therewith. By the loss of his father while he was still young, he could no longer receive paternal admonition, nor be subject to that watchful oversight and control which a religiously concerned father might have exercised. In early life ne too much allowed his naturally lively imagination and strong will to rule his conduct. It is believed that he was favored to witness preservation from gross and reproachful vices, though he deviated from the simplicity of the Truth, and turned aside from the way of the cross. Yet, when the Lord's Holy Spirit awakens the best and cleanest livers among unregenerate men to a sense of their lost and undone condition, how do they see that their whole life has been a polluted one! and how are they brought to repent, in dust and ashes, over past transgressions and inward and outward corruption!

He once, in his earnest, animated manner, gave a ministering Friend an account of the way in which he became a Quaker. His narrative was to this effect: At the time the English army, early in the Ninth month, 1777, after having landed at the head of Elk, were approaching Philadelphia, they passed near the place where he lived. He was out of his house, and a company of Hessians meeting him, appeared disposed to rob him. By some means they learned that he was a Quaker, whereupon they desisted from all acts of violence toward him, but carried him to the English officer in command. Here, too, probably, the reputation of the Society of which he was then but an unworthy member, cast a shield over him, and he was told that he should receive no harm. He must, however, remain with them for a time, as they were about to engage with the American army, and if he were released, he might carry to their opponents the knowledge of their position and their intentions. They treated him, however, kindly, and the chief officer of that portion of the army kept him near his person. As they were standing on the Brandywine hills, surveying the beautiful country around — beautiful although arrayed in the graver tints of early autumn — the British officer made many remarks on the loveliness of the scene. At last the firing commenced, and John, who was still near the officer, saw many fall around him. The awfulness of his situation, in the consciousness that he was unprepared for death, made him tremble. The officer perceived the uneasiness of his companion, and, smiling on him, inquired if he was afraid. To this John promptly replied, "Yes." As no object was to be gained by detaining him any longer, he was told he might go, and he soon reached his home in safety. As John in his old age related this circumstance, he added, "That day made me a Quaker. I never was one before."

It is probable that the view of death thus brought powerfully before him, was of essential service, and tended to drive him to seek for consolation where alone it could be found, even in Him, who, by taking away our sins, taketh away the sting of death. He had been made to *quake* for fear of death; — he was now made a *Quaker* indeed, in an awful sense of the power and presence of the Lord God of Hosts, visiting his soul as a refiner with fire, and as a righteous Judge with judgments. Witnessing his own will brought into subjection, a new heart was given him, and he no longer took delight in this world's pleasures. He submitted to the cross of Christ, and through the effectual working of the Lord's preparing Spirit, and a gift in the ministry of the Gospel committed to him, he was soon qualified for usefulness in the church of Christ. The prospect of entering into the ministry, was a very awful thing to him, and many deep baptisms were his portion. In relation to it, he said, "He felt so poor, so little, so rude and uninstructed in the work of religion, that he could hardly esteem it possible that the Almighty could condescend to make use of so mean an instrument for the promotion of his holy cause." Yet as he abode under the visitation and the baptisms allotted him, he was brought into submission to the Lord's will, and in due time was enabled in living authority to speak of that which he had known in himself, and to direct his hearers to the Lord Jesus Christ, the sanctifier and Saviour of his people.

John Parker was thoroughly convinced that the salvation of man was in and through the Lord Jesus Christ. He knew that through the offering of the dear Son of God — a lively faith in Him — and submission to his soul-cleansing baptisms, he had witnessed the forgiveness of sin — and therefore in the love which would have all saved, he pressed upon his hearers the necessity of obedience to that Spirit, and faith in the Lord Jesus, through whom there is forgiveness and remission of sins. He could speak from living experience, for he had himself tasted and handled of the good Word of life, and therefore he was prepared to proclaim with emphasis and energy, "These are not cunningly devised fables, but living, substantial truth."

The first time he opened his mouth in the way of public ministry, he uttered but four words. This act of dedication, notwithstanding the smallness of the offering, he said brought him the reward of peace. He was not for a time abundant in expression, for he knew the necessity of waiting closely on the Lord, and speaking only as he opened the way. Being concerned to close his communications at the Master's bidding, as well as to commence in his authority, and in obedience to his will, his growth was solid.

John Parker was no man's copy. He possessed a large share of natural ability, and although he had not been favored with much literary education, yet his cheerful temper, and his lively imagination, under subjection to the Truth, made his company and conversation agreeable to young and to old. Great, at times, were his earnestness and fervency of spirit, when in a loud, clear, and melodious voice, he was enabled to preach the Gospel of life and salvation. There was much solemnity in his manner, and his delivery was impressive, while his illustrations from common things of daily occurrence, connected with the business of life, were often exceedingly felicitous, and happily adapted to give to the mind of the hearer clear views of doctrinal truth and practical heart-cleansing religion.

It appears from an account preserved, that Joshua Evans was at times led to make comparisons in his ministry, some of which, although startling to his hearers while he was enunciating them, were found at the close to be exceedingly pertinent, and to leave valuable and lasting impressions. On one occasion, while on a religious visit in the limits of New York Yearly Meeting, he held a meeting, at which there were few Friends present, but many others, among whom were the most respectable and best-educated people of the neighborhood. After a time of silence, Joshua arose, and commenced speaking to this import: "Suppose a person eminent for wisdom among you, being about to perform a journey, should harness his horse behind his wagon! Would you not, if he were your friend, remonstrate against the measure, and if he persisted, would you not think him irrational, and that his undertaking would never be accomplished?"

As Joshua spoke these sentences, the congregation seemed astonished. Joshua then quoted the text, "Seek ye first the kingdom of God and his righteousness, and all these things shall be added unto you." "This," said he, "was an admonition or commandment of the blessed Saviour himself; but people generally, instead of obeying him, seek first the things of this world and the glory thereof, and appear to be under an apprehension that the kingdom and righteousness of God will be added, without their care or concern. When or how it is to be obtained seems a matter of indifference to them, although they think and say, 'It is desirable.' In this careless and unconcerned state, many are summoned to appear before the Great Judge who gave forth the command. These careless and unconcerned ones are more unlikely to accomplish the design of their creation, and to be saved with an everlasting salvation, than the man would be to accomplish his journey whose horse was hitched behind his wagon." The assembly, by this time, began to appreciate the fitness of the comparison, and appeared to feel the solemnity and importance of the subject. The baptizing power of Truth was manifested that day among them, and many tears of contrition were shed. The meeting was long remembered in that neighborhood, and was often spoken of by those who had attended it, who manifested a high degree of veneration and respect for the simple-hearted preacher.

After John Parker was acknowledged as a minister by his Friends, he sometimes paid religious visits within the limits of his own Yearly Meeting. Yet he went not much abroad. His Master, whose prerogative it is to call his servants to labor where and when he pleases, generally apportioned him his field of service at home. There he was best known, and there he was most beloved. His consistent walking among men had an influence for good on those around him, and opened the way for his ministry, and for the counsel and warning which he was at times led to administer to those who had departed, or were in danger of departing from the Truth. These reproofs, although at times solemn and very close, it is believed, being given in love, were generally received in love.

He was distinguished by genuine, plain hospitality, and his friends were ever wont to be received at his house with a cordiality that made them feel that they were welcome. He was a hearty sympathizer with those who were in affliction, and when sickness assailed, or death entered a family, he was a frequent and welcome visitant. In the hour of trouble and season of calamity, he was looked to by his neighbors for comfort and advice, and tender consolation and judicious counsel were often administered by him.

John Parker had received but a limited education in his youth, yet, by reading and observation, he had accumulated quite a fund of knowledge, and his judgment of men and things was in general good. His conversational powers were excellent, and his animated yet familiar manners made his company very pleasant to young and old. He was often enabled to draw from even trivial events lessons of instruction for his youthful visitors.

John was in limited circumstances when he began life, but, through industry and economy, he supported a large family with reputation. He continued to labor with his own hands until quite advanced in years, yet he was very careful, after he had submitted to the cross of Christ, not to allow his temporal affairs to prevent his attending his own meeting or to interfere with his other religious concerns. Our Christian duties ought to be attended to, however much we may in a pecuniary point of view suffer thereby, inasmuch as heavenly riches exceed in value mere earthly treasure; yet men seldom suffer loss by attending diligently their religious meetings.

The following anecdotes are in point: On a certain occasion the late Timothy Paxson closed his place of business in order that he might attend his week-day meeting. During the time he was absent for this purpose, a customer went to his store with the intention of purchasing five hundred barrels of flour for immediate shipment. Finding that the door was shut, the man turned into an adjoining store and made his purchase. When Timothy returned from meeting, his neighbor who had made the sale, came to see him, and informed him what he had lost by his going to meeting. Timothy quietly told him that religious duty must take precedence of worldly business. The next morning a vessel arrived from Europe, bringing information of a sudden advance in the price of breadstuffs, and Timothy sold his flour at a dollar a barrel more than he would have received if he had not been at meeting.

Another Friend of this city, who deceased some years since, said that it had always been the practice of himself and brothers, who were his partners, regularly to attend all their week-day meetings. He added, they thought that even in a pecuniary point of view, they had never lost one cent by it. He said that once, on meeting-day, one of their largest customers called, and, as the members of the firm were all absent, he, in a great hurry to procure his goods, went to another store, where he purchased his six months' supply. After meeting, they were informed of what had happened, and came to the conclusion that in this one instance they had been pecuniarily losers by attending to their religious duties. But the result proved otherwise. Before the time came round at which payment for the purchase would in common course have been made, the customer was a bankrupt, and they saved the whole amount of the bill which he would have bought of them had they been at the store. These instances are introduced to show that apparent losses in support of our duty are not always really so, and that while it is the business of a Christian to walk in the path his Master points out, without reasoning as to consequences, yet that our blessed Caretaker often causes outward prosperity to attend a faithful performance of duty.

John Parker continued laboring faithfully in his gift, and cheering his neighbors by his animated manners and kind interest in their welfare. One day, having been favored to preach the Gospel with an unusual degree of the demonstration of the Spirit and power, on leaving the door of Kennet meeting-house, he appeared very cheerful, as was frequently the case with him under such circumstances, shaking hands with and addressing some pleasant remark to each person as he passed along. One of his sober neighbors, not a Friend, who had been at meeting that morning, stood a little back from the crowd, with much solemn gravity expressed in his countenance, viewing John's cheerful progress among his Friends. When John reached the spot where he stood, the neighbor, taking his offered hand, said, "I do marvel how you can be so lively and pleasant, immediately after having been so favored as you have been this morning, while engaged in the solemn and awful work of the ministry." After a short pause, John said, "I find I can raise a variety of crops, and keep different kinds of animals on my small farm by keeping good strong fences between the different fields, so as to confine everything to its proper place." "I see," answered his neighbor, "that much depends upon good strong fences to keep everything in its proper place, and that there is, in fact, but a step from one field of labor to another."

In the winter of 1828-29, John Parker had a severe attack of catarrh, and never seemed fully to recover from its effects. During the time he was most afflicted by this disease, he was absent from his meeting but one day, being there when many a younger person would have esteemed himself excused from attending. But he loved to be at the religious assemblies of his Friends, and in social worship to wait upon the Lord for a renewal of spiritual strength. When he grew somewhat better, he paid a visit to his Friends in Philadelphia, and in New Jersey, and was often engaged in public ministry in the meetings which he attended, as they came in course. He appeared lively in the exercise of his gift, and it was animating to behold this aged warrior of the cross, now evidently failing in bodily powers, so green and vigorous in the spiritual life.

John Parker attended the Yearly Meeting in 1829, and took part in the concerns which claimed its attention. The impression was strong on his mind that it would be the last he should ever be at. On his return home, his bodily infirmities increased, but his mind seemed brighter; and in his visits among his friends, he manifested much of that character so beautifully drawn of him in the memorial issued by his Monthly Meeting. It says, he was "not very thoughtful of what he should eat, or wherewithal he should be clothed; and feeling happiness and contentment within himself, he seemed to spread a ray thereof where he went." His strength gradually declined, but he continued to get to his religious meetings, and to the dwellings of Friends near by, almost to the very close. He one day said to a Friend, "I think much of late about dying. It is a serious thing to die. 'If the righteous scarcely be saved, where shall the ungodly and the sinner appear?'"

As the days of this aged servant of the Lord drew toward a close, his cheerfulness continued, and his mind seemed clothed with serenity. His thoughts were on religious subjects — and his conversation tended to the edification of his listeners. His judgment seemed clear and strong, and a sweet, deep feeling of humility appeared to clothe his spirit. He remarked on one occasion, "I can remember the time in my youth, when I first fully gave in my name to serve the Lord. I was broken down and deeply contrited, and, in this lowly state, experienced inexpressible peace and sweetness of feeling. A renewal of this precious feeling I have felt at various subsequent periods." He then added with emotion, "And I think I have felt a measure of it now in my old age."

How full of heavenly sweetness and consolation must such a condition of mind be at such a moment! To be able to look with gratitude to the Lord, who hath redeemed us from evil, and given us to experience the peace of his children; to feel the warm gushes of thankfulness for the present assurance of his love, and to have a quiet, well-grounded hope of a blessed immortality through the redemption which is in Christ Jesus, must indeed be as a foretaste of that heavenly joy which is laid up in store for the righteous, in that kingdom which shall never have an end.

In the latter part of the Sixth month, 1829, John Parker attended a meeting for worship for the last time, after which he said, "This world has lost its charms for me. I have no wish to continue a moment longer in it, unless it might be that I could do some good to the Master's cause."

After this he was mostly confined to the house, and, though gradually decreasing in strength, continued calm and cheerful. He at one time expressed that his only hope was in Christ, and in his mediation and intercession with the Father, for being received in the end. At another time, when under great suffering, he exclaimed, "Oh, that I had the wings of a dove, that I might flee away, and be at rest. Be near me, O

Lord, in these times of great trial, when the soul is about to be separated from the body. O Lord, my trust is in thee; let me not be ashamed!"

Two days before his death he took an affectionate leave of his family, setting forth his faith in the dear Redeemer, who had given himself a ransom for all. He could say in the present feeling of living faith, "'I know that my Redeemer liveth;' and because he liveth, I shall live also."

He continued at times engaged in supplication until First-day morning, the 12th of Seventh month, 1829, when he was quietly released from the body, and, we reverently believe, was gathered into one of those mansions which our Saviour testified that he went before to prepare for those who, believing in God, believed also in Him. He was in his eighty-first year.

NICHOLAS WALN.

NICHOLAS WALN was the son of Nicholas and Mary Waln, and was born on the 19th of Ninth month, 1742, at Fair Hill, near Philadelphia. He was deprived of a father's care, when he was about eight years of age; but was tenderly and affectionately brought up by his mother, aided by his guardian, her brother.

Soon after his father's decease, he was placed at a school, founded by charter, granted by William Penn, under the care of Friends in Philadelphia. Here he passed through the English departments, studied the mathematics, and became a good Latin scholar — and what was of far greater importance upon his after life, he was educated in the principles and doctrines of the Christian religion.

Nicholas Waln used to relate in after life that he never wholly lost the early impressions of pure religion. When tempted to go with his companions into many vices and follies, incident to vain youth, he would peremptorily refuse; and when rallied for his parsimony, on the ground that sordidness and love of money was the cause of his refusal, he allowed himself to be accounted mean in this respect, instead of acknowledging to them, as he should have done, his regard for a governing principle in his own mind, that secretly restrained him from gross evils, and mercifully kept him from "many foolish and hurtful lusts, which drown men in destruction and perdition."

Immediately after leaving school, and while yet a mere lad, he commenced the study of the law; devoting a part of his time to obtaining a knowledge of the German language. In his close application to study, an important habit of industry was acquired; he was freed from the train of temptations and evils that wait upon idleness, and, in great measure, from the company and solicitations of idle young men. He was naturally vivacious, witty, and sarcastic, delighting in gayety and merriment, but suffered nothing to interfere with his studies; and, while yet a minor, was admitted to practice in the courts, where, it is said, "he met with great encouragement."

With a view of improving his knowledge of the law, he embarked for England, on the 10th of Tenth month, 1763, and proceeding to London, immured himself in the Temple, and entered upon his studies anew. Here his early habit of attention to the object of pursuit, had also a tendency to preserve him from the idle pastimes, diversions, and dissipations of a great city, and the absence of his old associates, in whose company he had at home delighted to spend the part of his time allotted to relaxation, in gayety and frolic, gave him leisure for reflection and retirement. Early religious impressions were here revived, he reviewed his past career, and seemed resolved to lead a different life. The following letter to his aunt, the widow of his guardian, shows the state of his mind at this time.

"London, 20th of First month, 1764.

"Dear Aunt,— I have entertained an opinion that it is my duty by this opportunity to write to thee, for whom I have a very great regard. I am sensible thou hast undergone a great deal of affliction, and hast been wounded with the most piercing sorrow — which has rendered it highly necessary for thee to sum up all thy fortitude and patience to bear up under them. There is something implanted within us by our Heavenly Father, which excites our grief for the death of our friends and relations, and that in proportion to the affection and esteem we have for them. This is a natural principle, and by no means inconsistent with Christianity. But, as the dispensations of Providence are always founded upon the highest wisdom, it is undoubtedly our duty to submit to them with patience and resignation, and to say, 'Thy will be done, O Father,' without murmuring. I am confident, dear aunt, it is a hard task for flesh and blood; but, nevertheless, if everything is duly considered, as, first, that we are born to know trouble, that we are placed here in a state of probation, and must necessarily expect to meet with trials — we shall then plainly perceive that we suffer nothing more than that we fall heirs to as men, and of course ought to be satisfied with our lot. But, this is not all. Let us consider the gracious promise of our Lord, the blessed Redeemer of mankind, who says, 'Come unto me, all ye that labor, and are heavy laden, and I will give you rest;' and again, 'Blessed are they that mourn, for they shall be comforted.' These are gracious promises, for which we can never be enough thankful, and which ought to cheer up the drooping spirits of the afflicted Christian, who, by applying to the great Physician of souls, will find relief and comfort in the most fiery trials. Let us then not despair, but place an implicit faith in Him, who is Truth itself, and can never have deviated from his blessed promise, but will always be with his children and people.

"I thank God, the Father of all mercies, that he has been pleased to visit my poor soul, and convince me of the errors of my conduct; and I hope I shall be enabled, by his blessed assistance, to experience a redemption from the things of this wicked world; for, really, the more I see of its vanities, the more empty they appear to me, and altogether incapable of affording any solid satisfaction. Cheer up, and rejoice, for the time is drawing nigh, when everlasting joy will be assigned to those who have fought the good battle of faith, and have worn the cross with resignation and patience. Amen.

"I am, etc.,
NICHOLAS WALN."

From other letters there is evidence that his stay in London was a time of religious impressions, though not a season of much religious improvement. After he had passed through his new course of study, and become a member of the Temple Society, he returned to Philadelphia, after an absence of little more than a year, and resumed the practice of the law.

The fluency with which he spoke the German language, his cheerful, pleasing, and amiable manners, together with their confidence in his integrity, soon made him a favorite with the Germans, and opened, in addition to his Philadelphia business, an extensive and profitable practice in the County Courts, particularly at Lancaster and Easton; and, during a period of nearly seven years, he seems to have devoted every faculty of his mind to his profession, and apparently with a view to make money.

He married Sarah, the only child of Joseph Richardson, of Philadelphia, on the 22d of Fifth month, 1771, who, as he many times bore testimony, was, through life, a true helpmeet to him.

In the course of a year after his marriage, he was mercifully favored with a renewed visitation. That good hand which had been with him from childhood, now seemed to lay hold on judgment, and bring all his sins into remembrance. He, by whom "God shall judge the secrets of men," even Jesus Christ, who, according to the apostle, is in all men, sat upon the judgment-seat, in his soul. The book was opened, and he was judged out of those things that were written in the book. His whole life, even every day of his life, as he long afterward used to describe this "judgment day," seemed to be laid open. Every thing that was covered, or past, was revealed; and through the power of conviction, he experienced judgment to pass upon the transgressing nature. He had many times consulted with flesh and blood, and reasoned himself from under strong convictions; but now, through the power of constraining grace, he gave up to the heavenly visitation. He was overwhelmed with sorrow and contrition. He was utterly disqualified from attending to business, or for seeing and conversing with business men. In this unsettled condition he remained, until he felt an impression of duty to go to the Youth's meeting, held for Divine worship, on the Third day of the week, at the Market Street house, on the 4th of Second month, 1772.

In this meeting he felt constrained to appear in public prayer to the Almighty. It was evidently an unexpected thing to the whole assembly; but his supplication, which seemed to be altogether on his own account, and was delivered with great deliberation, had a powerful effect upon all present; and, upon the minds of his acquaintances, as they heard of it, and indeed upon the citizens generally, (for he was known to almost every one,) it was scarcely less humbling and remarkable.

Leaving his seat in the middle of the house, and advancing to the preachers' gallery, he kneeled in the attitude of prayer. The congregation arose, but for some minutes the internal agitation of the young man seemed to preclude utterance. At last his lips opened, and with a tremulous, but powerfully melodious voice, these aspirations burst forth:

"O Lord God! arise, and let thine enemies be scattered! Baptize me — dip me — yet deeper in Jordan. Wash me in the laver of regeneration.

"Thou hast done much for me, and hast a right to expect much; — therefore, in the presence of this congregation, I resign myself, and all that I have, to thee, O Lord! — it is thine! And I pray thee, O Lord, to give me grace, to enable me to continue firm in this resolution!

"Wherever thou leadest me, O Lord, I will follow thee; if through persecution, or even to martyrdom. If my life is required, I will freely sacrifice it. Now

I know that my Redeemer liveth, and the mountains of difficulty are removed. Hallelujah!

"Teach me to despise the shame, and the opinions of the people of the world. Thou knowest, O Lord, my deep baptisms. I acknowledge my manifold sins and transgressions. I know my unworthiness of the many favors I have received; and I thank thee, O Father, that thou hast hid thy mysteries from the wise and prudent, and revealed them to babes and sucklings. Amen."

Slowly, sentence by sentence came forth, and while breathing the spirit of humble supplication, or bursting forth in a hallelujah of praise, they baptized the hearers into tears.

When meeting was over, he quietly went to his habitation, where he kept much retired for a time. He left the bar, gave up his briefs, put on the attire of the consistent Friend, and in fervency of spirit sought to fill up his measure of religious duty.

For several years he led a very retired life, mostly at home, and diligently attended meetings, as they came in course;—and, during this period, his appearances as a minister were seldom, and his sermons very short and weighty.

As a companion to James Thornton, in the Fifth and Sixth months, 1774, he visited some meetings in Philadelphia, Chester, Lancaster, and York Counties.

After which, meeting with John Churchman, at a Quarterly Meeting, held at Cecil, in Maryland, he accompanied him to some meetings in Delaware, in the Eleventh and Twelfth months following. But for several years, he was mostly at home, or near home, and grew in his gift, and in religious usefulness. He attended the Yearly Meeting, held at Newport, for New England — and also New York and Baltimore Yearly Meetings; and the two latter many times in the course of his useful life. But, it was in and near Philadelphia — in the Youth's meetings, held quarterly — and in those large general meetings, which, in those days, were held once a year, at suitable places through the country, that he was most frequently engaged in the exercise of his gift, which, at times, was attended in no ordinary degree with the influences of the Holy Spirit.

On Sixth-day, the 11th of Eighth month, 1797, he attended a Youth's meeting, held at Abington. After the meeting had been sitting awhile in silence, a tall, slender man, in the preachers' gallery, whose head had been, for some time, bent down between his knees, slowly rose. His form bent over, his silk cap, and white dress might have drawn a smile from the heedless stranger; but there was an earnestness about his countenance which bespoke attention and respect. He spoke briefly, yet forcibly. Apt at illustration, and felicitous in expression, he caught and enchained the attention of all, strangers, children, babes in the truth, and fathers and mothers in the church. Though not a writer of rhyme, he was yet a *poet*, and throngs of bright images, carrying forcible conviction, and Christian instruction, flowed from his lips. His name was James Simpson. He sat down, and a deep silence came over the heart-tendered assembly. After a solemn pause, Nicholas Waln rose on his feet. His heart seemed filled with Gospel love, to which his richly melodious voice gave utterance — while the baptizing power of the Holy Spirit accompanying the word preached, softened the hearts, and moistened the eyes of those there gathered. He stood and ministered for about an hour; after which, upon his knees, he lifted up the voice of prayer and praise. A solemnity very unusual covered those assembled, as he ceased to offer on their behalf supplication to the God of mercy and grace. The solemnity continued; and they remained sitting together, baptized into oneness of feeling. Those at the head of the gallery at last shook hands, in token that the meeting had closed. The solemnity was still unbroken — and no one seemed willing to depart. A pause ensued — Nicholas then spoke out, "Under the solemn covering we are favored with, perhaps Friends had better separate." A few young men near the door then rose on their feet, but the solemnity was still over them; and observing none follow their example, they sat down again. Sweet, awful silence continued, until Richard Jordan standing up, broke forth with the song of triumph, which greeted our Saviour's entrance into Jerusalem, "Hosanna! blessed is he that cometh in the name of the Lord!" A few sentences followed, setting forth the blessedness of these merciful visitations, these seasons of favor, wherein the Saviour makes himself known among his people. He sat down, and again shaking hands with the Friend by his side, the meeting ended. Most present were so solemnly tendered in spirit, that few words of conversation passed among them, as Friend separated from Friend.

Although Nicholas Waln was at times thus favored in his ministry, he was careful in the freedom of Gospel truth, to make way for the humble little ones, who were just beginning, in obedience to the call of the Lord, to deliver the message he gave them.

Oliver Paxson speaking of him, expressed his opinion in the following words: "As a great man, as a wise man, as a learned man, and as a rich man, I know none possessed of as much childlike humility and simplicity as Nicholas Waln." Others who knew him, thus bear testimony: "Although he was a man of no ordinary talents, and had great influence in society, he was remarkable for condescension." "He was an original, being no man's copy, and remarkable for independence of mind. He feared no one, in doing what he believed to be his duty, and sought not the applause of men. Faithful Friends, and even children, loved him, but hypocrites feared him. He possessed much of this world's goods, but lived a life of self-denial."

He had an exalted idea of the unity and harmony of religious society, as inseparable from its strength, considering it an evidence of Divine approbation. In reference to this subject, he wrote, "Though there may be a variety of prospects, and difference of sentiment, yet as we dwell in love, and keep low in the feeling state, we are sometimes favored with a sense of what is proper to be done, and so unite with the judgment of Truth; and which, when known, we dare not oppose."

The nature of that government in religious society, which we profess to be Divine, cannot perhaps be better described. "To dwell in love, and keep low in the feeling state," is the condition in which we arrive at "the judgment of Truth," which is the judgment of Christ — and "when this is known, we dare not oppose." When the unity is broken, and love is lost, in any, then there is an end of "keeping low in the feeling state" — "the judgment of Truth" cannot be known, though it may be professed; and without it our own judgment soon carries us beyond the bounds of charity and brotherly kindness! "By this shall all men know that ye are my disciples, if ye have love one to another!"

Nicholas Waln seldom made general visits of a religious character, apprehending it was not right for him to remain from home, and away from his home friends, long at a time. He used to say it was "better to go again, twice or thrice, than overstay one's time; for then we are liable to become bewildered, and not know when to return."

In the years 1783 to 1785, he visited most of the meetings in England, to his own, and greatly to the satisfaction of Friends. Ten years afterward, accompanied by David Bacon, of Philadelphia, an elder, he visited Friends in Ireland, and thence, passing through some parts of England, again returned home in the Tenth month, 1796, after an absence of one year and four months.

His natural peculiarities were of such a character as ever to distinguish him from others; yet he labored harmoniously in the ministry of the Gospel, with men of weaker intellects, and widely different temperaments from his own. Strong good sense distinguished his conversation; yet his keen sense of the ludicrous, and nervous constitution of mind, at times led him to actions inconsistent with his usual quiet, staid dignity of manners — actions which he afterward deeply regretted. Meek was he with the meek, but to the bombastic or hypocritical he was severe and sarcastic in no ordinary degree. Humor, at times, sparkled in his light eyes, and the reflection of ludicrous thought often flashed in changeable hues over his face. He was throughout life noted for quickness of repartee, and aptness of reply: in his facetious manner, he once rebuked one of his young friends, whom he found wearing an outside fashionable coat, hung round with several capes. Nicholas, taking hold of one of the capes, inquired, "What is this?" "Cape Hatteras," was the reply of the young man, who wished to turn aside Nicholas's reproof with assumed pleasantry. "And this?" continued Nicholas. "That is Cape Henlopen." "This, then, I suppose, is the *Lighthouse*," said his interrogator, placing his hand on the young man's head.

An anecdote of Nicholas Waln published shortly after his death, in some of the public papers, contains a narrative of a generous act, coupled with a little of his pungent wit. The account states that he noticed his wood-pile in the back of his yard rapidly and mysteriously diminishing, and on watching, found that a person living on a small street in the rear of his house was making free use of it. Believing that the man was really needy, the next morning Nicholas went to the wharf, bought a load of wood, and directed that it should be delivered at the door of his pilfering neighbor. The man came speedily round, demanding the reason of the gift. "I did not want thee to break thy neck off my wood-pile," was the reply.

As age advanced upon him, he became increasingly feeble, yet continued diligent in his attendance of meetings, even at times when his friends thought his bodily infirmities might excuse him from it. To one of them who kindly spoke to him on the subject, telling him he was not well enough to go to meeting, he replied, that he "would as lief die there, as anywhere else." As the end approached, a season of deep conflict was permitted to assail his mind, and prove his faith in the sufficiency of divine and saving faith; but a short time before his death, he said, with much emphasis, "To die is gain."

He deceased the 29th of the Ninth month, 1813, aged seventy-one years.

MOSES BROWN.

MOSES BROWN was born in Providence, Rhode Island, on the 23d of Seventh month, 1738. He was the son of James and Hope Brown, who instructed him in the tenets of the Baptist Society, of which they were members. He received a plain, moderate education, leaving school at thirteen years of age. As his father was deceased, he then went to reside with an uncle.

As Moses grew up to manhood, he manifested a strong mind, and his influence was felt in every body of men with whom he associated. From 1764 to 1771, he was a representative in the General Assembly of the Colony of Rhode Island; and such was the character he bore among his fellow-citizens, that, notwithstanding partizanship and political differences prevalent, he was elected without opposition. At this time he was an active, earnest man in all that he undertook — but, though bearing a good character among men, and honest and honorable in all his intercourse with his fellows, he was not a religious man; his duty to his heavenly Father was not the uppermost thought in his mind. The circumstances under which he first bowed in awful fear, and with deep reverence and prostration of soul, entered into covenant with his Maker, he related in after life in conversation with his friends. It was while travelling by water between Newport and Providence, when a storm came down on the boat in which he was. So violent was the tempest, that all hope of the vessel living through it was taken away, and the poor trembling sinner was brought to feel the apparent certainty of immediate death. He knew he was not prepared by living faith in the Lord Jesus, and the heart-renovating influence of the baptisms of the Holy Ghost and fire, to enter into rest with the redeemed children of God. Nought else remained but that his portion must be with the accursed, who have their perpetual habitation in the lake of fire, where the worm dieth not, and the fire is not quenched. In this fearful condition of mind, he was led to cry mightily for help, and to enter into covenant with the Lord God of mercy and strength, that if he would send deliverance, the life thus spared should be dedicated to his service. The storm abated — he reached his desired haven, and the covenant made in his hour of distress he was enabled in good measure to keep.

Moses Brown was married in the year 1764. He had the previous year entered into a commercial business in partnership with his three brothers, in which he continued actively engaged for ten years. At the end of that time having a sufficiency, and being in feeble health, he withdrew from business.

About the year 1773, Moses Brown was acknowledged as a member in the Society of Friends. His was no change made from a sudden, temporary impulse. He acted from a conscientious conviction of the truth of the doctrines advocated by Fox, Penington, and Barclay; and under a persuasion of duty, he applied for membership among the professors of those doctrines. Having been deeply grounded in these principles, he was prepared to advocate and defend them, and was soon esteemed by those he had joined as one of their faithful and prominent men.

Friends in Philadelphia, in 1775, were brought into sympathy with the poor in Boston, which was then in possession of the English, and blockaded by their vessels, while on land strictly invested by the American army. Knowing that much suffering must result to those of small means, from this state of siege, the sympathizers desired to administer some relief. For a time they could not see how to do it, without compromising their Christian testimony against war. They were anxious to alleviate suffering; but they did not wish, by anything they did, to appear as though they thought that emptying the tea into Boston harbor was right, or the best way of obtaining redress of colonial difficulties. A correspondence was opened by Friends of the Philadelphia Meeting for Sufferings, with some members of Salem Monthly Meeting, Massachusetts, relating to the condition of Friends in Boston. The Meeting for Sufferings then addressed a letter in the Fifth month of the same year, to the Yearly Meeting of Rhode Island, suggesting the propriety of that body appointing a committee on sufferings. This hint was well received by the Yearly Meeting held in the Sixth month, and such a committee was appointed. It consisted of twenty-two members, of whom Moses Brown was one.

In the Seventh month of that year, a committee of Friends of the Meeting for Sufferings in New England, which had been appointed to further the concern of Philadelphia Friends, took boat at Lynn, and went round to Boston harbor by water. Moses Brown was a member of this committee. Being taken before the British admiral, they told him the business which led them to endeavor to enter the town. The admiral had heard of divers Friends having joined the Continental army, and that a regiment of them had been raised at Philadelphia, and he seemed disposed to show the committee no favor. They told him that no consistent Friend had taken up arms, and that those who had done so, had been disowned by the Society. This explanation satisfied him, and permitting them to proceed, they entered Boston, and found the few members residing there were in low circumstances.

In the Eleventh month following, David Evans and John Parrish, two members of the Meeting for Sufferings in Philadelphia, feeling a concern to attend the newly organized Meeting for Sufferings of New England Yearly Meeting, left Philadelphia to fulfil their prospect. They carried with them, on behalf of Friends in Philadelphia, funds to the amount of two thousand pounds, most of it in gold, for the aid of the destitute in New England. The epistle, of which they were the bearers, which was to govern Friends in New England in the disbursement of the money, has this passage in it. "It is not our intention to limit the distribution to the members of our own, or any other religious Society, nor to the place of their present or former residence. It seems probable many who never lived in Boston may be as proper objects as those who have; and though we would not have our brethren in religious profession who are in real suffering, excluded from partaking of the contribution, yet we consider they are entitled to *your* immediate care, and will no doubt partake of the Christian brotherly assistance we have ever as a Society extended to such."

After receiving this contribution, an attempt was made to carry out the benevolent design of the donors, and in the Twelfth month a committee of five Friends, of whom Moses Brown was a member, was appointed by the Meeting for Sufferings for this purpose. In pursuance of their object, they presented an address to General Washington, commanding the American forces around Boston, desiring permission to enter the town; and a copy was also sent to General Howe, the officer in command of the British troops; an extract from which is as follows:

"The principle of benevolence and humanity exciting our brethren in Pennsylvania and New Jersey to contribute and send to our care a considerable sum of money, to be distributed among such sufferers as are by the present unhappy difficulties reduced to necessitous circumstances, without distinction of sects or parties, provided they are not active in carrying on, or promoting military measures, (so that our religious testimony against wars and fightings may be preserved pure;) and we being sensible there are many such within, as well as without the town of Boston — and being desirous of finding those that are most needy there, as well as without, desire thy favorable assistance in getting into the town."

Though kindly received by General Washington, the requisite permission could not be obtained, and difficulties being raised by those in possession of the town, a draft for one hundred pounds was sent to two Friends residing in Boston, and the committee turned their attention to relieving the destitute in other portions of New England.

In a letter written by Moses Brown, there is a brief account of the labors of this committee, from which the following is extracted:

At Marblehead, 18th of Twelfth month, 1775, "we went from house to house among the poor, seeing and inquiring into their circumstances. Where need required, and they were within the intention of the donation, we relieved them. . . . We found great poverty to abound; numbers of widows and fatherless, and wood and provisions greatly wanting among them. . . . When I have since reflected on divers necessitous states [we met with], I have been so affected, as to conclude, had I not been favored with an unusual fortitude, and guard upon the affections, the service we went through would have been too hard for me to have borne. Through Divine favor we were preserved through the whole in a good degree of satisfaction, having sometimes a word of consolation, counsel, and admonition, occasionally arising. We visited this day, and helped between sixty and seventy families, mostly widows and children."

At Cape Ann, he says, "The inhabitants were very necessitous, having been poor, when the fishery was carried on — which is now wholly stopped. You can have very little idea of their poverty, yet the children seemed healthy, though crawling into the ashes to keep themselves warm. I may say it hath been a sort of school to us, for we never saw poverty to compare with [that of] about one hundred families in this town, which we visited and relieved. Many expressed — some [of them] feelingly — a sense of gratitude. The name Quaker, though little known in these parts, will be remembered, and perhaps some may no more think it a reproach. I have thought of John Woolman's remark in his illness, of affluence relieving in times of sickness. ['How many are spending their time and money in vanity and superfluities, while thousands and tens of thousands want the necessaries of life, who might be relieved by them, and their distresses at such a time as this, in some degree softened by the administering suitable things.'] This has been, indeed, the case with some."

Further remittances were made by Friends of Philadelphia, making the amount contributed by them £2540. The names of three thousand and thirty families, consisting of six thousand nine hundred and twenty-three persons, who received aid from this sum, were recorded. Of the families more than eight hundred were those of widows. This charitable gift appears to have been of singular service, and carried the more weight as an act of public generosity, inasmuch as very few members of the Society of Friends received any benefit from it. The report sent to Friends of Philadelphia states the profession of religion, as well as the names of those relieved. The whole sea-coast of New England, from New Hampshire to Newport, was visited by some of the members of the committee, of whom Moses Brown appears to have been the most prompt and efficient. Nantucket and the Isle of Shoals also received help.

About the time that Moses became a member of the Society of Friends, his first wife, Anna Brown, died, making a remarkably peaceful close. On returning from her grave, and while meditating upon the Lord's mercies and favors to him, the query arose in his mind: "What shall I render unto Thee for thy loving-kindness and abundant mercy?" At this time his slaves passed in review before his mind, and he afterward said to those to whom he was relating it, "I saw them with my spiritual eye as plainly as I see you now, and it was given me as clearly to understand, that the sacrifice that was called for at my hands was to give them their liberty."

He liberated all his slaves, and from this time became a consistent and fervent advocate for the rights of suffering humanity, earnestly desiring to see slavery abolished, and the prejudice of caste done away. He acknowledged the black man as his brother, entitled to all the privileges of humanity, and an equal participator in its responsibilities.

Having cleared his own hands of the iniquity of holding his fellow-men in bondage, he was prepared, as the Lord led him, to labor availingly to induce those who still held slaves to give them their freedom.

He was an active member of committees of the Yearly Meeting and Meetings for Sufferings of New England, appointed at different times to petition those in authority in the States of Rhode Island and Massachusetts, to pass laws for the abolition of slavery in their respective territories.

In the Second month, 1784, Moses Brown had the satisfaction of seeing a law passed by both Houses of the Legislature in his own State, prohibiting the slave trade, and providing for the gradual abolition of slavery within its limits.

In the year 1786, Elisha Kirk, being on a religious visit in New England, made the following memorandum under date of Sixth month 27th: " We lodged at Moses Brown's, a Friend who was convinced, and joined our Society about ten or twelve years ago. He had formerly been a Baptist, and very active in the affairs of Government, but has given up to the cross, which crucifies to the world. He is a man of great parts and a large estate; he is also a very useful man in Society, though he makes but very little appearance. I think he is the most like Anthony Benezet of any I now remember. His wife is also one of the same stamp." Respecting his labors on the 7th of Seventh month, Elisha wrote: "Next day, in company with Moses Brown, made several family visits in Providence, leaving matters as they in simplicity arose. In one family I was led to speak on the danger of those who had known good beginnings, sitting down by the way, and taking up a rest short of the true rest, instancing the children of Israel formerly, the primitive church, and many gloriously begun reformations of such who, beginning in the Spirit, degenerated into externals, and sat down short of the true rest which was prepared by the Lord for those who were still pressing forward toward the top of the mountain of his holiness. While I was speaking, I observed a young woman present was much affected, which she endeavored to hide till I was done, by turning herself away, after which she left the room, and stayed out till she had a little recovered. On her return, Moses Brown tenderly spoke a few words to her in much brokenness, withal informing her that it was not our practice to give information beforehand of the state of any to Friends who were travelling. With this she was exceedingly overcome, so that she could not forbear crying out aloud. I was afterward informed she had been religiously inclined from her childhood, and when about twelve years old had joined the Baptists, and been baptized; but not finding full satisfaction, had latterly left them, and had not joined any religious society."

This ministry, by which a rightly authorized servant of the Lord Jesus is brought into sympathy with, and enabled to speak effectually to the condition of strangers, is not understood by the world, being indeed a mystery to the unregenerate mind. The apostle declared, that the Gospel which he preached "was not after man;" for said he, "I neither received it of man, neither was I taught it, but by the revelation of Jesus Christ." This is the ground of true Gospel ministry, and the openings and intimations of the Lord's Holy Spirit not only enable his servants to minister to individual states, but also at times, in a remarkable manner, to reveal his secret things.

In the year 1752, Catharine Payton was ill in Scotland, and a report spread in England that she had there deceased. Samuel Fothergill was at the time in London to attend the Yearly Meeting. He had heard the rumor, and one day a woman Friend came to bring him information which seemed to confirm the statement. On hearing it, Samuel was quiet for a time, when he felt an internal assurance which enabled him in humble confidence to bid the Friend tell her informer from him, that Catharine Payton was not dead. This assertion was speedily confirmed.

There is an anecdote recorded concerning that valuable minister, Joseph Gill, to this effect: He was travelling on a religious visit, when he felt a stay on his mind to proceeding, and a belief that it would be right for him to return directly home. He did so, and found his wife dying. How grateful must he have felt to his Almighty Caretaker, who had thus, through the directing influences of his Holy Spirit, brought him once more to see and to be with his beloved companion, before she was forever removed from this state of existence!

Gervase Johnson, a ministering Friend of Ireland, toward the close of the last century was liberated to pay a religious visit to America. Before leaving his native country, he attended a Quarterly Meeting, in which a Friend, in a religious communication, referred to a dear brother, who was going to a distant country, with his life in his hand. He expressed his faith that the Lord would be with him and lay out his work, day after day; that he would enable him to perform acceptably what was designed for him to do; and to return him to his family and friends with the reward of peace; giving him to experience Him who had been his morning light, to be his evening song. But he stated that in his absence, the sword would be near his house — the dead bodies lying in the streets — but neither hurt nor harm should befall his family; for the Lord would encamp about them and preserve them, as in the hollow of his hand, from the rage and fury of the enemy.

This opening was in a remarkable manner verified. Gervase Johnson's residence was in Antrim, and during the battle at that place, while he was in America, the insurgents planted their cannon before his door. His family endeavored to escape from the place, but owing to the crowd around they could not effect it. They all succeeded in returning to the house, excepting the son, who for a time took refuge in the stable. His sisters soon found where he was, and one of them venturing thither, brought him in safety to the house. The rebels being vanquished, the family were in great danger of being injured by the victorious party. Orders were issued that the part of the town in which they resided should be destroyed; but one of the daughters applying to the commanding officer to know if their house was to be burnt, he commanded that the houses around it should be sacked, and it saved. Many attempts were made to plunder them, but not a shilling's worth was taken from them, and none of them sustained the slightest injury.

In early life Moses Brown had been a member of a

Free Masons' Lodge — but left it soon after he was brought under serious conviction, and felt bound to walk consistently with the Gospel of Christ Jesus. He was admitted a member on the 4th of the Tenth month, 1758, was made secretary to the lodge in the Twelfth month following, and continued to fill that appointment until the year 1768, when he withdrew from all attendance at their meetings. In his ninety-third year he wrote, "If any have the curiosity to inquire why I left the lodge — I may state, that about that time, I became more engaged after improvement in the Christian religion, and its Divine precepts, than for the social company, precepts, or work of the lodge, as it used to be called; believing that the benevolence, the charity, the enjoyments and usefulness which Christianity affords to its votaries, are much more precious, valuable, and worthy to be sought after and enjoyed, than all that attends the Masonic system." "About five years after I left the attendance of the lodge, I became a member of the Society of Friends, whose discipline was and is against the members of our religious Society joining in the meetings or public entertainments of those called Free Masons." "It has long been known that Friends have been opposed to all oaths, secret combinations, and public parades — well knowing that the vanity and exaltation of the human heart are to be subdued or checked."

We have not sufficient information to enable us closely to follow Moses Brown in his private life, or to trace him in his manifold labors for the good of that religious Society of which he was a member. It may be safely said, that he was actively engaged in promoting the welfare of the human family, and was earnestly concerned that true Christian faith and the fruits of the Spirit should increase and abound.

He was remarkable for his uprightness and consistency. He was intrusted with a large share of this world's goods, which he was concerned to hold in due subordination to religious obligations; his philanthropy was proverbial, though not ostentatious, and he observed in an uncommon degree this injunction of our Lord: "When thou doest alms, let not thy left hand know what thy right hand doeth." His house was always open for the entertainment of Friends; and his hospitality in this respect was experienced by many. Being a man of good natural parts, and of large and varied information, he was interesting and agreeable in conversation beyond most, on which account his company and advice were much sought by men of all classes, not only within his own community, but beyond its limits; and his simplicity of manner, unassuming deportment, unbending integrity, and consistent adherence to his religious principles, won for him the respect and veneration of all who sought his acquaintance. For many years he occupied the station of elder in the Society of Friends; and during the latter part of his life he occasionally spoke in our religious meetings to the comfort and satisfaction of the right-minded.

A concern for the maintenance of the original doctrines of the Society of Friends, manifests itself in Moses Brown's last will. Having left some property for certain designated purposes to the Yearly Meeting of New England, he adds, "It is my will that the same, and all estates herein given to them, do vest in, and remain to the said Yearly Meeting, and to their successors holding the same Christian faith and doctrines as exemplified in the writings of George Fox, George Whitehead, William Penn, Robert Barclay, and others of our early Friends, professors of the Christian religion of our blessed Lord and Saviour — both as to his outward manifestations in the body, and inward Divine Light, Spirit, Grace, and Truth, for the conversion, regeneration, preservation, and sanctification of the mind and soul of man, and is truly taught in the Scriptures when opened by the same Divine Spirit which superintended the writers thereof."

A Friend has furnished the following sketch of Moses Brown, as he appeared in his extreme old age. "A few months previous to his decease, I enjoyed the privilege of spending an afternoon in conversation with him. He was then in his ninety-eighth year, yet apparently in the enjoyment of good health. Although his body was slightly bent, his step was firm, and I observed that he could read without the use of glasses. He was very abstemious, and his food was of the simplest character. So vigorous was his frame, that he regularly attended to his outward affairs, and was diligent in the attendance of religious meetings. In one for discipline, I heard him deliver an impressive exhortation to young persons, in which the necessity of inward and vital religion, was clearly set forth. Considering his age, the powers of his mind were truly astonishing — particularly his memory. Few persons, in the meridian of life, can recall to mind past events, with the accuracy which he could, after having lived almost a century. Whether he referred to occurrences of his early years, or to those of recent times, it was with equal clearness and precision. He appeared to be able to mention the day and year, in which any event took place, of which he was speaking; and to describe the smallest particulars respecting it. He must have been distinguished for order and method, for having occasion to refer to various letters received, at widely separated periods of time, he could tell, without a moment's hesitation, where each one was to be found.

"In conversation, he was very animated and instructive. His memory being stored with anecdotes, he was enabled to illustrate the various subjects of discussion, and to interest those with whom he conversed. With the history of the Society of Friends, he was very familiar, and was deeply interested in its welfare. He was a firm believer in the soundness of the doctrines and testimonies, into the profession of which Friends were originally gathered — and in their adaptation to all times, and all conditions of society. To those, who, he feared, were in danger of making shipwreck of faith, and of a good conscience, he pointed out the rocks upon which many who had sought an easier way had been lost, and faithfully warned them of the consequences of a departure from the true ground of old-fashioned Quakerism."

This aged patriarch having filled up a long life of usefulness — having dedicated the strength of youth, of manhood, and of age, to the service of his Divine Lord and Master — was sustained in a quiet, comfortable faith, as he approached the borders of the grave. His comfort sprang not from looking over his past life, and enumerating supposed good deeds! No! he felt, in himself, poor, and weak, and destitute of all claims on the kingdom of grace and glory; but in the Lord Jesus he had hope, he had peace, he had confidence of attaining the rest of the righteous. On the 23d of the Eighth month, 1836, he was taken unwell, and gradually, yet constantly, declined in strength. He felt that the issue was uncertain, and arranging all his temporal affairs, awaited in calmness the result. His mind continued vigorous, and no cloud of doubt appeared to overshadow his spirit, as he entered the valley of the shadow of death. On the 6th of the Ninth month, having nearly completed his ninety-eighth year, he was released from all the trials of time.

INDEX.

AMERICAN Revolution, Predictions of William Hunt and others in reference to the, 42.
    Brief allusion to troubles during the, 188.
    Labors of Jacob Lindley against war during the, 307.
    Observations on the feelings of Friends during the, 329.
    Relief afforded by Friends to the destitute in New England during the, 399.
Andrews Edward, Illustration by, of the importance of attending to impressions of duty, 134.
    Brief account of, 134.
Andrews Peter, Notice of, 351.
Atkinson Samuel, Short discourses by, in a religious meeting, 121.

Baker Richard, Testimony of, to the importance of attending to small impressions of duty, 120.
Barbadoes, Notice of a religious visit by Samuel Emlen and Daniel Offley to, 142.
Barclay Christiana, Brief notice of, 35.
Barclay Robert, Incident attending the convincement of, 120.
Barnard Hannah, Notice of, 165.
Bayley Solomon, Anecdote of spiritual sympathy of, with William Williams, 117.
Benezet Anthony, Sketch of the life of, 296.

418 INDEX.

Bettle Samuel, Divine intimation to, of the death of a daughter, 223.
Bible, Objection made to the, by an infidel, 317.
Blakey William, Meek endurance of robbery by, and its effects, 333.
Bownas Samuel, Counsel given by, after a religious meeting, to the younger and older members, 96.
Brown Moses, Sketch of the life of, 396.
Brown Thomas, First appearance of, in the ministry, 173.
Burrough Edward, Dying expressions of, 36.
Business, Religious duties not to be interfered with by worldly, 374.

Carping Spirit withstood by John Churchman, 75.
Carrington Thomas, Prophetic declarations of, respecting George Withy, 350.
Cash Thomas, Remark of, upon humility, 119.
Chalkley Thomas, Providential relief of, from starvation at sea, 16.
Christ, Observations on and illustrations of the spiritual appearance of, in the heart, 176, 178, 179, 198, 208.
Church, Observation on efforts to benefit the, 323.
   On government in the, 392.
Churchman George, Letter of, to Peter Yarnall, 284.
Churchman John, Sketch of the life of, 67.
Clark Samuel W., Brief notice of, 88.
Coale Elizabeth, Remarks of, to Jacob Lindley, upon religious scruples, 309.
Collins Comfort, Brief notice of, 27.
   Exercise of mind of, on account of David Ferris, 29.
Covetousness, Testimony of Anthony Benezet against, 300.
Creaturely Activity in Monthly Meetings, Observation of William Hunt on, 43.

Davies Richard, A spurious ministry detected and judged by, 269.
Dawes J. and A., Letter of Jacob Lindley to, 319.

Dicks Zachariah, Letter of William Hunt to, 38.
Dillwyn George, Sketch of the life of, 182.
Dillwyn George, Prophetic intimations to, 106, 219, 325.
    Apt illustrations and remarks of, 194.
Dillwyn's Reflections, Extracts from, 198, 199, 203, 208, 209, 210, 211.
Discernment, Anecdotes of Samuel Emlen illustrating spiritual, 47, 49, 51, 52, 105.
Dream of D. Ferris in relation to his call to the ministry, 25.
    Of Mary England conveying instruction in regard to the ministry, 72.
    Of William Savery on the necessity of passing through the fire of the Lord's judgments, 152.
    Of a young Carolina girl, related by William Williams, 155.
    The danger of spiritual pride made known to a minister through a, 211.
    Of Isaac Jackson respecting his settlement in America, 241.
    Of a minister about to set out on a religious visit, 363.
Dress, Observations and anecdotes on plainness of, 57, 161, 205, 206, 207, 345, 346.
    Remarkable encouragement given to a young woman in regard to plainness of, 208.
Drinker Henry, Remarks of, on the character of Anthony Benezet, 302.
    Letter of Samuel Emlen to, 191.
Dudley Mary, Prayer of, on behalf of a distant brother, made effectual, 364.
Dyer Mary, Joyful declaration of, at the time of her execution, 315.

Ellwood Thomas, Account of the proceedings of, in relation to marriage, 20.
    Remarks of, in reference to a plain appearance, 58.
Emlen Samuel, Sketch of the life of, 46.
    Remarks of Henry Drinker in reference to, 141.
    Short message of, remarkably encouraging to George Dillwyn, 188.

Emlen Samuel, Remarks of, in reference to George Dillwyn, 191.
  Encouragement given by, to an unknown auditor, 204.
  Remark of, in reference to the ministry of Richard Jordan, 249.
  Peter Yarnall effectually reached by the ministry of, 271.
  Message of, to Sarah Harrison, 353.
  Letter of, to Sarah Harrison, 364.
England Mary, Instructive dream of, 72.
"Eternity," Anecdote of the effect produced upon a gay woman by the word, 133.
Evans Jonathan, Account of the convincement of, 128.
Evans Joshua, Anecdote of a startling comparison made use of in the ministry by, 371.

Ferris David, Sketch of the life of, 9.
Fothergill Samuel, Remarkable participation of, in the spiritual exercise of his father, 116.
  Impressions made by the ministry of, on William Jackson, 244.
  Letter of, to Mary Yarnall, 260.
  The reported death of Catharine Payton contradicted by, 107.
  Remark on the humility and ministry of, 119.
Foulke Elizabeth, Notice of, 351.
Fox George, Anecdote of, concerning the necessity of prompt obedience to apprehended duty, 141.
  Narrative of the convincement of a young woman by, 178.
  A trooper sent to, for direction, 179.
Free Masonry, Testimony of Moses Brown respecting, 410.
Friends, On the privileges and responsibilities of the children of, 90.
  Prophetic declaration of Samuel Emlen respecting, 92.
Funeral, Account of a remarkable communication by Arthur Howell at a, 235.
Furniture of houses and simplicity of living, Advice of William Jackson upon, 253, 254.

Gawthrop Thomas, Whistling reproved by, 183.

Gibbons Abraham, Reply of, upon partisan feeling during the American Revolution, 331.
Gill Joseph, Anecdote of obedience by, to intimations of duty, 408.

Harrison Sarah, Sketch of the life of, 344.
    Extract from a letter of, 118.
    Letter of Samuel Emlen to, 61.
Haste, Reproof of Anthony Benezet to a person habitually in, 298.
Hatton Robert, Letter of, to Peter Yarnall, 276.
Haviland Daniel, Spiritual sympathy of the daughter of, with, 115.
Horne Susanna, Divine intimation to George Dillwyn of the safe arrival of, in England, 219.
Howell Arthur, Sketch of the life of, 227.
Hub-burner, Anecdote of religious impressions made on the mind of a, 308.
Hull Henry, Convincement of, through the instrumentality of Daniel Offley, and comments, 138.
Humility, Observations upon, 119, 211.
Humphreys Whitehead, a professed infidel, Account of the death of, 168.
Hunt William, Sketch of the life of, 33.

Incivility reproved by Samuel Emlen, 59.
Indian, Testimony of an, against war, 216, 219.
Indians, Interview of George Dillwyn and other Friends with a deputation of Cherokee, 214.
    Visit of Jacob Lindley and other Friends to attend a treaty with, 311.
Individual Example, Observations on the influence of, 139.
Infidel, Dying expressions of a professed, 164, 169.
    Testimony of a religious man against the conduct of an, 317.
Infidelity, Testimony of William Savery against, 161.

Jackson Isaac, Notice of, 240.
Jackson William, Sketch of the life of, 240.

Jacobs Isaac, Letter of, to Sarah Harrison, 352.
Jenkins Mehetabel, Anecdote of the effectual ministry of, 170.
Johnson Gervase, Prediction of the preservation of, and his family — its remarkable fulfilment, 408.
Jones Rebecca, Sketch of the life of, 80.
Jordan Richard, Observations on the powerful ministry of, 248, 249.
  Remarks of, on ministry, 361.

Kirk Elisha, Remarks of, on the character of Moses Brown 405.
  Anecdote of the ministry of, 405.
Kite Benjamin, Observation of, in reference to young men in meetings for discipline, 96.
Kite Thomas, Remark of, on his death-bed, 360.

Labor, Precept and example of Anthony Benezet in regard to, 297.
Language, Experience of William Lewis in regard to the use of the plain, 55.
  Peace felt by George Dillwyn for faithfulness in the use of the plain, 184.
  Peter Yarnall required to use the plain, 274.
Lewis Ellis, Short account of, 35.
Lewis William, Convincement of, in regard to the testimony of Friends to the use of the plain language, 54.
Lindley Jacob, Sketch of the life of, 305.
Lukens Joseph, Warning given to, through the ministry of Sarah Harrison, 347.

Marriage, Experience of D. Ferris in relation to, and comments, 18.
  Of Thomas Ellwood, Account of the, 20.
  Spiritual unity and fellowship of Eli Yarnall and his wife, 335.
Meetings Religious, A member among Friends reproved by his landlord for non-attendance of, 76.
  Consolation experienced by a child in, 88.

Meetings Religious, Observations and anecdote upon the indulgence of wandering thoughts in, 110.
    Remarks of George Dillwyn on the attendance of, 195.
    Observations on silent exercise in, 280.
    A member among Friends rebuked by Judge Hemphill for non-attendance of, 196.
    Maintenance of, in Philadelphia, during the prevalence of the yellow fever in, 319, 321.
    On the attendance of, in the middle of the week, 374.
Mercy, Remarkable illustration of the Lord's restraining and saving, 200.
Mifflin Warner, Remarks of, to General Washington, upon the Revolutionary War, 331.
Ministry, of women, Observations of David Ferris upon the, 13.
    The gift of, at times, committed to very young persons, 33.
    Anecdotes illustrating the necessity of being subject to Divine openings in the, 69, 71.
    Remarks upon a lifeless, 112.
    Melody of sentences and beauty of ideas, not Gospel, 170, 171, 172.
    The advice of elders to be taken by Friends in the, 197.
    A spurious, detected by Richard Davies, 269.
    Observations on the nature and authority of Gospel, 407.
Mitchell James and Ann, Letter of William Hunt to, 41.
Molleson Margaret, Holy rejoicing of, on the bed of death, 315.

Nesbitt Robert, Anecdote respecting inconsistency in dress related by, 58.
Newland George, Short account of, 34.
"No Cross, No Crown," Instrumentality of, in the convincement of Jonathan Evans, 129.

Obedience to manifested duty, On the danger of refusing, 231.
Offley Daniel, Sketch of the life of, 127.

Parker John, Sketch of the life of, 366.
Parnell James, Dying expressions of, 36.

INDEX.

Patrickson Anthony, Rejoicing of, under affliction of the body, 315.
Paxson Oliver, Testimony of, concerning Nicholas Waln, 391.
Paxson Timothy, Anecdote of the attendance of week-day meetings by, 374.
Payton Catharine, Letter of, to Rebecca Jones, 86.
Penn William, Remarks of, in reference to the ministry of illiterate Friends, 172, 173.
Pemberton John, Notice of, 262, 265, 283, 328.
    Letter of, to Peter Yarnall, 265.
    Letter of Eli Yarnall to, 329.
Philadelphia, Incidents connected with the appearance of the yellow fever in, 112, 137, 143, 228, 319, 320.
Popularity, Observations on the danger to ministers of, 286.
Price Peter, Brief account of, 250.
Pride, Remarkable dream upon the danger of spiritual, 211.
Priestley Joseph, Brief reference to, 222.
Privateering, Peter Yarnall required to make restitution of money obtained in, 275, 278.
Providential relief experienced by David Ferris in pecuniary distress, 15.
    Relief from starvation of Thomas Chalkley and companions, 16.
    Deliverance from shipwreck, 208.
    Warnings, 209, 210, 228, 232.

Removals of residence, Comments on, 23.
Resignation to the loss of friends and connections, On the duty of, 360.
Richardson John, Remarks of, in reference to the ministry, 174.
Rodman Sarah, Interview of Daniel Offley with, and death of, 145.
Ross Thomas, Anecdote of a prophetic intimation given by, 106.
Routh Martha, Divine intimation to, of the drowning of a nephew, 220.
    Visit of, to individuals in Philadelphia, with E. Foulke, 352.

INDEX.   425

Savery William, Sketch of the life of, 149.
    Dream of Peter Yarnall concerning himself and, 294.
Salkeld John, An admonition of, made instrumental in preventing a person from committing suicide, 280.
Sands David, Letter of, to Thomas Scattergood, 194.
    A person deterred from self-destruction through the ministry of, 281.
Scattergood Thomas, Remarkable confirmation of a religious concern of, through Rebecca Jones, 114.
    Interesting circumstance attending the acknowledgment of, as a minister, 186.
    Led to appoint a meeting in London for George Dillwyn, 192.
    Letter of, to George Dillwyn, 193.
Scott Job, Testimony of, concerning Samuel Emlen, 54.
Scruples, Anecdote and observations upon religious, 308.
Simpson James, Remark of, upon humility, 119.
    Remark of, upon a dependence on popular preachers, 287.
    Divine intimation to, in reference to Eli Yarnall, and its fulfilment, 339.
    Ministry of, in a youth's meeting at Abington, 389.
Slave-holding, Observations of William Hunt upon, 40.
    Apprehension of Jacob Lindley of an approaching judgment upon the land on account of, 324.
    Successful labor of Sarah Harrison against, 356.
    Moses Brown led to testify against, 404.
    Notice of the efforts of Friends against, in New England, 405.
Stanton Daniel, Brief notice of, 101, 104.
Steel John, Brief notice of, 172.
Swearing, Observations of George Dillwyn upon, 199.

Thomas Edward, Confirmation of, in his ministry, through the instrumentality of John Richardson, 174.
Thornton James, Remarks of on the death of Anthony Benezet, 303.
    Brief notice of, 388.
    36 *

Truxton Thomas, Observation of, in relation to Rebecca Jones, 107.

Universality of Divine Grace, Anecdotes and observations respecting, 198, 208.

Valentine Robert, Providentially restrained from proceeding on a religious visit, and led to speak at a funeral, 220.
Vision seen by Peter Price, Account of a, 250.

Waln Nicholas, Sketch of the life of, 381.
    Observation of Sarah Harrison respecting, 118.
    Labors of, against infidelity in Ireland, 163.
    Effectual testimony of, on the freedom of Gospel ministry, 279.
War, Anecdotes of sufferings endured by Friends on account of their testimony against, 158, 331.
    Testimony of an Indian against, 216, 219.
    Refusal of Eli Yarnall to collect taxes for purposes of, 327.
Wealth, Scruples of Anthony Benezet upon accumulating, 296.
Williams Sarah, Letter of, to Sarah Harrison, 357.
    Testimony of Sarah Harrison respecting, 358.
Wilson William, Anecdote of humility in, 120.
Wistar Thomas, Notice of, during the yellow fever of 1793, 147.
Withy George, Prediction of Thomas Carrington in relation to, 350.
    Divine intimation to, during a religious visit, to return home, 222.
Woman Friend in Canada, Remarkable incidents connected with the ministry of a, 121.
Women, Observations of David Ferris on the Gospel ministry of, 14.
    Incidents connected with the establishment of a Yearly Meeting of, in London, 108.
Woodward Increase, Brief notice of, 54.
Worship, On silent, 280.

Yarnall Eli, Sketch of the life of, 326.

Yarnall Mordecai, Brief account of, 259.
Yarnall Mordecai, Jr., Letter of, to Peter Yarnall, 283.
Yarnall Peter, Sketch of the life of, 259.
Yarnall Peter, Letters to, from Daniel Offley, 131, 136, 139.
Yarnall Priscilla, Spiritual sympathy and fellowship of, with her husband, 335.
   Dying expressions of, 337.
Yearly Meeting of Women Friends in London, Incidents connected with the establishment of, 108.
Yellow Fever in Philadelphia, Notice of the, 112, 137, 143, 228, 319, 320.

Zane Isaac, Brief notice of, 215.

THE END.

www.ingramcontent.com/pod-product-compliance
Lightning Source LLC
Chambersburg PA
CBHW050427240426
43661CB00055B/2295